T0305079

Failing to Compete

This book is dedicated to
Maya Lall
and
Giulio and Livia Pietrobelli

And to the memory of Julio Samper Vargas and his friendship

Failing to Compete

Technology Development and Technology Systems in Africa

Sanjaya Lall

Professor of Development Economics, Oxford University (at the International Development Centre, Queen Elizabeth House), UK

Carlo Pietrobelli

Professor of Economics, University of Rome III and Research Fellow of CEIS, University of Rome Tor Vergata, Italy

Edward Elgar

Cheltenham, UK • Northampton MA, USA

Published by
Edward Elgar Publishing Limited
Glensanda House
Montpellier Parade
Cheltenham
Glos GL50 1UA
UK

Edward Elgar Publishing, Inc.
136 West Street
Suite 202
Northampton
Massachusetts 01060
USA

A catalogue record for this book
is available from the British Library

Library of Congress Cataloguing in Publication Data

Lall, Sanjaya.
Failing to compete : technology development and technology systems in Africa/ Sanjaya Lall, Carlo Pietrobelli.
p. cm.
Includes bibliographical references and index.
1. Technological innovations—Economic aspects—Africa—Case studies.
2. Africa—Economic conditions—1960- I. Pietrobelli, Carlo, 1959- II. Title.

HC800.Z9 T455 2002
338′.064′096—dc21

2002024370

ISBN 1 84064 640 3

Printed and bound in Great Britain by MPG Books Ltd, Bodmin, Cornwall

Contents

List of figures vi
List of tables vii
List of boxes ix
Exchange rates x
Acronyms xi
Preface and acknowledgements xvi

1. Competitiveness and national technology systems: an introduction 1
2. The relative competitive and technological performance of Sub-Saharan Africa 12
3. Kenya 54
4. Tanzania 83
5. Uganda 109
6. Ghana 141
7. Zimbabwe 176

Annex: Attracting Manufacturing FDI to Africa 202
Bibliography 241
Index 259

Figures

2.1	UNIDO Industrial Performance Scoreboard	13
2.2	Skill indices (HMI), 1995	39
2.3	Tertiary technical enrolments, 1995	39
4.1	Senior management time spent negotiating with officials on regulations	107
6.1	The science and technology system in Ghana	152
7.1	Percentages of technically qualified personnel in total employment in manufacturing enterprises, 1993–94	181

Tables

2.1 Technological classification of exports 19
2.2 Growth and distribution of world exports, 1980–97 21
2.3 Growth and shares of manufactured exports by technological categories and country groups 23
2.4 Shares of regions in developing world exports by major categories 24
2.5 Shares of primary products in total exports 25
2.6 Manufactured exports, values and structure, SSA and selected developing countries 27
2.7 Manufactured export growth rates, 1980/81 to 1996/97 29
2.8 Manufacturing value added in case study and comparator countries 33
2.9 Enrolment ratios 35
2.10 Tertiary level enrolments and enrolments in technical subjects, 1995 36
2.11 Harbison-Myers Index (HMI) ranks, 1995 and 1957–58 38
2.12 Hourly labour costs in the apparel industry, 1990–95 40
2.13 R&D propensities and manpower in major country groups 42
2.14 ISO certificates at end 1999 in Africa and comparators 43
2.15 FDI Inflows, 1988–99 45
2.16 FDI inflows into Sub-Saharan African countries, 1987–98 46
2.17 Recent equipment imports 50
2.18 Technological capability index of sample manufacturing firms, 1995 52
3.1 Kenya, number of patents registered 62
3.2 Technology inflows into Kenya 63
3.3 Sectoral shares of R&D expenditure in public research institutions 1996–97 67
4.1 Recent manufacturing performance in Tanzania 86
5.1 Uganda: structure of the economy, 1987-97 110
5.2 Uganda: index of industrial production 111
5.3 Uganda: manufactured exports, 1993–97 113
5.4 Ugandan imports of capital goods, 1993–97 118
5.5 Investment approvals by sector by Uganda Investment Authority, 1991–98 120
5.6 Technical skills in 121 Ugandan enterprises, 1998 123
5.7 Makerere University enrolment and graduates by discipline, 1991–97 125

6.1 Ghana (1970–98) selected growth indicators 142
6.2 Manufacturing production and growth rates, Ghana, 1986–97 143
6.3 Estimated rate of capacity utilization in manufacturing, Ghana, 1984–93 144
6.4 Manufactured exports: Ghana and other SSA countries, 1980–95 145
6.5 Annual government budget allocations to MEST 155
6.6 Total government funding of CSIR, 1996–98 156
6.7 R&D funding released: multilateral donor and Ghana Government, 1996–98 157
6.8 'Commercialization' of CSIR activities, 1996–98 157
6.9 Ghana: payments for royalties and licence fees 158
6.10 Registered direct investments, Ghana, 1995–98 160
6.11 Training in Ghanaian manufacturing enterprises 161
6.12 Summary financial indicators of the Ghana Standards Board 163
7.1 Comparisons of various wages 184
A.1 Investment location decisions by MNCs 203
A.2 Host country determinants of inward FDI 206
A.3 Main economic determinants of FDI 207
A.4 Average processing time for FDI approvals in selected countries 218
A.5 Types of investment promotion activities 226

Boxes

3.1 Technological upgrading by Power Technics, Kenya 64
4.1 Tanzania Cigarette Company and upgrading via foreign direct investment 90
4.2 New Tanzania Investor Roadmap, 1999 92
5.1 Training and skill development by TNCs – Unilever Uganda 121
5.2 Weak enterprise-technology institution relationships constrain industry in Sub-Saharan Africa 132
5.3 Emerging exports and the lack of a technology system: rose exports from Uganda 135
6.1 Ghana Free Zones Board: two TNCs' experiences after liberalization 147
7.1 National Institute of Fashion Technology, India 185
A.1 Free trade and export processing zones in evolution 211
A.2 FDI promotion by Zimbabwe Investment Centre (ZIC) 228
A.3 Information provided by the Thai Board of Investment 231
A.4 The UK's approach to attracting Siemens 233
A.5 FDI in the Caribbean Basin: from low-wage assembly to high-tech clusters 234

Exchange rates

Units of national currency per US$, nominal current rates, yearly averages

	1990	1995	1996	1997	1998	1999	2000
Ghana	326.3	1200.4	1637.2	2050.2	2314.1	2647.3	5321.7
Kenya	22.9	51.5	57.1	58.7	60.4	70.3	76.2
Tanzania	195.1	574.8	580.0	612.1	664.7	744.8	800.4
Uganda	429.0	969.0	1046.1	1083.0	1240.3	1454.8	1644.5
Zimbabwe	2.4	8.7	9.9	11.9	21.4	38.3	43.3

Source: IMF, *International Financial Statistics*, various years.

Acronyms

GENERAL

ARIPO	Africa Regional Intellectual Property Organization, Harare
ARSO	Africa Regional Organization for Standardization
CIDA	Canadian Agency for International Development
CNC	Computer numerically controlled (machine tools)
COMESA	Common Market for Eastern and Southern Africa
DANIDA	Danish International Development Agency
DFID	Department for International Development, UK
EDB	Economic Development Board (Singapore)
EMPRETEC	Capacity Building Programme to Foster and Growth and Competitiveness of Small and Medium-Scale Enterprises in Developing Countries (UNCTAD)
EPZ	Export Processing Zone
EU	European Union
FAO	Food and Agriculture Organization
FDI	Foreign direct investment
GDP	Gross domestic product
HKPC	Hong Kong Productivity Council
IDRC	International Development Research Council, Canada
IFAD	International Fund for Agricultural Development
IFC	International Finance Corporation
IPA	Investment promotion agency
IPRs	Intellectual property rights
ISO	International Standards Organization
JITAP	Joint Integrated Technical Assistance Programme
MFA	Multi-Fibre Agreement
MNC	Multinational corporation
MSTQ	Metrology, standards, testing and quality
MVA	Manufacturing value added
NGO	Non-governmental organization
OECD	Organization for Economic Co-operation and Development
R&D	Research and development
S&T	Science and technology

SADC	South African Development Community
SITC	Standard International Trade Classification (UN)
SME	Small and medium enterprise
SSA	Sub-Saharan Africa
TNC	Transnational corporation
TRIPS	Trade related intellectual property rights
UDEAC	Central African Customs and Economic Union
UNCTAD	United Nations Conference on Trade and Development
UNDCP	United Nations Drugs Control Programme
UNDP	United Nations Development Programme
UNEP	United Nations Environmental Programme
UNESCO	United Nations Educational, Scientific and Cultural Organization
UNIDO	United Nations Industrial Development Organization
USAID	United States Agency for International Development
WHO	World Health Organization
WIPO	World Intellectual Property Organization
WTO	World Trade Organization

KENYA

ARIPO	African Regional Industrial Property Office
JKUAT	Jomo Kenyatta University of Agriculture and Technology
KARI	Kenya Agricultural Research Institute
KEBS	Kenya Bureau of Standards
KEFRI	Kenya Forestry Research Institute
KEMFRI	Kenya Marine and Fisheries Research Institute
KETRI	Kenya Trypanosomiasis Research Institute
KIPC	Kenya Investment Promotion Council
KIPO	Kenya Industrial Property Office
KIRDI	Kenya Industrial Research and Development Institute
NCST	National Council for Science and Technology
PCT	Patent Cooperation Treaties

TANZANIA

CDTT	Centre for the Development and Transfer of Technology
COSTECH	Commission for Science and Technology
IPC	Investment Promotion Centre
IPI	Institute of Production Innovation

NFAST	National Fund for the Advancement of Science and Technology
SIDO	Small Industries Development Organization
TASTA	Tanzania Award for Science and Technological Achievement
TBS	Tanzania Bureau of Standards
TCC	Tanzania Cigarette Company
TEMDO	Tanzanian Engineering and Manufacturing Design Organization
TIC	Tanzania Investment Centre
TIRDO	Tanzania Industrial Research and Development Organization
TNSRC	Tanzania National Scientific Research Council

UGANDA

ARIPO	Africa Regional Intellectual Property Organization
EPRC	Economic Policy Research Centre, Makerere University, Kampala
GOU	Government of Uganda
HIPC	Highly Indebted Poor Country Initiative
MAAIF	Ministry of Agriculture, Animal Industry and Fisheries
MOES	Ministry of Education and Sports
MOTI	Ministry of Trade and Industry
MTAC	Management Training and Advisory Centre
MTTI	Ministry of Tourism, Trade and Industry
MU	Makerere University, Kampala
NARO	National Agricultural Research Organization
NCDC	National Curriculum Development Centre
PERD	Public Enterprise Reform and Divestiture
PSF	Private Sector Foundation
UEA	Uganda Exporters' Association
UFEA	Uganda Flower Exporters' Association
UIA	Uganda Investment Authority
UIRI	Uganda Industrial Research Institute
UMA	Uganda Manufacturers Association
UMACIS	Uganda Manufacturers Association Consultancy and Information Services
UNBS	Uganda National Bureau of Standards
UNCCI	Uganda National Chamber of Commerce and Industry
UNCST	Uganda National Council for Science and Technology
URSB	Uganda Registration Services Bureau
USSIA	Uganda Small-Scale Industry Association
VTC	Vocational Training Centre, Nakawa

GHANA

AGI	Association of Ghana Industries
ARI	Animal Research Institute
ASSI	Association of Small-Scale Industries
BIRD	Bureau of Integrated Rural Development
BRRI	Building and Road Research Institute
BSS	Bio-Sanitation System
CDS	Centre for Development Studies
CRI	Crops Research Institute
CRIG	Cocoa Research Institute of Ghana
CSIR	Council for Scientific and Industrial Research
DAPIT	Development and Application of Intermediate Technology
EIA	Environmental Impact Assessment
EMP	Environmental Management Plan
EPA	Environmental Protection Agency
ERP	Economic Recovery Programme
FORIG	Forestry Research Institute of Ghana
FRI	Food Research Institute
GAAS	Ghana Academy of Arts and Sciences
GAEC	Ghana Atomic Energy Commission
GEPC	Ghana Export Promotion Council
GFZB	Ghana Free Zones Board
GGDP	Ghana Grains Development Project
GIMPA	Ghana Institute of Management and Public Administration
GIPC	Ghana Investment Promotion Centre
GOG	Government of Ghana
GRATIS	Ghana Regional Appropriate Technology Industrial Service
IIR	Institute of Industrial Research
INSTI	Institute for Scientific and Technological Information
ITTU	Intermediate Technology Transfer Unit
KNUST	Kwame Nkrumah University of Science and Technology
MDPI	Management Development and Productivity Institute
MEST	Ministry of Environment Science and Technology
MIST	Ministry of Industry, Science and Technology
MOFA	Ministry of Food and Agriculture
MOTI	Ministry of Trade and Industry
NARP	National Agricultural Research Project
NASTEP	National Science and Technology Press
NASTLIC	National Science and Technology Library and Information Centre
NBSSI	National Board for Small-Scale Industries

NLC	National Liberation Council
NRC	National Research Council
OPRI	Oil Palm Research Institute
PEED	Private Enterprise and Export Development (sponsored by World Bank)
PEF	Private Enterprise Foundation
PGRC	Plant Genetic Resources Centre
PNDC	Provisional National Defence Council
PSDP	Private Sector Development Project
RTSC	Rural Technology Service Centre
SARI	Savannah Agricultural Research Institute
SRI	Soil Research Institute
SSNIT	Social Security and National Insurance Trust
STEPRI	Science and Technology Policy Research Institute
TCC	Technology Consultancy Centre
TCPD	Town and Country Planning Department
TIP	Trade and Investment Promotion Programme (sponsored by USAID)
UCC	University of Cape Coast
UDS	University for Development Studies
UG	University of Ghana
WAIFOR	West Africa Institute for Oil Palm Research
WRI	Water Research Institute

ZIMBABWE

BESA	Business Extension and Advisory Services
CDTI	Clothing Design and Technical Institute
CZI	Confederation of Zimbabwe Industry
ESAP	Economic Structural Adjustment Programme
SAZ	Standards Association of Zimbabwe
SBSU	Small Business Support Unit (Zimbabwe National Chamber of Commerce)
SEDCO	Small Enterprises Development Corporation
SIRDC	Scientific and Industrial Research and Development Centre
UDI	Unilateral Declaration of Independence
VCCZ	Venture Capital Company of Zimbabwe
ZIC	Zimbabwe Investment Centre
ZIMPREST	Zimbabwe Programme for Economic and Social Transformation

Preface and acknowledgements

The woes of Sub-Saharan African manufacturing industry are well known. One basic problem is its inability to compete both at home, when exposed to direct import competition, and in export markets. Apart from niches - say, in resource-based industries or in activities serving small, localized markets - where it survives, there is little evidence of diversification or dynamism. In a world driven by rapid technical change, therefore, African industry is increasingly 'out of the loop', marginal to the global scene. The *World Industrial Development Report 2002* of UNIDO, in which one of the present authors is directly involved, finds that most African countries cluster at the bottom of the group of developing countries in an 'industrial performance scoreboard'. More worrying is that their lag vis-à-vis other developing regions in most drivers of industrial development is increasing rather than decreasing.

Liberalization and adjustment have not changed African industrial prospects. On the contrary, where carried through intensely they have often made matters worse. African enterprises are being devastated in simple industries like clothing, footwear and the like by competition from other developing countries. Deprived of these entry-level activities, they are finding it impossible to move into complex industries where international competitiveness entails advanced skills, organizations and technological capabilities. Only a cumulative process of learning and upgrading can produce these capabilities; the learning process itself is being curtailed, even strangled. Yet it would be defeatist to argue that 'Africa cannot industrialize': industrialization remains the main engine of structural transformation. While *not* neglecting other productive sectors, Africa *has* to industrialize if it is to develop in the long term, and for this its enterprises must become competitive.

One vital element of industrialization is 'national technology systems' - the superstructure of institutions linked to industry that allows enterprises to access, deploy and improve imported technologies efficiently. National systems interact intimately with industrial enterprises; where both are weak, it is very difficult to promote sustained industrial growth. This is unfortunately the case in much of Africa - technologically weak enterprises coexisting with weak technology support institutions, with little interaction between the two. This aspect of development has not been adequately studied, and this book is a preliminary attempt to explore the issues.

The analysis here brings together fieldwork and desk research by the authors, funded by different agencies at different times. The work in Kenya, Tanzania, Uganda and Kenya took place in 1999 and 2000 and was financed under JITAP (Joint Integrated Technical Assistance Programme) by UNCTAD, WTO and the International Trade Centre. The Commonwealth Secretariat and the Government of Zimbabwe funded the work in Zimbabwe in 1997–98, in the context of an analysis of export competitiveness. The World Bank sponsored the paper by Lall on FDI in Africa in 1999, reproduced here in the Annex (with some amendments).

The fieldwork involved interviews with enterprises, business associations, government officials and major institutions dealing with industrial technology. Sanjaya Lall prepared the studies on Kenya, Tanzania and Zimbabwe, and Carlo Pietrobelli those on Ghana and Uganda.

We wish to thank the sponsors of the studies and all the people who gave generously of their time, effort and knowledge during the fieldwork. We cannot, for obvious reasons, thank them all individually, but this does not in any way diminish our gratitude. We also acknowledge our thanks to colleagues in Africa who organized the fieldwork and provided background information and analysis. Geoffrey Ngugi Mokabi collaborated with us in Kenya, Godwill George Wanga in Tanzania, Paul Sagala in Uganda and Joseph Oko Gogo in Ghana. The work in Zimbabwe benefited immensely from the involvement of Peter Robinson (of Zimconsult).

Our sincere thanks are due also to the UNCTAD staff who managed the JITAP project. In particular, we would like to acknowledge our debt to Khalil Hamdani, Menelea Masin, Bonapas Onguglo and Taffere Tesfachew, who provided guidance, encouragement, comments and administrative support. In the Commonwealth Secretariat, we would like to thank Rumman Faruqi and Ganeshan Wignaraja for their support of and participation in the analysis. In the World Bank, Miria Pigato commissioned the FDI paper and provided vital inputs for its preparation.

We have tried to make the analysis policy-oriented, but we believe that the book will also be useful for researchers into industry and technology in Africa. We hope that the cross-regional perspective will provide new insights into African problems, highlighting some problems that globalization poses for industrial 'latecomers'. We hope most of all that the book will encourage further work on the institutional framework for technology development. The issues it raises tend to be neglected by economists and assigned low priority by policy-makers; this bias has to be corrected.

Oxford and Rome
October 2001

1. Competitiveness and national technology systems: an introduction

This book analyses national technology systems supporting manufacturing in five African economies: Kenya, Tanzania, Uganda, Ghana and Zimbabwe. The first reaction of many readers is likely to be as follows. 'Why look at industrial technology systems in Africa? Surely industrial development at this level does not need a "technology system"? And, given the rather parlous state of manufacturing in these countries, doesn't technological effort take fairly low priority?' The contention here is that 'technology' is vital to industrialization at all levels. This has always been so - but the new technological and competitive environment makes it even more important, and in many ways more difficult, to build the local capabilities needed. Technology 'systems' (the term is defined below) are vital to building industrial capabilities at the enterprise level - and such systems are extremely weak and fragile in most African countries. What is worse is that they are neglected and so are increasingly lagging behind technology systems in competing countries. The structural base of African industrial development is thus being weakened, and this should be an important consideration for development strategy in the region.

The analysis seeks to illustrate the technology situation in African countries at different levels of industrialization. It draws upon fieldwork done in a fairly short period in each country. It cannot, therefore, provide detailed institutional analysis - the intention is more to describe the 'technology system' in broad comparative terms and to suggest directions of policy reform. Given the relative neglect by researchers of this subject, even a study of this sort is useful: little is known about the nature of technology systems in Africa (an important exception is Enos, 1995).

The remainder of this chapter spells out the analytical framework for the empirical analysis. Chapter 2 provides some background on the competitive performance of manufacturing industry in Sub-Saharan Africa relative to other developing regions. Chapters 3 to 7 deal with technology systems in the selected countries, and make policy recommendations to strengthen the systems in each. An Annex treats an important related issue: the attraction of foreign direct investment (FDI) in manufacturing to Africa, with a focus on export-oriented activities.

THE PREMISES

Despite its disappointing performance in the last decade, industry remains vital to growth, employment and structural change in Sub-Saharan Africa. Manufacturing is still the main engine for transforming the economic structure of low-income countries, letting them shift from slow-growing, low-return activities to activities with high productivity and strong growth potential (Chenery et al., 1986). It is the most potent user and carrier of technology to the economy, the main agent for the creation, transfer and application of new technologies. It provides the hardware of production (machinery) to all economic sectors and catalyses new methods of management, organization, ownership, financing and governance. It creates new jobs, skills and entrepreneurship, and often promotes social mobility. It is a powerful magnet for attracting foreign resources. It can play a vital role in upgrading agriculture and services, providing new inputs, knowledge and skills as well as new demand for their products. It stimulates the development of new institutions and legal structures.

If we accept that revitalization of industrial growth will be a crucial element in African development, we should also bear in mind that, with rapid technical change, globalization and policy liberalization, the *context* for industrial development is changing radically. It is becoming imperative for enterprises (whether they serve domestic or foreign markets) to be internationally competitive. Many things matter for competitiveness, but one of the most important is the ability to access new technologies, deploy them efficiently, and improve them in line with technical change. This ability cannot be taken for granted and it is not easily acquired, even in countries with simple industrial sectors that rely heavily on imported technologies. African enterprises may not need to create new technologies; they do need to build capabilities, organizations and industrial structures to master, adapt and improve on foreign technologies. All the evidence suggests that these elements are deficient in Africa, even in comparison with other developing regions (Biggs et al., 1994, 1995; Lall, 1995, 1999; Lall et al., 1994; Pietrobelli, 2001).

Building industrial capabilities in developing countries is often a difficult, prolonged, costly and risky task. Since it faces numerous market and institutional failures, it cannot be assumed that efficient capabilities will arise automatically in response to liberalization of trade, technology and foreign direct investment (FDI) policies. Rapid liberalization with a weak base of capabilities can devastate industrial enterprises, as they are exposed to competition from firms with much stronger capabilities. Opening up to inflows of technology and FDI does not mean that they will come to economies without the complementary capabilities needed to make them technically efficient. Yet much of liberalization in Africa seems to have been premised on the assumption that capabilities do not matter or will arise by 'getting prices right'. One economy after another is exposing their industries to global market forces without any strategy or effort to discover capability needs and meet those needs. As a result, there has been considerable hardship, dislocation and closure in industry (Lall et al., 1994; Lall, 1999c), and few signs of the emergence of competitive new manufacturing activities.

Industrial capabilities develop largely within individual enterprises, but the pace and depth of this development depend significantly upon the economic, policy and institutional environment in which the enterprises operate. Firms do not build capabilities in isolation but in close interaction with each other, factor markets and support institutions, and in response to signals arising from markets and policy-makers. Many of these elements have systematic relations with each other and so are described as forming a 'technology system'. Weak systems lead to deficient capabilities, the inability to use technology effectively and so to uncompetitive firms. The causation also runs the other way around: technologically slothful firms do not demand strong support systems and do not feed into technological effort by other firms and institutions. This book deals, not with the entire technology system, but with the *main institutions involved* in technology import, creation and diffusion.

THE COMPETITIVENESS CHALLENGE

International competitiveness has always mattered for industrial growth, though its significance has varied by country and stage of development. Most countries - including the mature industrial powers today - launched industrialization behind protective barriers, but the extent and duration of protection varied. The early industrializers (in Europe and North America) enjoyed fairly high levels of 'natural' protection from foreign competition arising from high transport costs, poor communications and differing demand patterns. Policy-imposed protection was, nevertheless, also significant. High import tariffs, widespread quantitative restrictions and more subtle barriers (for example from bans on equipment export and migration, government procurement or technical standards) were common among industrial economies (Reinert, 1995). And this was at a time when competitive gaps in technology, skills and institutions were relatively small.

The post-Second World War period saw a widespread dismantling of trade barriers in the mature countries. It also saw the launching of a deliberate development strategy in the developing world, generally with the promotion of industrialization behind high barriers to import competition. In part this strategy was a reaction to the liberal trade and investment setting of the colonial era, when little industrial development took place. In part it reflected development thinking at the time, with a strong emphasis on planning and other forms of strong government intervention. For several decades thereafter manufacturing industry in most developing countries grew with little or no exposure to international competitive pressures.

There were some exceptions. A few developing countries - entrepôt centres, tax havens and small industrializing economies like Hong Kong and Singapore - maintained liberal trade regimes. Of these, only the two economies mentioned were able to build large and competitive industrial sectors, the former because of unique initial conditions and the latter by virtue of pervasive industrial policy (Lall, 1996). Some others, most notably Korea and Taiwan, succeeded dramatically by combining import protection and other forms of industrial policy with export orientation, forcing their enterprises to compete in global markets (ibid.). By contrast, the vast majority of developing countries, including those in Africa, sheltered their industries for long periods, their governments often owning firms and directing resource allocation. Many countries also restricted inflows of technology via FDI, licensing and capital goods. One result, now universally accepted, was the fostering of technical inefficiency, technological lags, poor capabilities, and uncompetitive firms.

This setting is changing rapidly and irreversibly as industry the world over moves into a more open environment. Part of the reason is technological. New transport, communication and information technologies are reducing natural protection, forcing economies closer together and spreading demand patterns. Industrial firms are increasingly transnational, taking their operations into the domestic markets of most countries and confronting domestic firms with direct competitive pressures. Part of the reason lies in policy reform. Governments are (willingly or reluctantly) removing interventions in trade and investment, disillusioned with import-substitution policies and state ownership, or giving in to powerful external pressures. Whatever the reason, most remaining policy barriers are set to disappear. Africa is part of this trend, and its industrial firms will face the global competitive economy more or less openly by 2010.

Needless to say, in this setting industrial growth - and indeed survival - in every country will depend on the ability of its enterprises to compete fully with international counterparts. Some new forces make it easier to become competitive: market signals are clearer and stronger, and technology is more mobile than ever before. Transnational companies (TNCs) are growing in size and spread, transferring new technologies across the world with unprecedented speed and effectiveness (UNCTAD, 1999a). Similarly, many technologies are also readily available to local firms (in the form of capital goods, licensing, consultancy or subcontracting). Other forms of information also flow far more easily and cheaply, making it possible for enterprises to access new markets, technologies and collaborators.

At the same time, some forces make it more difficult to achieve industrial competitiveness. The technological demands of efficiency are rising apace, with a host of new skill, organizational and institutional needs, and the rate of change is accelerating (Lall, 2001a). Some technologies and markets are more effectively controlled by giant TNCs, who are unwilling to part with them without taking a large equity stake. There are limits to the involvement of developing countries in the globalization of technology (Archibugi and Pietrobelli, 2001). Many of the tools of industrial policy apart from import restrictions (local content rules, export subsidies, directed credit, reverse engineering and so on) are being constricted or forbidden by international rules and agreements.

The pace and ubiquity of technical progress mean that all activities have to improve their technologies and the skills needed to operate them if they are to compete. With the liberalization of trade and investment, even non-traded activities are increasingly exposed to international competition, and have to improve their competitive base to survive and grow. Skill needs rise with the level of development, but even the least developed countries have to improve their human capital base if they are to grow and prosper. To quote ILO (1998, p. 32),

> In both developed and developing countries, employment of skilled workers has been on the rise ... The rate of growth of employment in the period 1981–96 in advanced countries has usually been highest for professionals and technicians... In developing countries, too, this occupational category has witnessed a high growth rate, though one less disproportionate to other categories in comparison to developed countries. In contrast, the rate of growth of employment for the production and related workers category (which contains skilled manual and craft workers but mainly the unskilled and semi-skilled) has been very low, often negative, for developed countries. In the developing countries for which data are available, with some exceptions (e.g. Philippines), this group has witnessed much lower employment growth than the highly educated and trained group of professionals and technicians.

Maintaining a competitive edge with rising wages requires advanced skills, even in simple labour-intensive activities. For instance, in the clothing industry, it requires sophisticated design, quality control, layout, delivery and so on as product cycles become shorter and more reliable, and high quality and rapid delivery become vital to winning orders. In fact, the skill needs of high value added activities in labour-intensive industries may be even more demanding where automation is possible. Skills are, moreover, subject to constant change. Thus,

> the demand for professionals and technicians has increased in all countries, as their

> analytical, cognitive and behavioural skills equip them better to adapt to more sophisticated technology. However, even within these high-skilled jobs the trend is increasingly towards multi-skilling - combining specialised professional expertise with business and management skills ... [Even for production workers] the trend is towards up-skilling and multi-skilling. A study of 56,000 production workers over an eight-year period shows that skill requirements in production jobs have changed across the board. It is not only that each job has experienced up-skilling, but the overall distribution of production jobs has shifted away from the less skilled to the more skilled. (ILO, 1998, p. 47)

Analysts like Best (1990) note that the nature of competition itself is changing. Traditional modes of competition, based on low costs and prices, are being replaced by 'the new competition' driven by quality, flexibility, design, reliability and networking. Firms are specializing increasingly in different segments of the production chain, outsourcing processes and services to reap economies of scale and specialization. Tapping information flows and networking, very skill-intensive functions, are the new weapons in the competitive armoury. As much as 50 per cent of the value of a new car now lies in its 'information content' - design, process management, marketing, sales and so on. As *The Economist* (1996, p. 48) noted, 'over three-quarters of the value of a typical manufactured product is already contributed by service activities such as design, sales and advertising'. The rise in the share of high value services strengthens this trend.

While Africa faces the same international context as other regions, the fact that it is the least developed industrially exacerbates the competitive challenge. Import substitution has provided African enterprises with the smallest base of industrial capabilities. Its technology base is the lowest, its attractiveness to manufacturing TNCs the weakest and its ability to respond to world market opportunities the most constricted. Its enterprises have furthest to go in building basic competitive capabilities. Thus, liberalization is likely to have the most damaging effects in Africa. The structural weaknesses are taken up in the next chapter; let us now consider why capabilities are necessary.

THE NEED FOR INDUSTRIAL 'CAPABILITIES'

Much of the conventional policy literature in development assumes away the need for industrial capabilities as a determinant of industrial success, by presuming that 'latecomers' can simply import appropriate technologies from advanced countries and use them in production without further effort, cost or risk. If technology were transferable like a physical product (that is, embodied in equipment, patents and blueprints), then indeed no further learning or capabilities would be called for - getting prices right would ensure that developing countries optimized their technological choice and use. Industrial capacity (the physical plant) becomes equivalent to industrial capabilities.

A large body of empirical research on developing countries suggests that this depiction is over-simplified and misleading (for summaries see Lall, 1992a, 2001a; Pietrobelli, 1997). Based on the evolutionary tradition pioneered by Nelson and Winter (1982), it argues that firms do not have a clear knowledge of the available set of technologies or of how to operate any new technology efficiently. Finding the right technology at the right prices involves cost and risk (particularly in a developing country). Using the technology involves further effort: search, experimentation, induction of new information and learning. Making the technology work efficiently under new conditions involves further effort, to adapt it to local demand, scales of production, worker skills and raw materials (Battisti and Pietrobelli, 2000). Technologies, in other words, have large 'tacit' elements that have to be mastered by the recipient and cannot be sold by the technology supplier like a physical product. Without considerable additional effort to learn various aspects of the technology, no enterprise can reach the levels of efficiency required to compete in world markets.

Technological effort does not end with mastering a given version of the technology. All technologies can be improved by minor adjustments, which calls for further effort and new capabilities. If the international frontier in the technology shifts - it always does - firms have to induct and master the new versions to stay competitive. As technologies in use grow more complex and involve new skills and larger scales of production, formal research and development (R&D) often becomes necessary, not so much to recreate the technology as to monitor, understand, adapt and improve it. Much of R&D, even in developed countries, is used to keep track of, copy and adapt innovations outside the firm (Cohen and Levinthal, 1989). In developing countries, the main function of R&D is to master, adapt and improve imported technologies; only at some relatively mature stage does it become truly innovative.

While using any new technology involves building new capabilities, the degree of uncertainty and difficulty varies according to the technology and, within it, the specific functions undertaken. The more complex the technology involved, and the more advanced the functions undertaken, the more difficult it is for a newcomer to build the capabilities. How difficult it is depends on three things: the initial capabilities of the enterprise, the support it can draw upon from its environment, and the novelty of the technology relative to its existing stock of knowledge. The same technology may be almost costless to absorb for a firm in a relatively industrialized country but very costly and difficult to master for a firm in an unindustrialized one.

These efforts can occur almost anywhere in the firm, on the shop floor, in process or product engineering departments, procurement or marketing, or R&D. In-house efforts can draw upon information, assistance and skills from outside. In fact, a great deal of technological information comes from other firms: equipment and material suppliers, contractors, competitors or buyers (particularly foreign buyers). Some comes from institutions like technical extension services, technology institutions, universities or financial intermediaries. Then there are informal sources of information like trade fairs, conferences, journals and the like. Ultimately, however, capability building is a collective action within the firm: to be effective, it has to involve the whole firm and be accessible to all its members. A few skilled technicians or engineers do not make for a capable and competitive enterprise. A very similar process of capability building occurs in non-technical functions like marketing, procurement, training or financial management. Technical and other processes have to interact with each other, since building capabilities involves changing institutional processes or routines and launching new ways of managing information and people (Nelson and Winter, 1982).

The way in which knowledge is used differs, of course, by the level of development. In mature industrial countries, the competitive use of technology is largely a matter of *innovation* - the ability to create new products and processes. In developing countries, innovation is less important than *the ability to use and adapt existing technologies at competitive levels of cost and quality*. How difficult this is and how long it takes depends on the country and the technology, but learning is always necessary. Even routine capabilities, say for quality management or process optimization, take years to build in industrial newcomers. More advanced capabilities, for modifying, improving or generating technologies, can take longer to build. The pattern of industrial success in the developing world reflects to a large extent the effectiveness with which countries have undertaken learning (Lall, 1996; Pietrobelli, 1994b). Some have reached the frontiers of advanced technologies, and are competing with mature countries on their home turf. At the other extreme, many, as in Africa, have not been able to build even the basic operational capabilities needed to compete internationally in simple technologies.

The rise of globalized production under the aegis of TNCs reduces the need for building domestic capabilities in some ways. Since TNCs provide affiliates with intangible assets (skills, technology, production expertise, training and so on), the host economy needs to offer correspondingly fewer 'ready-made' capabilities and invest less in subsequent absorption. Considerable industrial and export growth has taken place on this basis in countries with relatively low local technological capabilities. The growth of global production systems does not, however, do away with the need for local capabilities (see Guerrieri et al., 2001, on the complementarity between local and global capabilities). The countries that have attracted export-oriented FDI have offered a base of basic skills and infrastructure for simple manufacturing operations. Subsequent upgrading into more complex activities has involved investments in skill and institution building, supplier development and modern infrastructure.

The diffusion of TNC technology to local enterprises has also involved strong support for developing their technological capabilities. The transfer of the most advanced functions like R&D has only taken place in host countries that have advanced capabilities and research institutions. In other words, FDI can reduce the need for local capabilities and institutions in the early stages and for very simple activities. Beyond this stage, countries still need to build local capabilities. In any case, there are many industries where TNCs are not very active. African countries in particular cannot rely on foreign firms to lead growth in a range of simple processing activities using low technologies at small scales of production. There is no alternative to building local capabilities in these activities. Finally, there is the fact that all countries, even the least developed, have a myriad of small and micro enterprises in existence. These have to be helped to survive and grow: in the new competitive environment this necessarily involves the building of new capabilities.

NATIONAL TECHNOLOGY SYSTEMS

We noted that firms do not learn or innovate on their own but in intense interaction with other firms, factor markets, support institutions and governments. They respond to rules on trade, competition, employment, intellectual property or the environment, and they behave in ways fashioned by their history, culture and environment. The interaction of economic, social and political factors provides the system within which firms learn and innovate, and so compete in global markets. There is a substantial recent literature on 'national innovation systems' which deals with these systemic aspects of technological performance, focusing mainly on the creation of new technologies in advanced industrial economies (Lundvall, 1992; Nelson, 1993; Edquist, 1997).

Similar systemic considerations apply to developing countries, where frontier innovation is not important but other forms of technological effort are. Technological effort is similarly embedded in the specific economic, policy and institutional context of each country. We use the slightly different term, 'national technology systems', to describe the environment within which developing countries build industrial capabilities. The idea is very similar to the 'national innovation system', but in developing countries the emphasis is different. There is greater stress on the incentive regime (like trade and competition policies, which differ more than in developed countries) and market and institutional failures in learning (again more pervasive and stringent than in developed countries).

What determines the effectiveness of national technology systems? In the simple neo-classical world that informs most development analysis, firms optimize under free market conditions by choosing, from a known array, the techniques appropriate to their relative factor prices and costlessly using these at 'best practice'. In an evolutionary world like the one posited here, with complex learning processes and externalities, the ability to select and deploy technologies efficiently cannot be taken for granted in this way. Many requirements of learning involve serious market failure. It cannot be assumed that over time enterprises will move automatically and efficiently into more difficult technologies (or taking on more complex tasks) in response to changing prices and factor endowments. Technological upgrading and deepening requires enterprises to invest in more advanced - and so more costly, uncertain and prolonged - learning processes. In the presence of externalities and deficient factor markets, such investments will be deficient in free markets. Policy interventions are then needed to overcome market failures - to tackle learning costs, promote externalities and linkages, coordinate factor market improvements with needs, and develop institutions. In the final analysis, therefore, *national technology systems depend on the effectiveness of industrial policy*.

The general trade and other policy needs of industrial development have been extensively debated in the literature and it is not relevant for us to review that debate. Our focus is on two aspects of national technology systems: *technology policies in the narrow sense* and *technology institutions*. Technology policies cover such areas as technology import by licensing and FDI, incentives for local R&D and for training. 'Technology institutions' are used here in the narrow sense to refer to bodies such as quality, standards, metrology, technical extension, R&D, and technology training. They may be government-run, started by the government but run autonomously, or started and managed by industry associations or private interests. The technology literature (for instance, country studies in Nelson, 1993) stresses the significance of such institutions for supporting enterprise efforts to innovate and build capabilities. Mowery and Rosenberg (1989) describe the historic evolution of technology policies and institutions in mature industrial countries, in particular in the USA.

The technology institutions analysed here include those for *MSTQ* (metrology, standards, testing and quality), *public research* and *university research* concerned with industry, and *technical support and extension* for SMEs. Many of their services are the essential 'public goods' of technological effort, difficult to price on market terms. Public research institutes and universities undertake basic research that does not yield commercial results in the short term, but provides the long-term base of knowledge for enterprise effort. Quality, standards and metrology institutions provide the basic framework for firms to communicate on technology and keep the basic measurement standards to which industry can refer. Extension services help overcome the informational, technical, equipment and other handicaps that SMEs tend to suffer. The provision of these services faces market failures of the sort that every government, regardless of its level of development, has to remedy.

CONCLUSIONS

Africa needs to industrialize but in the near future it will have to do this in a much more demanding setting than in the first bout of industrialization. Most of its enterprises will face the full force of international competition, with aggressive firms from other low-wage developing countries seeking to penetrate their domestic markets and keep them out of export markets. Their competitors will often have higher levels of skill, stronger technological capabilities, denser supply networks and better physical and institutional infrastructure than they do. To compete with these firms in a world of pervasive and rapid technical change, African firms will need a much more advanced and broad-based set of skills and capabilities.

Simply liberalizing on trade, getting the macroeconomic and political situation right, promoting FDI and domestic competition will not be enough to meet these needs and to catalyse the flagging industrial sector. There is a need for comprehensive and proactive policies to build industrial capabilities, and without using traditional tools of policy like protection and subsidization. The brunt of future needs has to be met by technology and skill-creating institutions acting on the 'supply side' of industry.

All African countries have most of the necessary institutions in name. Most have copied the institutional structures of former colonial powers, the UK in the case of our sample countries. The dynamic Tiger economies of East Asia have very similar institutional structures, charged with similar functions. How effective in comparison are the African institutions? Are they capable of meeting the technological needs of the firms they serve in the new global setting? How can they be improved?

These are some of the questions which subsequent chapters try to answer.

2. The relative competitive and technological performance of Sub-Saharan Africa

THE RECENT BACKGROUND

The weaknesses of African manufacturing are well known, but it is useful to review its broad dimensions. Growth in the past two decades has been low, in several cases negative. Over 1990–97, manufacturing value added (MVA) in Sub-Saharan Africa (SSA), excluding South Africa, grew at only 0.1 per cent per year. This poor performance occurred in the context of rapid industrial growth in other developing regions, with many countries using manufacturing to drive a rapid transformation of their production and export structures. The share of Africa, including South Africa, in global MVA has remained constant since 1980, at under 0.4 per cent (UNIDO, 1999). Even this low level of activity is highly concentrated. In 1998, South Africa by itself accounted for 55 per cent of total SSA's MVA, and the next seven countries for another 22 per cent (ibid.).

SSA is lagging not just in terms of the volume of manufacturing activity, but also (increasingly) in the *technological content* of this activity. This is at a time of unprecedented technological progress, when new technologies, skills, organizational methods and modes of networking are transforming the nature of economic activity. In some (largely traditional) activities, it is possible to remain competitive with unskilled cheap labour and processing natural resources. However, this base is eroding steadily. In an increasing number of industrial activities, competitiveness involves technological change, flexible response, greater networking and closely integrated production systems across firms and regions (what Best, 1990, calls the 'new competition'). The new competition requires better technological capability in every country, regardless of its resource base and location, even in countries that are not innovating at the frontiers.

African manufacturing does not show many signs of such upgrading. Its structure remains backward, dominated by (simple, low level) processing of natural resources and the manufacture of simple consumer goods aimed at domestic markets. Food, tobacco, textiles and footwear together contribute 55 per cent of manufacturing output in 1998. There are few supply linkages between large and small enterprises. Productivity growth has been poor (UNIDO, 1999). Capacity utilization has fallen and remains below its peak of many years ago. In fact, a significant part of recent growth comes from utilizing this capacity rather than building new plant. Technological efficiency is relatively low, with little sign of technological dynamism or innovation (Lall and Wangwe, 1998). African firms are well below international 'best practice' technical levels, and below levels reached by other developing countries (Biggs and Srivastava, 1996).

UNIDO (2002) has produced (with the close collaboration of one of the present authors) an index ranking developing countries and regions by four indicators of industrial performance. Called the 'Industrial Performance Scoreboard', this index comprises four indicators: MVA per capita, manufactured exports per capita, the share of medium and high technology products in MVA and the same share in manufactured exports. The index captures the extent and competitiveness of industrial activity along with its technological complexity, so indicating the ability of manufacturing to survive and grow in the emerging international setting. Figure 2.1 shows the regional ranks in 1985 and 1998. The regions are: mature industrial countries, transition economies, East Asia (including China), Latin America and the Caribbean, SSA1 and SSA2 (including and excluding South Africa), and the Middle East and North Africa. The poor and deteriorating industrial performance of Africa is evident from the figure.

Largely as a result of weak competitive performance, manufacturing has become a drag on growth rather than the engine of growth for development in

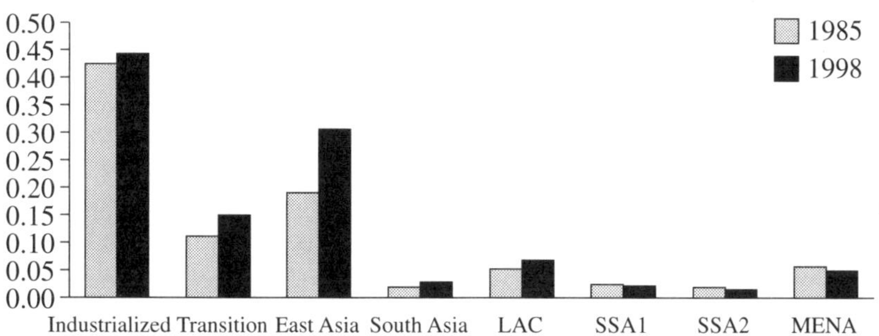

Note: The TC index is a normalized average of scores assigned to a range of technological functions, and ranges between 0 and 1.

Source: UNIDO (2002).

Figure 2.1 UNIDO Industrial Performance Scoreboard

much of the region. Manufactured exports have not grown significantly; indeed, non-traditional exports as a whole have done poorly. To quote a recent analysis, 'Yet, despite an evidently increasing need for it, Sub-Saharan Africa appears to have achieved remarkably little diversification of its traditional primary export base over recent years' (Helleiner, 1999, chapter 1). In a world of accelerating technical change, intensifying competition and globalizing production, Africa is not only failing to improve its international competitive position - it is fast falling behind. What is perhaps more worrying, there is no other sector apart from manufacturing that appears able to act as the catalyst of economic development and modernization. As in other countries through economic history, Africa must industrialize efficiently if it is to sustain growth and competitiveness, and reap the benefits of modern technology.

UNDERSTANDING POOR INDUSTRIAL PERFORMANCE

Some of the weaknesses of African industrial development are traceable to bad luck (conflicts, droughts and so on) and external shocks (declining terms of trade, debt, falling aid inflows). Some are traceable to policy failures. There was often poor macroeconomic management and inadequate investment in infrastructure. On the industrial front, there were evident policy errors. Most African governments fostered industry behind high and indiscriminate protection. Given the small and weak indigenous base of industrial entrepreneurship, many gave the lead to state-owned enterprises that had even less managerial and technological capabilities. There was often rampant rent-seeking and political interference. Some governments nationalized enterprises run by foreign firms or entrepreneurs of non-African origin, further affecting efficiency. The business environment was often inhospitable to local entrepreneurs, with high transaction costs, corruption and uncertainty.

Even taking all this into account, African industry performed worse than other developing regions that had similar inward-oriented policies with a strong role for the state, rent-seeking and high transaction costs (Lall, 1992a). African enterprises clearly lagged in building up and deepening technological capabilities during the period of import-substitution. The structure of industry remained very simple, and remarkably few firms achieved international competitiveness in using these simple technologies. There were clearly *structural factors* at work that held back the growth of efficient industrial capabilities.

Surprisingly, the 'capability explanation' has been relatively neglected in the mainstream literature on African development and in World Bank analysis. The result is that attention continues to focus on general policy failures and the weaknesses of the African state.[1] While policy failures certainly played an important role, excessive emphasis on these - with an accompanying stress on minimizing the role of government and maximizing that of free markets - can lead to the wrong policy conclusions (Lall, 2000b). The argument here is that policy mistakes were indeed made in the past and have to be corrected, with greater outward orientation, lower transaction costs and more welcoming attitudes to FDI. However, this has to be combined with strong policies to correct the market and institutional failures that hold back the building of industrial capabilities. A market friendly state in the 'Washington consensus' mode is unlikely to be able to catalyse sustained and competitive industrial growth in Africa. The reasons why this is so will become evident as we go through the empirical evidence in this book.

As events turned out in Africa, economic stresses, disillusionment with past strategies and intense pressure from donors led most governments to liberalize economic policies, some rapidly and willingly, others slowly and reluctantly (Husain and Faruqee, 1994). However, most did so on the expectation of a revival of growth in manufacturing output, exports and employment. The dominant model of policy reform - stabilization and structural adjustment as proposed by the IMF and World Bank - was applied uniformly across countries regardless of their level of industrial development (Stein, 1992). Adjustment was supposed to improve productive sectors by removing inefficient interventions and exposing enterprises to international competition, in the belief that such exposure would lead to greater efficiency and technological dynamism. Almost the entire burden of policy reform was laid on 'getting prices right' - liberalization was considered not just *necessary* but also *sufficient* for better performance (Lall, 1995). There was, at least in the early days of adjustment, even an expectation that liberalization would lead Africa to replicate the success of export-oriented Tiger economies of East Asia.

The reality, as noted, turned out to be very different. Import liberalization devastated most industries exposed directly to import competition, largely as a result of entry by more competitive products from other developing countries rather than from developed ones. The African enterprises that are surviving are those with a natural cost advantage (based on local primary resources) or with niche markets that do not face direct import competition (small enterprises making low-quality, low-price products not served by imports or those making customized products for local customers). They are not growing in activities that are competitive purely on the basis of productive efficiency, even in simple labour-intensive areas where Africa now has an advantage because of its low relative wages. The share of machinery production in total manufacturing has practically halved, from 12.2 to 6.5 per cent, over 1980–96 (UNIDO, 1999). The industries that initially led export-oriented growth in Asia - labour-intensive assembly - are the ones worst affected. FDI is not responding to the labour cost advantages of Africa by setting up export-oriented operations. There is a trickle of FDI going into resource extraction, the privatization of state-owned utilities and some food activities. The constraints to FDI attraction in Africa are discussed in the Annex to this book.

The dynamic processes driving manufacturing growth and exports in many developing countries are conspicuously absent in Sub-Saharan Africa. What is more worrying, the divergence in the 'drivers' of industrial growth is widening rather than narrowing between Africa and most of the developing world.[2] *The main structural problem of African industry appears to be its weak base of technological and managerial capabilities.* The revival of growth in a competitive setting has to be based on greater technology inflows into Africa and, more importantly, much better abilities of enterprises to absorb, adapt and improve upon imported technologies. It cannot be taken for granted that either will follow as a natural result of adjustment. Let us compare some of the main indicators and drivers of industrial performance across the regions.

MANUFACTURED EXPORT PERFORMANCE

A useful point with which to start the comparison is manufactured exports, looking at the technological structure and dynamism of such exports. These can provide useful indicators of the underlying technological strength and specialization of national industrial sectors (though there are qualifications, noted below). They obviously cannot capture trends in activities that do not enter trade, but in a liberalized trade setting they do provide a good picture of underlying technological activity in the industrial sector as a whole. This section places the performance of Africa and of the case study countries in the international context.

Note that in standard theory, export structures are incidental and uninteresting. Countries specialize in activities where they have relatively abundant resources (in the most common models these include only physical capital, labour and human capital). Over time, they switch to different activities as factor endowments, and so relative factor prices, change. Thus, developing countries start by exporting low-skill, labour-intensive products and switch to more skill and capital-intensive products as they grow and capital becomes more abundant relative to labour. The export structure at any point of time does not matter, since it simply reflects reigning factor prices; over time it adjusts automatically and without lags or constraints to these prices. Given efficient markets - the basic assumption - no structure can be more desirable than another, since all markets clear and all factor returns are equalized at the margin (that is, there are no externalities, economies of scale, learning or agglomeration effects). In this setting, therefore, export structures do not raise any economic or policy issues.

A more realistic analysis of how firms develop technological competence suggests that *export structures can and do matter*. These structures are *path dependent* and *difficult to change,* being the outcome of slow, incremental capability development processes. They are not, however, rigid. They change in response to market signals, new technologies and external catalysts (like FDI), new policies and the accumulation of new capabilities. Even so, structural change takes time and effort. Moreover, different technological structures have *different growth and development implications*. They face different market prospects and potential for the application of new knowledge. For developing countries relying on imported technologies, different structures can offer different opportunities for further learning. In general, *technology-intensive structures are expected to be more beneficial* because:

- Activities with rapid product or process innovation enjoy *faster growing demand* vis-à-vis technologically stagnant activities. They also grow faster because they substitute for other final or intermediate products, and stimulate demand for other technology-based products. Throughout the world, *technology-intensive activities are growing faster* in terms of production, employment and exports.[3]
- Technology-intensive activities are *less vulnerable* to entry by competitors compared with low technology activities where scale, skill and technology requirements are low. A low-technology export structure is a good starting point for a developing economy with ample unskilled labour, but over time, as wages rise, it can sustain growth only by taking shares from other low-wage exporters. In relatively slow-growing markets, this is possible but difficult. For instance, in garments, entry into high quality, brand-conscious segments needs considerable technical effort and high levels of design and marketing skill: the 'tacit' element of enhanced competitiveness is very large and very difficult to acquire. In fact, it may prove more difficult than upgrading technologies in more complex products where automation in response to rising wages is easier.
- Technology-intensive activities offer higher learning and productivity potential as well as greater spillover benefits to other activities. Thus, they lead to faster growth in capabilities, greater diffusion and higher quality capabilities. A technology-intensive structure is thus likely to offer *greater systemic benefits* in terms of learning and innovation.
- Capabilities developed in technology-intensive activities are more attuned to technological and market trends, giving the *ability to respond*

more flexibly to changing conditions. In the emerging global environment, therefore, they provide more valuable competitive skills.

We can distinguish *four technological categories* of manufactured exports (Table 2.1). The major groups conform to general perceptions of technology intensity based on R&D expenditures or employment of scientists and engineers in technology activity (Lall, 1998). Each has subsets of products, based on differences in materials, technologies or emerging global production systems.

The technological features of the main categories are as follows:

- *Resource-based* (RB) products tend to be simple and labour-intensive (for example simple food or leather processing), though there are segments using capital, scale and skill-intensive technologies (for example petroleum refining or modern processed foods). Competitive advantages in these products arise generally - but not always - from the local availability of natural resources. We draw a distinction between *agriculture/forest-based* products and *others*, mainly mineral-based.
- *Low-technology* (LT) products tend to have stable well-diffused technologies mainly embodied in capital equipment, with low R&D expenditures and simple skill requirements. Labour costs tend to be a major element of cost and barriers to entry are relatively low. The market as a whole tends to grow slowly, with income elasticities generally below unity, though there are exceptions for particular products like fashion garments. Products tend to be undifferentiated and bought mainly on the basis of price competitiveness; however, there are high quality segments where brand names, skills, design and technological competence are vital. However, products of major interest to developing countries are in the lower quality segments. We distinguish between the *textile*, *garment*, *footwear* ('fashion') cluster and *other low-technology products*. The former has undergone massive relocation from developed to developing areas, with the simpler assembly operations shifted to low-wage sites and complex design and manufacturing functions retained in advanced countries. This relocation has given rise to a dynamic international production system that has served as an engine of export growth for many countries. However, location in textiles and clothing has been influenced not just by cost but by market access, as for example the Multi-Fibre Agreement, offshore assembly provisions offered by the USA and Europe and regional trade agreements like NAFTA.
- *Medium-technology* (MT) products are the heartland of industrial activity in mature economies, comprising the bulk of skill and

Table 2.1 Technological classification of exports

Classification	Examples
Primary products	Fresh fruit, meat, rice, cocoa, tea, coffee, wood, coal, crude petroleum, gas
Manufactured products	
Resource-based manufactures	
Agro/forest based products	Prepared meats/fruits, beverages, wood products, vegetable oils
Other resource based products	Ore concentrates, petroleum/rubber products, cement, cut gems, glass
Low-technology manufactures	
Textile/fashion cluster	Textile fabrics, clothing, headgear, footwear, leather manufactures, travel goods
Other low technology	Pottery, simple metal parts/structures, furniture, jewellery, toys, plastic products
Medium-technology manufactures	
Automotive products	Passenger vehicles and parts, commercial vehicles, motorcycles and parts
Process industries	Synthetic fibres, chemicals and paints, fertilizers, plastics, iron, pipes/tubes
Engineering industries	Engines, motors, industrial machinery, pumps, switchgear, ships, watches
High-technology manufactures	
Electronics and electrical products	Office/data processing/telecom equip, TVs, transistors, turbines, power generating equipment
Other high technology	Pharmaceuticals, aerospace, optical/measuring instruments, cameras
Other transactions	Electricity, cinema film, printed matter, ‘special’ transactions, gold, art, coins, pets

scale-intensive technologies in capital goods and intermediates. They generally have complex technologies, with moderately high levels of R&D, and advanced skill needs. Most require lengthy learning periods and considerable interaction between firms to reach 'best practice' technical efficiency. We divide them into three sub-groups. *Automotive* products are of particular export interest to newly industrializing countries. *Process industries*, mainly chemicals and basic metals, are different in their technological features from *engineering products*. The former tends to have stable and undifferentiated products and to stress the control and optimization of complex processes. The latter two, mainly machinery manufactures, emphasizes product design and development as well as supplier and subcontractor networks. Barriers to entry tend to be high where there are large capital needs or strong learning effects in operation, design, and product development. The relocation of labour-intensive processes to low-wage areas is possible but not as widespread as in low-technology activities: products are heavy and technological capabilities are needed to meet world standards.

- *High technology* (HT) products have advanced and fast-moving technologies, with high R&D requirements and an emphasis on product innovation. Many technologies require advanced technology infrastructures and close interactions between firms, and between firms and research institutions. However, certain electronic products have labour-intensive final assembly; their high value-to-weight ratios make it economical to relocate these processes in low-wage areas. We separate high technology *electronic and electrical* products from *other high-tech* products, like aircraft, precision instruments, and pharmaceuticals that tend to be rooted in economies with highly developed skills, technology and supplier networks.

Global Trends

Table 2.2 shows the global trends in exports. The main features are as follows:

- World exports growth was anaemic in 1980–85, a consequence of the second oil shock, followed by five years of rapid expansion and then a slowing down. Manufactured products drove growth throughout the period. *Primary products lost their share of world exports by over one-half over the period.* There was a sharp fall in the growth rate of manufactured exports in 1995, which persisted till 1997, and hit East Asia particularly hard.
- Of the broad technological categories, the *fastest growing set was*

Table 2.2 Growth and distribution of world exports, 1980-97

	Rates of growth (% pa)					Percentage distribution		
	1980–85	1985–90	1990–95	1995–97	1980–97	1980	1990	1995
Total exports	1.3	12.7	9.1	2.3	7.0	100	100	100
Primary products	1.1	1.0	5.3	1.5	2.3	23.0	13.1	11.0
Manufactures	1.6	15.2	9.4	2.9	7.9	73.7	83.4	85.5
Manufactured products								
Resource-based	−0.2	12.3	7.4	1.1	5.7	24.4	19.7	17.9
Agro/forest based	−1.1	14.0	8.9	−1.5	6.1	7.4	6.2	6.1
Other resource based	0.2	11.6	6.6	2.4	5.6	17.0	13.5	11.9
Low technology	0.9	16.5	9.3	0.8	7.8	19.3	19.8	19.7
Textile, clothing, footwear	2.5	17.0	8.7	2.1	8.4	7.8	8.9	8.6
Other low-tech	−0.2	16.2	9.7	−0.3	7.3	11.5	11.0	11.1
Medium technology	1.5	15.0	8.4	2.0	7.4	41.9	41.4	39.5
Automotive	4.7	14.1	7.5	4.2	8.2	10.9	12.0	11.1
Process	0.3	14.6	9.7	−0.6	6.9	10.4	9.5	9.6
Engineering	0.3	15.8	8.3	2.1	7.2	20.5	19.8	18.8
High technology	5.4	17.5	13.3	7.5	11.4	14.4	19.2	22.9
Electronic/electrical	7.4	18.8	15.6	6.7	13.0	8.5	13.1	17.3
Other high-tech	2.3	15.0	7.5	10.0	8.4	5.9	6.0	5.5

Note: Special transactions like electric power, art works, gold bullion, miscellaneous transactions and so on are not shown here.

Source: Calculated by Lall from Comtrade database.

high-technology products, with a rate double that of the *slowest growing, resource-based products*. High-tech exports maintained their growth best in the recession periods in the early 1980s and mid-1990s. Of the 50 most dynamic products in world manufactured trade in 1985–95, the largest share in 1995 (47 per cent) came from HT products, most of them electronics. These 50 products accounted for about 40 per cent of total manufactured exports.

- Low and medium-technology products grew at fairly similar rates over the period. Medium-technology products dominated world trade, and, despite some slippage, remained at around 40 per cent of the total. Low-technology products kept around 20 per cent, while resource-based products were the main losers.
- In the narrower sub-categories of manufactured exports, electronics and electrical products had the highest growth over the whole period, and were the only set to maintain double-digit growth rates during 1990–95. At the other end, both groups of RB products had the lowest rates. In low-technology products, the textile cluster did somewhat better than other products, which were worse hit in the 1995 slowdown. In the MT group, the best overall performer was the automotive industry, largely because of the massive expansion of Latin American auto exports since 1985, mainly from Mexico to the USA and Brazil and Argentina within the Mercosur.
- Export growth reflects a mixture of *innovation* (raising final demand and the competitive position of innovative products) and *relocation* of production from high to low-cost sites. Low-technology products grew because of the latter, high-tech products because of the former *and* the latter.

How did the developing world fare? Table 2.3 shows export growth and shares for industrial and developing countries. Developing countries have uniformly higher growth rates, which is to be expected given their smaller initial base. However, what is less expected is that their lead rises with technological complexity. According to received theory, the comparative advantage of developing countries lies in technologically simple activities. Are the data a statistical artefact, reflecting the relocation by MNCs of simple processes in high-technology industries? Or do they reflect genuine local capabilities, which imply considerable skill formation and technical effort? The explanation is a mixture. A significant part of the growth of high-tech exports reflects the spread of low-technology assembly. At the same time, such assembly in the developing world is highly concentrated, so that the figures reflect the success of a few countries. Among these, there are two groups. First are those that depend almost wholly on TNCs to export

Table 2.3 Growth and shares of manufactured exports by technological categories and country groups

	Growth rates 1980–97 (% p.a.)				Developing country shares (%)		
	World	Industrialized countries	Developing countries	Difference: Developing–Industrialized	1985	1995	Change in share
All exports	7.0	6.5	8.5	2.0	25.0	26.9	1.9
RB	5.7	5.1	8.1	3.0	22.4	24.0	1.6
Agro-based	6.1	5.6	7.8	2.2	22.0	23.8	1.8
Other RB	5.6	4.9	8.3	3.4	22.6	24.0	1.5
Low-tech	7.8	6.2	12.4	6.2	25.8	37.0	11.2
Textile cluster	8.4	6.3	11.9	5.6	38.7	50.8	12.1
Other LT	7.3	6.2	13.5	7.3	15.7	26.5	10.8
Medium-tech	7.4	6.6	16.4	9.8	7.4	16.8	9.4
Auto	8.2	7.5	22.3	14.8	2.4	9.6	7.2
Process	6.9	5.8	15.7	9.9	10.5	23.3	12.8
Engineering	7.2	6.4	15.3	8.9	9.0	17.7	8.7
High-tech	11.4	9.8	21.2	11.4	10.2	27.1	16.9
Electronic	13.0	10.9	21.7	10.8	13.4	33.1	19.7
Other HT	8.4	7.9	17.3	9.4	4.3	8.3	4.0
Total manufactures	7.9	6.8	13.5	6.5	14.7	24.0	9.3

Notes: Industrialized countries include Israel and Central and Eastern Europe. Developing countries include Turkey and South Africa.

Source: As Table 2.2.

sophisticated products as part of integrated global production; these include Malaysia, Thailand, the Philippines, Mexico and China. Second, there are a few that have built up competitive capabilities in domestic enterprises and spawned their own international networks, led by Korea and Taiwan.

African Performance

Table 2.4 shows the regional breakdown by technological categories for six

Table 2.4 Shares of regions in developing world exports by major categories

	1985	1990	1995
Total manufactures			
East Asia	66.5	74.0	75.3
South Asia	5.2	5.0	3.7
LAC	19.4	13.9	15.2
MENA	4.9	4.6	3.6
SSA1	1.2	0.8	0.5
SSA2	4.0	2.5	2.2
Resource-based			
East Asia	44.6	51.7	53.3
South Asia	5.0	5.6	5.3
LAC	33.8	25.3	27.8
MENA	10.1	12.3	7.5
SSA1	2.3	1.8	1.4
SSA2	6.6	5.1	6.1
Low technology			
East Asia	76.9	78.4	77.3
South Asia	8.9	8.7	7.3
LAC	10.0	8.0	9.4
MENA	2.2	3.0	4.6
SSA1	0.7	0.7	0.6
SSA2	2.1	1.9	1.5
Medium technology			
East Asia	72.3	73.9	73.3
South Asia	2.3	2.2	1.6
LAC	18.7	18.8	20.2
MENA	3.1	2.7	2.8
SSA1	0.8	0.6	0.3
SSA2	3.6	2.3	2.1
High technology			
East Asia	90.1	94.2	90.5
South Asia	1.2	1.1	0.6
LAC	5.8	4.1	8.0
MENA	0.7	0.3	0.6
SSA1	0.2	0.1	0.0
SSA2	2.2	0.4	0.3

Note: LAC stands for Latin America and the Caribbean; MENA for North Africa and the Middle East (including Turkey but excluding Israel, which is counted as part of the industrial world); SSA stands for Sub-Saharan Africa; SSA1 excludes South Africa, SSA2 includes it.

Source: As Table 2.2.

regions: Sub-Saharan Africa with and without South Africa, East Asia, South Asia, Latin America, Middle East and North Africa. There is a surprising degree of regional concentration. East Asia dominates all categories, its dominance rising over time and by 1995 reaching three-quarters of total manufactured exports by developing countries. Its share is lowest in the RB category, but even here its share is rising, reaching 53 per cent by 1995. Its largest share is in HT products, where it accounts for 90 per cent; however, this is a decline from 94 per cent in 1990, due to the rapid growth of such exports by Latin America. This is, in turn, due primarily to Mexican border *maquiladoras* and the advent of NAFTA; the rest of Latin America has done relatively poorly in HT products.

Sub-Saharan Africa without South Africa is practically absent from the manufactured export scene, with the minor exception of RB products. Over

Table 2.5 Shares of primary products in total exports (percentages)

	1980	1985	1990	1997
World	24.3	19.5	15.4	12.1
All developing	58.3	54.8	28.6	19.1
SSA2*	68.5	67.2	70.4	43.9
E. Asia	29.0	24.6	13.4	8.3
S. Asia	34.1	31.2	20.6	18.0
MENA	94.2	94.0	70.6	60.3
LAC	56.4	47.6	50.8	31.7
Kenya	45.9	64.1	47.5	52.8
Tanzania	89.0	81.4	82.6	82.6
Uganda	94.9	99.1	99.0	99.5
Ghana	82.5	77.2	72.5	N/A
Zimbabwe	N/A	60.4	59.6	55.3
South Africa	14.6	37.8	18.7	17.0
Egypt	79.1	74.7	44.3	31.4
India	32.3	28.9	19.9	20.0
China	N/A	60.8	20.6	9.5
Korea	6.2	3.9	3.4	2.7
Malaysia	52.3	44.6	25.5	11.0
Thailand	61.6	47.3	23.7	15.1

Note: *Excluding South Africa but including Mauritius.

Source: As Table 2.2.

time, it loses world market shares in every category. The dynamics of export growth and its technological upgrading are completely bypassing the region. One indicator of technological slack is the *share of primary products* in total exports. Table 2.5 shows how these products dominate African exports. Apart from the Middle East and North Africa, with its huge oil-exporting base, Africa is the region with the highest reliance on primary products. At the other extreme is East Asia, with the share falling from 29 to 8 per cent over 1980–97. Latin America lies in between, with a clear declining trend. While the 1997 figure suggests a sharp decline in African reliance on primary products since 1990, this is an illusion. Many African countries did not file data with the UN on exports in that year, and the total is distorted by the inclusion of Mauritius, whose manufactured exports have grown rapidly and which accounts for over half of manufactured exports by the region. If this is corrected for, the extent of reliance on primary products is likely to be constant (or higher, since liberalization has stimulated primary exports). In general, therefore, Africa has been unable to break the traditional mould of specialization in unprocessed materials, the slowest growing segment of world trade that also offers least by way of structural, entrepreneurial, skill and technology upgrading.

Case Study Countries

At the country level, the five countries studied here, led by Uganda, show the preponderance of primary exports. There is little change in this trend over 1980-97, when other countries show sharp declines. South Africa is a partial exception, as its share is relatively low through the period. China, the largest exporter in the developing world, reduces the share from 61 per cent in 1985 to below 10 per cent in 1997.

The value and structure of manufactured exports show technological strengths more directly. Table 2.6 gives the data for the case study and comparator countries, as well as for the main regions for the early 1980s and the late 1990s (Ghana data are not available for the latter period). Several interesting facts emerge from this evidence.

- World trade has shifted strongly from resource-based to technology-based products. East Asia shows this trend most strongly among the regions, with a higher share for HT products than even the industrialized world. Sub-Saharan Africa has the lowest share for high-technology, and the highest for resource-based, manufactures. While the African share of resource-based exports has come down sharply since 1980, with strong growth in labour-intensive manufactured exports, this is largely the result of Mauritian performance. The

Table 2.6 Manufactured exports, values and structure, SSA and selected developing countries ($ million)

	1980/81					1996/97				
	Total	RB	LT	MT	HT	Total	RB	LT	MT	HT
Kenya	706.7	606.0	58.0	31.0	11.8	913.1	519.5	257.0	103.5	33.2
Tanzania	56.7	38.4	14.5	1.9	1.9	99.1	71.1	19.1	2.2	6.7
Uganda	12.0	9.9	0.1	1.8	0.2	29.4	5.1	12.7	9.0	2.6
Ghana	144.3	135.4	3.0	2.6	3.2	N/A	N/A	N/A	N/A	N/A
Zimbabwe 1985 and 1998	360.5	97.2	84.4	173.6	5.3	873.6	336.7	229.2	290.3	17.4
South Africa	6 490.4	4 059.6	1 096.0	1 224.3	110.5	15 907.7	7 930.2	2 730.8	4 294.2	952.5
Egypt	666.3	400.1	252.3	9.0	4.9	2 669.2	1 343.3	1 048.7	215.5	61.7
India	4 901.9	1 431.3	2489.9	779.5	201.1	27 178.4	8 201.1	13 227.5	3 956.2	1 793.6
China	N/A	N/A	N/A	N/A	N/A	164 209.3	17 979.6	84 998.2	32 593.3	28 638.1
Korea	16 314.5	2 156.7	8 124.0	4 286.8	1 746.9	126 053.3	13 798.7	25 568.9	49 111.0	37 574.8
Malaysia	6 121.3	3 943.5	432.0	462.8	1 283.0	68 995.2	12 393.9	7 693.0	13 718.3	35 189.9
Thailand	2 258.4	944.5	709.7	564.6	39.7	47 190.4	9 127.9	11 961.5	9 662.8	16 438.2
			Distribution (%)							
Kenya	100	85.8	8.2	4.4	1.7	100	56.9	28.1	11.3	3.6
Tanzania	100	67.7	25.7	3.3	3.3	100	71.7	19.3	2.2	6.8
Uganda	100	82.7	1.1	14.7	1.6	100	17.3	43.2	30.6	8.8
Ghana	100	93.9	2.0	1.8	2.2	N/A	N/A	N/A	N/A	N/A
Zimbabwe 1985 and 1998	100	27.0	23.4	48.1	1.5	100	38.5	26.2	33.2	2.0

Table 2.6 Continued overleaf

Table 2.6 Continued

South Africa	100	62.5	16.9	18.9	1.7	100	49.9	17.2	27.0	6.0
Egypt	100	60.0	37.9	1.3	0.7	100	50.3	39.3	8.1	2.3
India	100	29.2	50.8	15.9	4.1	100	30.2	48.7	14.6	6.6
China	N/A	N/A	N/A	N/A	N/A	100	10.9	51.8	19.8	17.4
Korea	100	13.2	49.8	26.3	10.7	100	10.9	20.3	39.0	29.8
Malaysia	100	64.4	7.1	7.6	21.0	100	18.0	11.2	19.9	51.0
Thailand	100	41.8	31.4	25.0	1.8	100	19.3	25.3	20.5	34.8
		Memo item: distribution by regions (%)								
World	100	25.4	18.8	41.9	13.9	100	18.4	18.6	39.0	24.1
Industrialized	100	22.6	17.8	44.6	15.0	100	17.2	16.1	43.0	23.7
All developing	100	40.9	32.5	17.0	9.5	100	17.8	27.6	25.7	28.9
SSA2	100	89.3	6.3	3.0	1.4	100	40.8	44.2	13.0	1.9
East Asia	100	30.5	37.7	19.1	12.8	100	13.1	28.2	23.9	34.7
South Asia	100	31.0	52.0	13.6	3.4	100	24.0	57.4	13.4	5.2
Latin America	100	71.9	15.6	10.2	2.2	100	27.6	18.7	37.3	16.5
MENA	100	75.9	11.6	11.8	0.7	100	36.5	36.9	22.3	4.3

Source: As Table 2.2, and national sources for Uganda.

remainder of the region remains heavily dependent on slow-growing resource-based exports.

- The African countries in this study are tiny exporters of manufactures and their performance has been weak over time (Table 2.7). Zimbabwe is the only country that recorded significant growth rates over a decade. Liberalization has not sparked off growth or diversification in manufactured exports. While there are exceptions at the enterprise level in Africa (Wangwe, 1995), there is none of the vigour and dynamism seen in many other regions. More recent data are not reassuring.

Table 2.7 Manufactured export growth rates, 1980/81 to 1996/97

	Total	RB	LT	MT	HT
Kenya	1.6	−1.0	9.8	7.8	6.7
Tanzania	3.6	3.9	1.7	0.9	8.2
Uganda	5.8	−4.1	35.4	10.6	17.4
Zimbabwe 1985–98	5.7	8.1	6.4	3.3	7.7

Source: Calculated from Comtrade database.

- In terms of export structure, Tanzania is overwhelmingly specialized in resource-based products, and it has further strengthened its specialization in the last decade. Kenya, with a larger manufacturing base, has a more diverse export structure, but with a dominance of resource-based products. Its medium-technology exports are likely to be simple engineering products to neighbouring countries, while high-tech exports are re-exports (for instance, of pharmaceuticals where local production has been displaced by import and marketing of products made elsewhere) rather than domestic manufacture. The Uganda figures show some promising sign of structural change, but the values involved are so low, with total manufactured exports of under $30 million, that it is premature to think of structural propensities. Zimbabwe has always had the most diversified export structure among the sample countries. However, its share of RB exports has recently risen to replace MT exports.

Implications

World trade is increasingly technology driven, but innovation is not the main engine of export growth for the developing world. How can we explain such divergent export performances across the developing world? Much of the recent success recorded by some developing countries is due to the relocation of simple processes, in both high and low-technology activities, from high to low-wage countries. There has certainly been enormous upgrading of technologies in the latter: export competitiveness could not grow unless there was a matching rise in the ability to manufacture to international standards, albeit with technologies from the industrial countries. However, different products have very different technological needs, and there are different ways to access, use and build upon foreign technologies. The developing world displays a range of different strategies. We may distinguish four broad strategies for building technological competitiveness in manufacturing, mainly drawing on examples from Asia and Latin America (Lall, 1998):

- *Strategic FDI dependent*, driven by FDI and exports to MNC global networks. There was strong effort to upgrade MNC activity according to strategic priorities, directing investments into higher value added activities and inducing existing affiliates to upgrade their technologies and functions. This strategy involved extensive interventions in factor markets (skill creation, institution building, infrastructure development and supplier support), encouraging R&D and technology institutions, and in attracting, targeting and guiding investments. The best example is Singapore.
- *Passive FDI dependent*, also driven by FDI but relying largely on market forces to attract FDI and to upgrade the structure over time. The main determinants have been a welcoming FDI regime, strong incentives for exports, with good export infrastructure, and cheap, disciplined and trainable labour. There are two sub-groups here. The first is a small handful of countries that were able to attract FDI into export-oriented assembly of high-technology products, mainly electronics (for example, Malaysia, Thailand, Philippines and the *maquiladoras* of Mexico). The second is a larger, but still limited, group of countries that attracted FDI into the assembly of simple consumer goods, led by clothing and footwear and strongly influenced by the availability of export quotas under the Multi-Fibre Agreement. This group includes countries like Bangladesh, Sri Lanka, Mauritius, Morocco and some Caribbean economies. Over the years, the high-technology assembly group has shown much greater upgrading of export capabilities than the latter. With rising wages, low-technology assembly has tended to move on to other locations, while high-technology assembly has moved into more capital and skill-intensive processes. Moreover, the latter has led to more diversification, as electronics assembly has attracted suppliers and related products; the

skills created have had wide applications. In contrast, garment or footwear assembly has been relatively self-contained, with less learning or technological spillovers to other activities; however, it did lead to a blossoming of domestic entrepreneurship in simple export-oriented activities. A large part of garment exports from developing countries is now made by domestic enterprises. Both FDI dependent strategies face sustainability problems, the high-tech one in building the set of advanced skills and supply capabilities needed to deepen and localize TNC activity, the low-tech one in moving into more complex activities as they lose wage competitiveness.

- *Autonomous*, based on the development of technological and marketing capabilities in domestic firms, starting in simple activities and deepening over time. This strategy entailed extensive industrial policy, reaching into trade, finance, education, training, technology and industrial structure. It also involved selective restrictions on FDI with technology imports encouraged in other forms. The interventions were carried out in a strongly export-oriented trade regime, with favours conditional upon good export performance. The prime examples are Korea and Taiwan.
- *ISI restructuring*, with exports growing from established import-substituting industries where competitive (or nearly competitive) capabilities existed. The main stimulant to export growth was trade liberalization (sometimes within regional trade agreements), that led to considerable investment in upgrading, restructuring and expansion. In some countries the main agents were domestic enterprises, in others TNCs. The main difference from the 'autonomous' strategy was the lack of clear and coordinated industrial policy to develop export competitiveness, with haphazard (or weak) support for skills, technology, institutions and infrastructure. China, India and the large Latin American economies are good examples, but elements of this strategy are present in many other economies.

These strategies are not 'pure' types; most economies have a mixture. In technological terms, the main issue is to combine rapid access to new technology with the ability to use it effectively for global markets (Pietrobelli, 2000). Most new entrants – without large import substitution industrial sectors or the ability to mount the comprehensive industrial policies of Korea and Taiwan – have relied on the 'passive FDI dependent' route. However, sustaining competitiveness with all strategies has required policies to build technological capabilities locally, within TNC affiliates, local firms and related institutions.

What are the implications for Sub-Saharan Africa? SSA has been 'out of the loop' of all the strategies to build technological competitiveness. It has attracted little FDI into activities that stimulate technological learning; the boom in low-wage export-oriented FDI has so far passed the region by (Mauritius is the exception). It has not been able to devise or mount coherent industrial policies (Soludo, 1998), and its import substituting industries have not developed the minimal base to react competitively to trade liberalization. The dismal showing of the region on the world trade scene is a reflection of these policy failures.

INDUSTRIAL PERFORMANCE

Table 2.8 shows manufacturing value added (MVA) and one indicator of technological complexity: the share of capital goods (machinery and transport equipment) in MVA. Manufacturing contributes 10 per cent or less to national income in four of the five sample countries, which is very low by developing country standards. In Kenya and Tanzania the share has declined over time while in Ghana it has practically stagnated. In Zimbabwe manufacturing is more important, but there has been a fall in the MVA share from 21.6 per cent in 1980 to 17.7 per cent in 1997. The rise in Uganda reflects the very adverse conditions in the base year; capacity utilization even by 1999 had not reached its earlier peak. Growth rates of MVA are also anaemic in the case study countries (Uganda shows high rates because of the low base), as in Zimbabwe and South Africa. Per capita MVA figures confirm the low level of industrialization in the five countries. Only Zimbabwe has larger figures, but much smaller than in the East Asian tigers. Its evolution is especially worrying. While in 1980, $197.5 per capita was a satisfactory figure by developing country standards (higher than in China or Thailand), in 1996 $119.7 was a much smaller figure in relative terms. During this period, Thailand increased its level of per capita MVA fivefold, and China threefold.

These data suggest that technological capabilities, which largely explain the dynamism of the manufacturing sector, were also relatively low and stagnant. The figures on the share of capital goods in MVA strengthen this interpretation. It is generally accepted that the capital goods sector is the leading hub of innovation and the main source of diffusion of new technologies to other industries. Not only is the share very low, but it has declined in most case study countries. The contrast with Asia is striking.

Table 2.8 *Manufacturing value added in case study and comparator countries*

	Share of MVA in GDP		MVA value ($ m.)		Growth (%)	MVA per capita ($)		Growth (%)	Equipment % MVA	
	1980	1997	1980	1997	1980–96	1980	1997	1980–96	1980	1995
Kenya	12.8	10.1	796	883	0.3	47.8	30.8	−2.5	14.7	10
Tanzania	8.1	7.3	555	392	−3.1	15.9	12.9	−5.9	7.7	6
Uganda	4.3	8.2	53	489	12.7	4.1	24.0	9.7	2.5	-
Ghana	7.8	9.1	347	623	3.4	32.3	34.6	0.3	1.9	2.3
Zimbabwe	21.6	17.7	1 385	1 373	0.1	197.5	119.7	−2.7	8.2	11.2
South Africa	23	24	16 607	27 489	3.4	602.2	677.0	1.7	21	20
India	18	19	27 376	67 492	4.8	39.8	70.1	2.7	25	25
China	41	37	81 836	336 136	7.6	83.4	273.9	6.1	22	25
Korea	29	26	17 686	113 696	12.6	463.9	2 472.1	9.0	17	41
Malaysia	21	34	5 054	34 030	11.2	367.2	1 610.6	8.4	20	40
Thailand	22	29	6 960	44 379	12.8	149.0	732.3	11.1	9	8

Note: * Nearest year when given year is not available.

Sources: World Bank, *World Development Indicators 1999*, Washington DC; UNIDO, *Industrial Development Global Report 1997*, Vienna.

THE HUMAN CAPITAL BASE

Regional Educational Enrolment Rates

The links between skills and technological activity are close and intense. With the pace of technical change, the spread of information technologies and intensifying global competition, skill needs are growing and changing. Traditional methods of education and training often prove inadequate, even in developed countries; in developing countries the gaps between skill needs and provision are greater. Traditionally, industrial development required simply improving the quantity and quality of primary schooling and basic technical education and encouraging *all* in-firm training. In the new competitive setting, this is inadequate. There has to be greater emphasis on high-level and specialized training, with close interaction between education and industry to assess and communicate evolving needs. The greatest need is to create information technology-based cognitive skills (Bresnahan et al., 1999).

Comparisons of skill systems across countries are difficult, since skills arise in many different ways. The most convenient measure is enrolment at the three general levels (primary, secondary and tertiary) of formal education. However, there are significant differences in quality, completion rates and relevance of education that cannot be corrected for. Moreover, enrolment data ignore on-the-job and other forms of training. More importantly, they ignore experience-based learning from handling and mastering new technologies. Nevertheless, general education enrolment data are the only information available on a comparable basis, and they are relevant to the extent that they show the national base for *absorbing* skills at all levels. Let us consider the evidence.

Table 2.9 shows average (unweighted) enrolment at the main levels as shares of the relevant age group over 1980–95.[4] Enrolment rates in all regions have risen over the period, but there remain large disparities. Sub-Saharan Africa (including South Africa for this purpose) lags at all - particularly the tertiary - levels and the gap appears to increase over time. The four mature Tiger economies of Asia lead the developing world at higher levels, slightly lagging behind the developed economies. The four new Tigers, Latin America and MENA are roughly similar in their secondary and tertiary level enrolments, just behind the levels reached in the transition economies. South Asia and China have low levels of tertiary enrolment, but China is considerably stronger at the secondary level. To the extent that these simple indicators of skill formation are valid, they show large gaps in the education base for competitiveness.[5]

Tertiary enrolments in technical subjects are more relevant for assessing high-level capabilities to absorb technological knowledge. Table 2.10 shows

Table 2.9 Enrolment ratios (average, unweighted, as percentage of age groups)

	Enrolment ratios (1980)			Enrolment ratios (1995)		
	1 level	2 level	3 level	1 level	2 level	3 level
Developing countries	**88**	**34**	**7**	**91**	**44**	**11**
Sub-Saharan Africa	**74**	**17**	**1.3**	**78**	**23**	**2.9**
MENA	88	42	9.7	92	59	14.3
Latin America	102	45	14.1	103	53	18.1
Asia	95	44	7.4	99	54	14.4
4 Tigers *	106	72	13.0	100	82	36.4
4 new Tigers **	103	43	12.3	102	60	17.3
S. Asia	75	28	4.0	93	42	4.8
China	112	46	1.3	120	69	5.7
Others	96	37	3.7	98	35	5.9
Transition economies	100	77	14.6	95	76	22.2
Developed economies	**102**	**84**	**27.2**	**104**	**113**	**50.6**
Europe	101	82	24.5	104	113	44.6
N America	101	91	49.1	102	102	92.0
Japan	101	93	30.5	102	99	40.3
Australia, N Zealand	111	84	27.0	106	132	65.0

Note: * Hong Kong, Korea, Singapore, Taiwan Province; ** Indonesia, Malaysia, Thailand, the Philippines

Source: Calculated from UNESCO, *Statistical Yearbooks*, various.

the total numbers enrolled in tertiary education and in the three main technical subjects (science, mathematics/computing and engineering) by region in 1995. This time we use population (not the relevant age group) to weight regional averages. There is much wider dispersion in skill creation than the general enrolment rates. The Asian NIEs enrol over 33 times the proportion of their population in technical subjects than in Sub-Saharan Africa (again including South Africa). The ratio is twice that of industrial countries, nearly five times Latin America and the new NIEs, and over 10 times South Asia and China.

The leading three countries in terms of total technical enrolments – China (18 per cent), India (16 per cent) and Korea (11 per cent) – account for 44 per cent of the developing world's technical enrolments, the top ten for 76 per cent and the top 20 for 93 per cent. *Engineering enrolments* in the developing world are also highly concentrated, but the leaders differ. China continues to lead, accounting by itself for 23 per cent of the developing world's total

Table 2.10 Tertiary level enrolments and enrolments in technical subjects, 1995

	3 level enrolment		Technical enrolments, numbers and % of population							
	Total no. students	% pop.	Natural Science numbers	%	Maths, computing numbers	%	Engineering numbers	%	All technical subjects numbers	%
Developing countries	**35 345 800**	**0.82**	**2 046 566**	**0.05**	**780 930**	**0.02**	**4 194 433**	**0.10**	**7 021 929**	**0.16**
Sub-Saharan Africa	**1 542 700**	**0.28**	**111 500**	**0.02**	**39 330**	**0.01**	**69 830**	**0.01**	**220 660**	**0.04**
MENA	4 571 900	1.26	209 065	0.06	114 200	0.03	489 302	0.14	812 567	0.22
Latin America	7 677 800	1.64	212 901	0.05	188 800	0.04	1 002 701	0.21	1 404 402	0.30
Asia	21 553 400	0.72	1 513 100	0.05	438 600	0.01	2 632 600	0.09	4 584 300	0.15
4 Tigers	3 031 400	4.00	195 200	0.26	34 200	0.05	786 100	1.04	1 015 500	1.34
4 new Tigers	5 547 900	1.61	83 600	0.02	280 700	0.08	591 000	0.17	955 300	0.28
S Asia	6 545 800	0.54	996 200	0.08	7 800	0.00	272 600	0.02	1 276 600	0.10
China	5 826 600	0.60	167 700	0.02	99 400	0.01	971 000	0.10	1 238 100	0.13
Others	601 700	0.46	70 400	0.05	16 500	0.01	11 900	0.01	98 800	0.08
Transition economies	2 025 800	1.95	55 500	0.05	30 600	0.03	354 700	0.34	440 800	0.42
Developed economies	**33 774 800**	**4.06**	**1 509 334**	**0.18**	**1 053 913**	**0.13**	**3 191 172**	**0.38**	**5 754 419**	**0.69**
Europe	12 297 400	3.17	876 734	0.23	448 113	0.12	1 363 772	0.35	2 688 619	0.69
N America	16 430 800	5.54	543 600	0.18	577 900	0.19	904 600	0.31	2 026 100	0.68
Japan	3 917 700	0.49					805 800	0.10	805 800	0.10
Australia NZ	1 128 900	5.27	89 000	0.42	27 900	0.13	117 000	0.55	233 900	1.09

Source: Calculated from UNESCO (1997) and national sources.

enrolments. It is followed by Korea (14 per cent) and Mexico (7 per cent); these three account for 44 per cent of the total. India drops to sixth place, after these three, Indonesia and Philippines. The top ten account for 78 per cent and the top 20 for 94 per cent.

Sub-Saharan Africa accounts for 4.4 per cent of the developing world's total tertiary, 3.1 per cent of technical tertiary, and 1.7 per cent of engineering enrolments, while containing about 12 per cent of its population. The total numbers of engineers enrolled in the whole of Africa (about 70 000) are only 12 per cent of the numbers enrolled in Korea by itself (577 000). The spectacular industrial and competitive development of Korea owes in large part to its enormous investments in creating technical manpower.

National Enrolment Rates

An instructive way to evaluate skills at the national level is to trace the evolution over time of an index of skills based on the classic work of Harbison and Myers (1964). These authors derived an index for skill levels (Harbison-Myers Index, HMI) for 65 countries, using data for 1957–58. Their index was based on secondary school enrolments plus tertiary enrolments multiplied by five (both as percentages of the age group); they stressed the secondary and tertiary levels, as they regarded these as most important for development.

Table 2.11 shows the countries covered by HMI ranked by skill levels in 1995 and 1957–58. The ranks and changes in position are interesting. The rich industrial countries hold the top 9 places. Of these, Canada, Finland and Norway improve their ranks significantly, while the UK and Netherlands deteriorate. The first developing country on the list is Korea, which improves its rank significantly. Taiwan comes next, with a slight improvement. Of the large countries, China and Brazil retain their previous ranks exactly, while Argentina, Mexico, India and Pakistan deteriorate. Of the new Tigers, Malaysia and Thailand remain at their original ranks, while Indonesia improves. A more detailed analysis of skill formation and rankings is given in Lall (1999b). Figure 2.2 shows the HMI scores for Sub-Saharan Africa, with the US and Korea as benchmarks. South Africa, as expected, leads SSA. Of the sample countries, Ghana leads and Tanzania brings up the rear (and ranks lowest in the region and in the world).

The five countries in this study are near the bottom, and each deteriorates over time. Only Zimbabwe marginally improves its ranking, and is the second highest ranked African country after South Africa. Figure 2.3 shows enrolment rates in SSA with Korea and USA as benchmarks. The skill gaps faced by the region appear strikingly clear in these charts. Of the five case study countries, Tanzania comes last by both measures. Zimbabwe does best in both measures, and records a fourth and a third place respectively in SSA.

Table 2.11 Harbison-Myers Index (HMI) ranks, 1995 and 1957–58

1995		1957–58	1995		1957–58	1995		1957–58
1	Canada	9	23	Argentina	14	45	Malaysia	45
2	Australia	3	24	Poland	20	46	Indonesia	53
3	USA	1	25	Peru	37	47	Brazil	47
4	Finland	11	26	Uruguay	18	48	China	48
5	N. Zealand	2	27	Lebanon	44	49	Jamaica	39
6	Belgium	5	28	Chile	27	50	Paraguay	45
7	Norway	17	29	Costa Rica	29	51	Zimbabwe	60
8	Netherlands	4	30	Czech	19	52	India	34
9	UK	6	31	Hungary	25	53	Congo	59
10	Korea	23	32	S Africa	31	54	Myanmar	52
11	France	8	33	Yugoslavia	21	55	Nigeria	57
12	Spain	32	34	Egypt	30	56	Côte d'Ivoire	61
13	Sweden	15	35	Thailand	35	57	Ghana	46
14	Denmark	16	36	Colombia	46	58	Pakistan	42
15	Germany	12	37	Ecuador	43	59	Senegal	56
16	Russia	10	38	Bolivia	51	60	Kenya	58
17	Japan	7	39	Turkey	38	61	Afghanistan	64
18	Italy	22	40	Cuba	33	62	Sudan	54
19	Greece	26	41	Iran	49	63	Uganda	55
20	Israel	13	42	S Arabia	63	64	Ethiopia	65
21	Taiwan	24	43	Mexico	36	65	Tanzania	62
22	Portugal	28	44	Tunisia	50			

Source: Calculated from UNESCO (1997) and national sources.

Comparing Figure 2.2 to Figure 2.3 shows how Ghana does better in HMI, but very poorly in tertiary technical enrolments. While it used to fare much better than all African countries (except for South Africa) in 1957–58, its slide back has been remarkable in 1995. Kenya does better in technical enrolment ratios. In general, however, all do poorly in the global scene.

A recent paper analyses the impact of skills on productivity in Ghana, Kenya and Zimbabwe (Pack and Paxson, 2001). It finds that most firms have little involvement in world markets and import little technology (see below). Managerial skills are found to have no significant impact on costs. This may seem surprising in view of the overall skill constraints in these economies, but may be explained by the protected regimes and other constraints to productivity, such as infrastructure, uncertainty, and high business costs. As

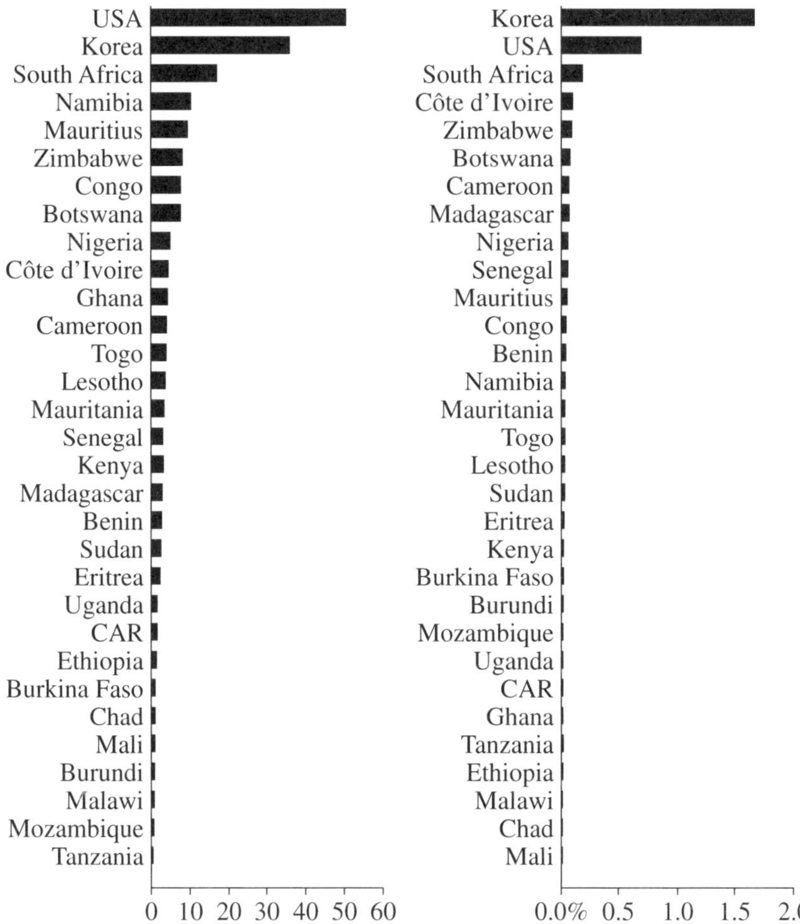

Figure 2.2 Skill indices (HMI), 1995

Figure 2.3 Tertiary technical enrolments, 1995 (% pop)

the authors conclude, 'in non-competitive industrial sectors with very little inflow of new technology, the contribution of technological abilities, however measured, is limited'.

Wage Costs

African countries have long had high wages compared to other developing countries. This was partly due to natural resource endowments (when these yielded high income) and partly to high salaries paid by governments. In

Table 2.12 Hourly labour costs in the apparel industry, 1990–95

	Country	1990	US$ 1993	1995	Annual growth (%)
1	Switzerland	14.19	18.08	22.42	9.6
2	Japan	6.34	10.64	20.95	27.0
3	Germany	7.23	17.22	20.35	23.0
4	Italy	12.50	12.31	13.68	1.8
5	USA	6.56	8.13	9.62	8.0
6	Spain	7.08	6.41	7.78	1.9
7	Greece	4.33	5.85	7.19	10.7
8	Taiwan	3.41	4.61	5.18	8.7
9	Hong Kong	3.05	3.85	4.32	7.2
10	Singapore	2.43	3.06	4.01	10.5
11	Portugal	2.30	3.03	3.85	10.9
12	Korea	2.46	2.71	3.29	6.0
13	Costa Rica	1.09	1.08	2.23	15.4
14	Hungary	0.92	1.62	1.68	12.8
15	Mexico	0.92	1.08	1.61	11.8
16	Malaysia	0.56	0.77	1.59	23.2
17	South Africa	1.07	1.12	1.58	8.1
18	Czech Rep	2.79	1.29	1.55	−11.1
19	Jamaica	0.91	0.78	1.55	11.2
20	Turkey	1.35	3.29	1.52	2.4
21	Dominican Rep.	0.67	0.63	1.52	17.8
22	El Salvador	0.69	0.63	1.431	5.7
23	Poland	0.50	0.44	1.42	23.2
24	Guatemala	0.45	0.78	1.3	23.6
25	Mauritius	N/A	1.04	1.28	N/A
26	Morocco	0.92	1.06	1.22	5.8
27	Thailand	0.63	0.71	1.11	12.0
28	Philippines	0.46	0.53	0.72	9.4
29	Egypt	0.34	0.43	0.51	8.4
30	Zimbabwe	N/A	0.35	0.45	N/A
31	Sri Lanka	0.24	0.35	0.41	11.3
32	Kenya	0.47	0.23	0.34	−6.3
33	Indonesia	0.16	0.28	0.33	15.6
34	India	0.33	0.27	0.29	−2.6
35	Pakistan	0.24	0.27	0.29	3.9
36	Vietnam	N/A	0.26	0.29	N/A
37	China	0.26	0.25	0.25	−0.8
38	Nigeria	0.2	0.27	0.24	3.7
39	Bangladesh	N/A	0.16	0.20	N/A
40	Tanzania	N/A	0.18	N/A	N/A

Note: Costs include social and fringe benefits.

Source: *Apparel Hourly Labour Cost*, Werner International, New York (1996).

recent years, with decline and liberalization, wages in Africa have fallen. In many cases they are about the same as in low-income Asia.

A good indicator of relative wages for export-oriented activity is in *garment production*. Table 2.12 shows data for 1990–95 for 40 countries, including five from SSA, and three from our case studies. The data confirm that cheap labour should be a source of competitive advantage in Africa. The fact that it is *not* suggests that labour quality is low, complementary factors are lacking or political and policy factors are holding back its exploitation. In addition, low skill and productivity are clearly an important factor. For instance, Biggs and Ratauri (1997) find that in men's casual shirts, task level efficiency in Kenya was around 55–68 per cent, and in Ghana 55 per cent, of that of good Chinese firms. With such low levels of productivity, it is not surprising that the industry is being devastated by liberalization rather than leading export-oriented growth (Lall, 1999c).

TECHNOLOGICAL ACTIVITY

The normal measure of national technological activity is formal R&D as a share of national income. This can be misleading since it includes R&D in public institutions, often unrelated to productive sectors and particularly to manufacturing industry. A better measure is R&D financed by productive enterprises as a share of income; however, the available data suggest that by this measure all the five countries spend practically *nothing* on technological activity domestically. Table 2.13 gives regional figures for R&D expenditures and numbers of scientists and engineers employed in R&D across the world in 1995. Not unexpectedly, SSA lags well behind other developing regions.

Another measure of technology – at least of that part related to quality management, and that may serve as an approximate indicator of technological activities in developing countries – is the number of ISO 9000 certificates obtained by countries. Such certificates are given to service firms and institutions, not just manufacturers; nevertheless, they are a good indicator of competitiveness because they are particularly important for export activity. Table 2.14 shows the total number of certificates for African countries by the end of 1999. In spite of the recent increases, little more than 1 per cent of ISO 9000 certificates in the world were granted to SSA – including South Africa (ISO, 2000). Uganda does not appear in the ISO data, presumably because none of its enterprises had been certified by this date. Kenya ranks second and Zimbabwe third in the region after South Africa, in line with the rankings yielded by the trade, industry and skill indicators. All point to very low levels of technological capability by international standards in all the case study countries, but with Kenya ahead of the others, and Zimbabwe slightly behind.

Table 2.13 R&D propensities and manpower in major country groups (simple averages, latest year available)

Countries and regions[a]	Scientists/engineers in R&D		Total R&D (% of GNP)	Sector of performance (%)		Source of financing (% distribution)		Source of financing (% of GNP)	
	Per mill. population	Numbers		Productive sector	Higher education	Productive enterprises	Government	Productive enterprises	Productive sector
Industrialized market economies[b]	**1 102**	**2 704 205**	**1.94**	**53.7**	**22.9**	**53.5**	**38.0**	**1.037**	**1.043**
Developing economies[c]	**514**	**1 034 333**	**0.39**	**13.7**	**22.2**	**10.5**	**55.0**	**0.041**	**0.054**
Sub-Saharan Africa (exc. S Africa)	**83**	**3 193**	**0.28**	**0.0**	**38.7**	**0.6**	**60.9**	**0.002**	**0.000**
North Africa	423	29 675	0.40	N/A	N/A	N/A	N/A	N/A	N/A
Latin America & Caribbean	339	107 508	0.45	18.2	23.4	9.0	78.0	0.041	0.082
Asia (excluding Japan)	**783**	**893 957**	**0.72**	**32.1**	**25.8**	**33.9**	**57.9**	**0.244**	**0.231**
NIEs[d]	2 121	189 212	1.50	50.1	36.6	51.2	45.8	0.768	0.751
New NIEs[e]	121	18 492	0.20	27.7	15.0	38.7	46.5	0.077	0.055
S. Asia[f]	125	145 919	0.85	13.3	10.5	7.7	91.8	0.065	0.113
Middle East	296	50 528	0.47	9.7	45.9	11.0	51.0	0.051	0.045
China	350	422 700	0.50	31.9	13.7	N/A	N/A	N/A	0.160
European transition economies[g]	1 857	946 162	0.77	35.7	21.4	37.3	47.8	0.288	0.275
World (79-84 countries)	1 304	4 684 700	0.92	36.6	24.7	34.5	53.2	0.318	0.337

Notes: a. Only including countries with data, and with over 1 million inhabitants in 1995; b. USA, Canada, West Europe, Japan, Australia and N Zealand; c. Including Middle East oil states, Turkey, Israel, South Africa, and formerly socialist economies in Asia; d. Hong Kong, Korea, Singapore, Taiwan Province; e. Indonesia, Malaysia, Thailand, Philippines; f. India, Pakistan, Bangladesh, Nepal (g) Including Russian Federation.

Source: Calculated from UNESCO (1997).

Table 2.14 ISO Certificates at end 1999 in Africa and comparators

Country	ISO 9000	ISO 14000
	No. of certificates	
Sub-Saharan Africa		
Botswana	4	–
Cameroon	5	–
Congo	2	–
Côte d'Ivoire	8	–
Gabon	3	–
Ghana	3	–
Guinea	2	–
Kenya	419	–
Madagascar	1	–
Malawi	1	–
Mali	5	–
Mauritius	92	3
Mozambique	3	–
Namibia	19	1
Nigeria	20	–
Senegal	4	–
Seychelles	5	–
Sierra Leone	1	–
South Africa	3 316	82
Sudan	1	–
Swaziland	7	–
Tanzania	2	–
Zaire	1	–
Zambia	4	2
Zimbabwe	112	4
Total SSA	4 030	92
% of world total	1.17 %	0.65%
(excl. S. Africa)	714	82
Other developing countries		
India	5 200	111
Sri Lanka	82	–
China	15 109	222
Korea	11 533	309
Malaysia	1 921	117
Thailand	1 527	229
World total	343 643	14 106

Note: ISO9000 = Quality management system standards; ISO14000 = Environmental management system standards.

Source: ISO (2000)

The ISO 14000 certificates are primarily concerned with environmental management - what the organization does to eliminate harmful effects on the environment. Thus, they represent a further sophisticated form to measure technology - of a specific nature. According to this measure, the African lag is even more pronounced. By all these measures, the level of technological efforts in Africa is lower than in most developing countries, but with Zimbabwe ahead of the others, and Kenya slightly behind.

TECHNOLOGY INFLOWS: LICENSING, FDI AND CAPITAL GOODS

This section concludes the general background with data on technology inflows into the countries. The main forms of technology inflow recorded are in the form of licence payments (royalties and fees), FDI, and capital goods imports.

Licence Payments

As far as licence payments are concerned, (patchy) data collected by UNCTAD show that in 1997 the developing world as a whole paid $5.8 billion for imported technology. Sub-Saharan Africa as a whole, excluding South Africa, paid $84 million; of this, Kenya accounted for $39 million and Swaziland for another $39 million (South Africa spent $258 million). The other sample countries did not record any significant payments on this score, so it can be assumed that royalty and technical fee payments were very low. By comparison, Korea spent $2413 million, Thailand $813 million, India $150 million and China $543 million. Thus, licences are clearly not a major channel of foreign technology inflow into SSA.

There is considerable evidence that technology imports are very low in Africa (Lall, 1995; Lall, 1997c; Pack and Paxson, 2000). Liberalization does not seem to have raised the general propensity of firms to buy new technologies, though there are exceptions. This clearly implies that local technological capabilities are so far behind world frontiers that full exposure to liberalization leads most enterprises to withdraw rather than upgrade.

Foreign Direct Investment

Table 2.15 shows FDI inflows by region and into the least developed countries as a subgroup, with African LDCs shown separately. The developing world as a whole maintains its share of world FDI flows over the 1990s. Within this group, Latin America increases its share, at the expense of South

Table 2.15 FDI inflows, 1988–99

	Inflows ($m)							Inflows (shares) (%)	
	1988–93 ann.average	1994	1995	1996	1997	1998	1999	1988–93	1999
World	190 629	255 988	331 844	377 516	473 052	680 082	865 487	100.0	100.0
Developed countries	**140 088**	**145 135**	**205 693**	**219 789**	**275 229**	**480 638**	**636 449**	73.5	73.5
West Europe	80 974	82 967	119 012	114 940	138 986	259 924	315 123	42.5	36.4
North America	50 117	53 302	68 029	94 091	117 249	208 021	300 594	26.3	34.7
Developing countries	**46 919**	**104 920**	**111 884**	**145 030**	**178 789**	**179 481**	**207 619**	24.6	24.0
North Africa	1 388	2 312	1 207	1 215	2 356	2 300	2 992	0.7	0.3
Sub-Saharan Africa	**2 084**	**3 320**	**3 493**	**4 307**	**4 540**	**5 220**	**5 958**	1.1	0.7
Latin America, Caribbean	13 136	30 091	32 816	45 890	69 172	73 767	90 485	6.9	10.5
West Asia	1 996	1 756	14	2 429	4 979	6 206	6 711	1.0	0.8
Central Asia	745	896	1 655	2 053	3 079	3 141	2 762	0.4	0.3
South and East Asia	27 113	65 954	71 654	87 952	93 518	87 158	96 148	14.2	11.1
Central and Eastern Europe	3 623	5 932	14 267	12 697	19 034	19 963	21 420	1.9	2.5
Memo Item									
Least Developed (43)	1 361	1 168	2 001	2 394	2 524	3 715	4 527	0.7	0.5
African LDCs	822	844	1 641	1 632	1 772	3 062	3 798	0.4	0.4

Source: UNCTAD, *World Investment Report* (2000).

Table 2.16 *FDI inflows into Sub-Saharan African countries, 1987–98 (period averages and changes on previous period, $m)*

Country	Period averages 1987–90	1991–94	1995–98	Changes 1987–90	1991–94	1995–98
Sub-Saharan Africa	**1455**	**1807**	**5583**	**385**	**352**	**3776**
Angola	29	395	570	−285	367	175
Benin	1	8	10	1	6	3
Botswana	73	−87	89	20	−160	176
Burkina Faso	4	16	36	3	12	20
Burundi	1	1	2	0	−1	2
Cameroon	2	148	102	−112	146	−46
Cape Verde	1	1	21	1	0	19
Central African Republic	3	−8	−1	−3	−11	7
Chad	7	11	14	−16	4	3
Comoros	4	0	1	4	−3	0
Congo, Democratic Rep. of	0	0	0	0	0	0
Congo, Republic of	−2	131	361	−34	133	231
Côte d'Ivoire	51	20	255	12	−32	235
Djibouti	0	2	3	0	2	1
Equatorial Guinea	2	22	314	6	20	292
Eritrea	-	0	26	-	-	26
Ethiopia	0	0	0	0	0	0
Gabon	66	−113	−95	5	−179	18
Gambia, The	7	9	8	6	2	−1
Ghana	10	100	92	6	90	−9
Guinea	15	70	52	13	55	−18
Guinea-Bissau	0	0	0	0	0	0
Kenya	40	8	26	16	−32	19
Lesotho	14	11	148	11	−3	137
Liberia	10	-	-	−4	-	-
Madagascar	9	14	16	9	5	2
Malawi	0	0	22	−1	0	22
Mali	3	4	42	1	0	39
Mauritania	3	8	1	−2	4	−7
Mauritius	29	−2	31	24	−32	33
Mozambique	6	29	99	−33	23	70
Namibia	7	85	127	7	78	42

Table 2.16 Continued

Country	Period averages 1987–90	1991–94	1995–98	Changes 1987–90	1991–94	1995–98
Niger	16	0	0	13	−16	0
Nigeria	865	618	984	557	−248	366
Rwanda	15	4	3	1	−12	0
Sao Tome and Principe	0	2	2	0	2	0
Senegal	24	20	104	31	−4	85
Seychelles	21	7	45	10	−14	38
Sierra Leone	18	11	14	59	−7	3
Somalia	0	–	–	6	–	–
South Africa	−81	124	1528	−82	205	1404
Sudan	1	–	–	−1	–	–
Swaziland	51	38	19	41	−13	−18
Tanzania	0	37	138	0	37	101
Togo	12	10	12	8	−2	2
Uganda	0	3	116	0	3	113
Zambia	134	10	160	103	−124	150
Zimbabwe	−18	44	85	−19	62	42

Source: Pigato (1999) based on IMF and World Bank staff estimates.

and East Asia. The gradual increase in inflows into SSA is not sufficient to raise its small share in world inflows. African LDCs remain marginalized, in spite of recent surges.

Table 2.16 shows World Bank and IMF (balance of payments) data on FDI inflows into Africa by country. The figures are higher than in the UNCTAD data, but the periods are not the same and there may be differences in sources and definitions. The surge in FDI in 1995–98 may be explained by the large inflows into South Africa and the privatization of public enterprises in manufacturing and utilities in other countries. Privatization has in fact played a larger relative role in attracting FDI in Africa than in other countries. As Pigato (1999, p. 12) puts it,

> Foreign exchange raised through privatisation (in the form of both FDI and portfolio flows) represented about 44% of total revenue generated by privatisation in developing countries during 1990–97 (up from only 8% in 1980). In SSA the foreign exchange contribution to privatisation revenue was 59% in the 1990–97 period and 44% in developing countries. In the last year for which data are available, foreign exchange represented 83% of privatisation revenue in SSA

> compared with only 43% in developing countries. Partial information suggests that some 80–90% of this foreign exchange is in the form of FDI. In other regions, notably East Asia, the proportion is much lower – around 50% . . . The latest round of privatisation involves large enterprises, particularly utility industries: power, railways, electricity, water and especially telecommunications. Foreign investors with the necessary capital and technical skills are attracted by large equity stakes and management control.

The distribution of FDI inflows is changing over time. Fuel exporting countries (Angola, Congo Republic, Equatorial Guinea and Nigeria) accounted for 41 per cent of inflows during 1995–98, down from 61 per cent during 1987–90. South Africa increased its share to 28 per cent while a group of 15 reforming countries[6] attracted 29 per cent of FDI inflows, a marginally higher share than in the previous period. The contribution of the rest of Africa declined sharply from 19 per cent to 2.3 per cent. In terms of the changes in inflows between 1995–98 and 1987–90, South Africa contributed more than 40 per cent, and the fuel exporting countries and the 'best performers' accounted for one-third of the change.

Of the case study countries, Uganda has the largest recent value of and increase in FDI inflows, followed by Tanzania and Zimbabwe, though the latter is down from 1991–94. Ghana suffers a decline after a rise in the earlier period. The average value of inflows during 1995–98 varies between a high of $138 million for Tanzania and a low of $26 for Kenya. By international standards these are very low figures, but for the region they are reasonable.

What do FDI inflows signify for technology inflows? Unfortunately not very much, in that much of the FDI is 'either in the primary sector, particularly petroleum, or in infrastructure. And, with the exception of South Africa, other SSA countries have seen very little inflows in the manufacturing sector in recent years' (Pigato, 1999, p. 11). While FDI in primary and infrastructure activities is desirable and economically beneficial, in terms of transfer of technology it does not add much to industrial capabilities or efficiency.

The region still has a poor image with international investors. Conversations with Asian investors suggest an undifferentiated perception of the region as unstable, poor and economically stagnant. There is little knowledge of how countries differ from each other, even of what or where they are, and there seems relatively little interest in finding out.[7] This is partly due to the fact that Asian investors have historically had low exposure to Africa. However, even investors with long historical links with Africa – from Europe – tend to invest less in researching investment opportunities there than in Asia or Latin America. Risk ratings of many African countries tend to be high.

Thus, the ratings of 150 countries by *Euromoney* give South Africa forty-eighth position in 1997, the highest in Sub-Saharan Africa. Ghana is next at 84, Zimbabwe 95, Kenya 96, Côte d'Ivoire 101 and Uganda 105. Apart from obviously risky and hostile countries, African countries come lowest in the world. We can compare these to Singapore at 3, Malaysia at 28, Thailand at 34, Chile at 33 and India at 50. A survey of UK and Hong Kong investors, conducted by Zimbabwe Trade and Investment Consultants for the Commonwealth Secretariat in 1997, is illustrative. It shows that while Zimbabwe is regarded by UK investors as better than most other destinations in Africa apart from South Africa, they rank it unfavourably with other developing regions (Lall et al., 1998). Many of these countries, say in South Asia, have worse infrastructure and more cumbersome and opaque approval procedures.

Pigato (1999) reports two other indicators of political and financial risk. The creditworthiness ranking produced by *Institutional Investor* assigns SSA the lowest rank in the world. The *International Country Risk Guide Index* measures political risk and is based on views expressed by banks, MNCs and institutional investors. This gives a more mixed picture: while its index on 'rule of law' ranks SSA about the same as South Asia and Latin America (but below East Asia), that of 'corruption' ranks Africa poorly. Pigato notes that privatization has been associated with a sharp rise in corruption in Africa.

A recent report for the Cross-Border Initiative (which includes all the countries in our study apart from Ghana) is clear on the reasons for low FDI inflows in the region. 'The main reason is the absence of one or more of the essential conditions for attracting investment: political stability, good governance, macroeconomic reform and stability, free trade and open foreign exchange systems, investment deregulation, and (for large investors) sufficient market size ... In addition, there is the problem of perception'(CBI, 1999, p. 3).

Capital Goods Imports

The final category of technology imports is in the 'embodied' form of capital goods. Table 2.17 shows values of machinery and equipment as well as electronic and electrical equipment imports by the case study and comparator countries for the last available year. While the data for Uganda and Ghana are rather out of date, the general trends are clear. All the five countries import relatively little embodied technology in the form of new capital goods, either as a share of total imports or on a per capita basis. Local data sources for Uganda show that industrial machinery imports have fallen from 1995 to 1997, when they accounted for a tiny 4.7 per cent of total imports (see Chapter 5). The only comparator country that does worse is India, which still has a highly protected and inefficient capital goods industry. China, also with a huge local manufacturing capacity, imports relatively large amounts of equipment. The highest imports of capital goods are by Malaysia, much of it going into

Table 2.17 Recent equipment imports ($ millions and percentages)

Country	Year	Machinery and equipment ($m)	Electronics and electricals ($m)	Total equipment imports ($m)	Total imports ($m)	Equipment as % of total imports	Machinery imports per capita ($)	Electronics imports per ($)	Total equipment imports per capita ($m)
Kenya	1998	427.8	218.9	646.7	3 301.8	19.6	23.8	12.2	35.9
Tanzania	1998	215.4	69.1	284.5	1 416.3	20.1	8.0	2.6	10.5
Uganda	1988	76.6	14.5	91.1	907.0	10.0	2.6	0.5	3.0
Ghana	1992	367.0	98.4	465.4	2 145.4	21.7	18.4	4.9	23.3
Zimbabwe	1998	641.5	240.1	881.6	3 157.8	27.9	16.9	6.3	23.2
South Africa	1998	4 884.0	4 343.2	9 227.2	26 624.1	34.7	444.0	394.8	838.8
India	1998	4 674.1	2 252.8	6 926.9	42 491.9	16.3	4.9	2.4	7.3
China	1998	24 371.8	27 821.8	52 193.6	140 236.8	37.2	20.1	22.9	43.0
Korea	1998	11 000.5	19 147.2	30 147.7	93 280.9	32.3	171.9	299.2	471.1
Malaysia	1998	9 700.6	24 375.8	34 076.5	57 759.4	59.0	461.9	1 160.8	1 622.7
Thailand	1998	8 562.4	9 100.4	17 662.8	42 684.1	41.4	142.7	151.7	294.4

Source: UN Comtrade database.

new infrastructure and TNC driven export-oriented activities. South Africa is also a major importer, and on a per capita basis it comes second to Malaysia.

IN SUM . . .

The picture of technology development in SSA that emerges from this overview is rather gloomy. The region as a whole - with the exception of South Africa - does poorly in industrial competitiveness. Its exports are specialized in primary products that face slow growing markets and offer few beneficial learning or spillover effects. Despite low wages, it has not made a dent in the fast growing global production system for low-technology consumer products like clothing or footwear. It is virtually absent in exports of more sophisticated products, where many other developing countries have established themselves as dynamic competitors. Its industrial base is eroding in response to liberalization and adjustment rather than becoming the engine of growth and structural transformation. Much of this has to do with the *weak technological base* in the region.

The region performs badly in terms of technological dynamism, as it lacks many of the basic ingredients of technology development. The skill base is very weak and the educational system is generally not geared to meeting the skill needs of industrial competitiveness. Inflows of technology, measured by contractual transfers, FDI or equipment imports, are very low. Local technological activity is weak. As a result, there is little mastery by 'best practice' standards of the simple technologies where other developing countries have established strong positions, and are competing strongly with African firms. The ability to enter more sophisticated technologies, the cutting edge of industrial dynamism and competitiveness, is conspicuously absent. The region is completely 'out of the loop' of the transnational production systems that increasingly dominate world trade in manufactures. While this may not come as a surprise – it is accepted in the region that industry suffers serious technological lags – the extent and nature of the problem are not well understood. A comparative evaluation, even a preliminary one of the type done here, is therefore useful. It illustrates how far the region is lagging behind others in an increasingly demanding competitive setting: note that some of the now successful developing countries were poorer than some of the case study countries in the 1950s.

These generalizations mask large differences between the five countries studied here. A comparison of technological capabilities in a sample of garment and engineering firms in 1995 in Kenya, Tanzania and Zimbabwe is illustrative (Table 2.18). It shows that Zimbabwean firms have the strongest capabilities in both industries, followed by Kenya and with Tanzanian firms

Table 2.18 Technological capability index of sample manufacturing firms, 1995 (means)

	Engineering	Clothing
Kenya	0.40	0.32
Tanzania	0.34	0.28
Zimbabwe	0.56	0.66

coming last. In clothing, for instance, Zimbabwean firms achieve double the score of their Kenyan and even more than double that of their Tanzanian counterparts. Even the highest scores, however, are well below international frontiers. Another exercise conducted by the World Bank measures technical efficiency (rather than capabilities) in Zimbabwe, Kenya and Ghana, and gives similar results, with Ghana coming last among these countries (Biggs et al., 1995).

This suggests that Zimbabwe, with the largest and most diverse manufacturing sector, leads the case study countries followed by Kenya. It is difficult to rank the others, but Ghana is likely to come next given the size of its MVA and manufactured exports, and larger stocks of skills. Tanzania and Uganda appear to be similar in terms of industrial capabilities. Once again, we need to recall that all of them are very far from the average of developing countries' frontiers of industrial efficiency and performance.

NOTES

1. Collier and Gunning (1999a) provide a good example. They attribute poor African performance (in general, not just in industry) to four factors: lack of openness to international trade, a high-risk environment, low levels of social capital and poor infrastructure. In another paper, Collier and Gunning (1999b) also address the issue of poor industrial performance in Africa. They accept that 'African manufacturing has been in a low-productivity trap' (p. 18) and attribute it to import-substitution that oriented firms to small domestic markets and protected them from international competition. In addition, poor infrastructure and other transaction costs held back productivity. The ability to deploy technology efficiently - and all the factors that affect the development of this ability - are ignored. Presumably, with liberal trade and competition policies, better infrastructure and a minimal government, all the necessary capabilities would arise automatically. This typifies the neo-classical approach, with its simplified view of technology, that informs the mainstream analysis of industrial development and the African experience. For a detailed theoretical critique see chapter 3 of Lall (2001a). On the World Bank approach to African adjustment see Stein (1992, 1994).
2. For analyses of competitiveness, dynamic comparative advantage and industrial strategies see Lall (1999a) and Pietrobelli (1997).
3. Evidence on the faster growth of technology-intensive industries and exports in 68 economies is provided in NSF (1998). 'The global market for high-tech goods is growing at a faster rate than that for other manufactured goods, and economic activity in high-tech industries is

driving national economic growth around the world. Over the 15-year period examined (1980–95), high-tech production grew at an inflation-adjusted annual average rate of nearly 6 per cent compared with a rate of 2.4 per cent for other manufactured goods ... Output by the four high-tech industries - those identified as being the most research-intensive - represented 7.6 per cent of global production of all manufactured goods in 1980; by 1995, this output represented 21 per cent' (NSF, 1998, chapter 6).

4. Since the ratios are for the relevant age groups, it is possible to get figures of over 100 where enrolments at a particular level include children from different age groups.
5. While we cannot correct satisfactorily for quality differences in schooling, it is instructive to consider one indicator of the *mathematics* and *science* training: the TIMSS (Third International Mathematics and Science Study) scores for 8th Grade students. Of the 41 countries in which half a million 13 year olds were tested, the position of Asian Tigers was as follows: Singapore reached first place in both mathematics and science; Korea came second in mathematics and fourth in science; Hong Kong came fourth in mathematics and twenty-fourth in science. Japan was the best of the developed countries, coming third in both. Of other developing countries, Thailand was halfway down in both, while Iran did poorly in science but better than Thailand in mathematics. Kuwait, Colombia and South Africa took the last three places in both subjects. No other African countries apart from South Africa were in the test, but the figures suggest large quality differences in schooling in the two subjects of critical importance to technological skill development. The TIMSS results are reported in NSF (1998).
6. These countries are Botswana, Cameroon, Côte d'Ivoire, Ghana, Guinea, Lesotho, Mauritius, Mozambique, Namibia, Senegal, Seychelles, South Africa, Tanzania, Uganda, Zambia and Zimbabwe (Pigato, 1999).
7. The main exception is Malaysia, which is mounting an investment drive in service and resource-based activities.

3. Kenya

INTRODUCTION

The Kenyan government clearly regards industrial development as a cornerstone of development, with competitive activities becoming the engine for export growth, employment creation and income generation. However, its plan and strategy documents show that it is fully aware of current technological shortcomings (Republic of Kenya, 1996, 1997). To quote some relevant passages:

> Kenya's industrialisation process will not be easily achieved in practice. Unlike the NICs, which industrialised under protected domestic markets, Kenya is attempting to achieve the same result with a liberalised market. Markets are also rapidly being globalised and the new information technologies are creating new uncertainties and opportunities. In addition, whereas the current NICs industrialised in high growth regions, Kenya is attempting to industrialise in a region with a tradition of low growth. To industrialise in such an environment, Kenyan manufacturers will have to produce goods and services that are internationally competitive in both quality and price ... The process of industrialisation will include a 'deepening' of the industrial sector by creating core and linkage industries, as well as acquiring and adapting relevant technologies to enhance factor productivity. (Republic of Kenya, 1997, p. 23)

It goes on to emphasize the role of R&D in industrial development:

> Research and development (R&D) plays a key role in industrialisation by facilitating the identification, characterisation and development of material bases, new products and new processes for industrial activities. Its application in generating improved technologies will influence the effective utilisation of local resources ... The vision to transform Kenya into a NIC by the year 2020 ... calls for a critical re-examination of the country's R&D policies and strategies ... Kenya's industrial enterprises are characterised by obsolete technologies and inefficient machinery, often over 20 years old. Information on available sources of technology is poor; indeed, some firms have continued royalty payments long after patent protection has expired. Moreover, domestic engineers have had little success in adapting imported technologies to the domestic environment. There is little evidence of technology deepening or adapting foreign technologies to produce improved or new products. Kenya today lacks well-developed capacities to provide advice and information to technology users, has inadequate

> capacity to screen foreign technologies and is unable to formulate adequate technology-related policies or plans. There will be need for significantly increased skills at the enterprise level and in government institutions to address these shortcomings.

This awareness is encouraging; the government clearly understands the need to upgrade the competitive structure and technical base of its industrial sector. This need is increasingly pressing. By regional standards, Kenya already has a relatively strong industrial and technological base; the only countries that appear stronger are South Africa and Zimbabwe (Lall 1999c). However, in the new setting these are not the only – or even main – competitors for Kenyan industry. With liberalization and falling transport costs, the 'real' competition is likely to come from countries further afield. In low-technology products it will come from low-wage economies in South and Southeast Asia. In medium and high-technology products it will come from the OECD countries and East Asia. In resource-based products it will come from Southeast Asia and Latin America. The technological capabilities that Kenya must muster have therefore to match those provided by its global competitors.

It appears, however, that despite ambitious plans for reform and improvement, Kenyan technology and capabilities lag behind those of many countries in Asia and Latin America. There is little sign of technical dynamism: the private sector invests little in R&D and does relatively little to upgrade the technology it imports. It also has few links with the official technology infrastructure. Government efforts in science and technology tend to lack coherence; more importantly, they do not carry much credibility with industry. The institutions providing basic services and inputs into enterprise technological activity are weak. Policy continues to focus on the supply side of technology rather than ensuring that productive enterprises are induced to demand it and to invest more in it. In general, the technology structure does not provide Kenyan industry with the capabilities it needs to sustain growth and competitiveness in the future.

There are exceptions, of course: there are some 'good' firms that do invest in competitive technologies and the capabilities needed to use them. But these are few and relatively isolated, and will not provide the locomotive to pull the industrial sector as a whole. The rest of manufacturing can grow, but mainly by confining itself to activities where it does not come into direct competition with foreign producers - resource-based products or small niche markets. This does not promise a base for sustained growth. It certainly does not promise the diversification and upgrading of exports Kenya needs for its long-term development. Before coming to technology policy and institutions, however, let us review the background to industrial development in Kenya.

INDUSTRIAL BACKGROUND

In the mid-1960s Kenya launched an import-substituting industrialization strategy, with high levels of protection for manufacturing and a large role for the public sector in industry. Fuelled by rising rural incomes and the trade agreement with Tanzania and Uganda, it enjoyed rapid growth till the late 1970s (UNIDO, 1999, p. 54). By the 1980s it had achieved a reasonable level of industrialization by regional standards - the share of manufacturing in GDP averaged 12.3 per cent in 1975–80 compared to about 10.0 per cent for SSA as a whole. Food and beverages (37 per cent of MVA in 1993) dominated the industrial structure. However, manufacturing growth began to slow down in the 1980s, as did manufactured exports (Wignaraja and Ikiara, 1999). The share of manufacturing in GDP stagnated at 13 per cent and fell to 10 per cent in 1997. Over the entire post-independence period (1963–96) its MVA growth was 3 per cent, lower than the rate of population increase. Employment growth in manufacturing was below 2 per cent per annum in the 1990s, far less than the addition to the labour force.

Much of the blame for the slowdown in manufacturing growth lay with the inward-oriented strategy in a small market, though other factors were also to blame.[1] High levels of protection distorted resource allocation, constricted foreign competition and restricted technology inflows from abroad. The protection was indiscriminate and open-ended, providing few incentives for enterprises to build technological capabilities and upgrade imported technologies. The large and inefficient parastatal sector in manufacturing became a drag on growth. Recognizing the need for change, the government introduced import liberalization in 1980–84 (part of a World Bank structural adjustment programme), one of the first countries in SSA to do so. The liberalization was, however, halting and intermittent until the 1990s, when the government began to show more commitment. The latest episode of opening up has removed most quantitative restrictions to imports and lowered and simplified tariff rates. Tariffs now range from 5 to 25 per cent, with lower rates (5–10 per cent) for most capital and intermediate goods, and higher rates for various agricultural and textile products and finished consumer electronics.[2] Foreign exchange transactions are now largely left to the market.

Despite this, economic performance has continued to falter in the 1990s. GDP growth fell from 4.3 per cent in 1990 to 2.3 per cent, 0.5 per cent and 0.2 per cent in 1991, 1992 and 1993 respectively. The government introduced further structural reforms in 1993, including the removal of price controls, import licensing and foreign exchange controls, and reforms to investment incentives, public enterprises and financial institutions. These policies bore some initial fruit, with GDP growing at 3.0 per cent in 1994, 4.8 per cent in 1995 and 4.6 per cent in 1996. However, there was a relapse thereafter, with growth falling to 2.4 per cent in 1997 (Central Bureau of Statistics, 1999). The industrial sector's growth in 1998, only 1.4 per cent, was 'a result of the sector's inability to compete with low priced imports into the local market, depressed local market demand and a combination of infrastructural constraints' (ibid., p. 142).

The latest round of policy reforms has removed the anti-export bias; in fact, the Sessional Paper No 1 of 1994 calls for an 'export bias' (UNIDO, 1999, p. 56). Along with the promotion of the small scale and '*jua kali*' (informal) sector, trade policy reform has become the centrepiece of industrial policy in Kenya. However, trade liberalization has not only failed to stimulate manufactured exports, it has led to retrenchments in activities directly exposed to import competition. Non-traditional exports based on agriculture are growing, as are manufacturing activities that serve sheltered or niche local and regional markets. The quantity index of manufactured exports in 1998 was actually 13.8 per cent *below* that of 1994 (Central Bureau of Statistics, 1999, p. 95). In the preceding period, weak export performance was traceable to the trade regime, lack of credibility in liberalization, macro instability and the failure to develop competitive capabilities. Most recently, however, it can be accounted for largely by weak domestic capabilities and the failure to attract foreign export capabilities in the form of inward FDI, with a few exceptions. The 'Asian model' is not being replicated in Kenya; one of the main reasons is the weak base of technological capabilities.

SCIENCE AND TECHNOLOGY POLICIES

Antecedents

Early science and technology efforts by the colonial government focused on the agricultural sector, supporting cash crops like coffee, tea, sisal, wheat and livestock.[3] The 1940s also saw the creation of specialized institutions to conduct research for Kenya, Uganda and Tanzania (see also Chapters 4 and 5). The only research for industry in Kenya was conducted in public works by the materials branch of the Ministry of Works. Isolation during the Second World War led the colonial government to set up the East African Industrial Research Board in 1942 and its affiliate the East African Industrial Research Organization (the predecessor to the present Kenya Industrial Research and Development Institute, KIRDI). After the war, however, technological efforts declined and the economy again became heavily dependent on imported technologies and skills.

After independence, the National Development Plan of 1970–74 advocated a National Research and Scientific Council to launch scientific research in support of economic and social development, and to set national priorities for scientific research. In 1975, the government set up, with the assistance of a UNESCO mission, a nucleus secretariat consisting of a Secretary and two assistant Secretaries. The Bill for the creation of the National Council for Science and Technology (NCST) was introduced in Parliament and became law in March 1977. NCST was officially inaugurated in October 1977. The Science and Technology Act was amended in 1979 to provide for the establishment of semi-autonomous National Research Institutes and Advisory Research Committees. The institutes set up were the Kenya Agricultural Research Institute (KARI), the Kenya Trypanosomiasis Research Institute (KETRI), the Kenya Forestry Research Institute (KEFRI), the Kenya Industrial Research and Development Institute (KIRDI), and the Kenya Marine and Fisheries Research Institute (KEMFRI). The Ministry of Regional Development, Science and Technology was created in 1982, followed in 1987 by the Ministry of Research Science and Technology. The Ministry now oversees all science and technology activities in Kenya.

Policy-Making Structure

Technology policy in its various aspects is spread over three ministries in Kenya. The relevant institutions and departments under them are as follows:

1. *Ministry of Education, Science and Technology*
   Promotion of Research, Science and Technology
   Technical Training Institutes
   Commission for Higher Education
   Technical Education
   National Polytechnics
   Research Authorization, Coordination, Inventory and Dissemination
   Liaison with Research Institutes
   National Council for Science and Technology
   Centre for Research and Technology

2. *Ministry of Tourism, Trade and Industry*
   Export Processing Zone Authority
   Kenya Industrial Training Institute
   Kenya Industrial Estates
   Kenya Investment Promotion Council
   Quality Control including Standards
   Kenya Bureau of Standards
   Kenya Industrial Research and Development Research Institute
   Patents

Trade Marks
Kenya Industrial Property Office

3. *Ministry of Labour and Human Resources Development*
Youth Polytechnics
Institutes of Technology
Informal, Micro and Small-Scale Enterprise Development
Directorate of Industrial Training
Directorate of Applied Technology.

In addition, there are technology-related activities carried out in the railways, parastatal enterprises and university departments.

Policy-making on technology in Kenya is widely dispersed over ministries and departments. There are many overlapping jurisdictions and considerable scope for 'territorial' conflict, along with the risk that there is no institution that can provide coherence and coordination to strategic decision making that concerns the economy as a whole. There is no mechanism for analysing Kenya's competitiveness relative to other countries, in order to derive practical technology policy needs. While technology and higher education are now under the same ministry, the departmental distinctions inherited from previous ministerial identities remain. The relations between the technology bodies under the Ministry of Tourism, Trade and Industry and those under Education, Science and Technology are not strong. The Kenya Investment Promotion Centre (KIPC) does not seem to be concerned about technology issues, though its FDI attraction function deals with the main channel for technology transfer into the country.

On broader policy issues, the reform of the trade regime clearly has direct effects on industrial restructuring and technological activity. However, liberalization is not related to technology policies, in the sense that there is little or no coordination between the pace of opening up in different activities and the mounting of technology support policies to boost competitiveness. Nor is liberalization related to strategies for creating competitive skills.

Such lack of coherence and coordination in technology and other economic policies is a result of the historical evolution of government functions. It is common to many other countries, but it renders them unable to mount strategic responses to liberalization and globalization. One important policy implication of this study is that the government should review and improve its strategy making capabilities, possibly through the creation of a body capable of analysing technology needs at the broad economic level and designing and implementing strategies that cut across many ministerial and departmental lines. Much of the success of the Asian Tigers lies in their ability to mount such a coordinated strategic effort, often with inputs from the private sector and in some cases transnational investors.

Intellectual Property Regime

The intellectual property rights (IPR) regime is important for technological activity, and covers a number of legal devices to protect intellectual property, led by patents and trademarks. However, the importance of IPRs varies by country, particularly between the major innovators and countries that are predominantly users of technology. In the former, patents tend to spur innovation by granting temporary monopolies in the exploitation of the property. In the latter, they also reward innovators and facilitate the transfer of technology. As the innovators are overseas, however, and local markets may be quite small, investments in innovation may not be strongly affected by local protection. At the same time, IPR protection can raise the costs to developing countries of buying technology and prevent local copying of technology (potentially an important way to build technological capabilities). Thus patents represent a trade-off: a market distortion (with raised costs to users) is created in exchange for disclosure of the information relating to the technology. This disclosure benefits society by disseminating new technologies and, indeed, encouraging competitors to invent around it, stimulating a second round of innovation.

A stronger IPR regime assumes that the positive impact of appropriability for the innovator and disclosure for competitors outweigh the negative impact of the market distortion, making IPR protection beneficial to society as a whole. This is nearly impossible to test in practice, and remains a highly controversial subject. Most developing countries see themselves as users of technology rather than makers of new technology and consider it premature to adopt the Western models of IPR protection. In fact, it is feared that technological catch-up may be constrained if stronger IPRs are enforced in developing countries. This argument has some merit. Historically, there has been a U-shaped relationship between GDP and IPR protection. The very low-income countries possess strong IPR regimes, in the absence of a domestic industry lobby in favour of lax rules (that would allow them to imitate and reverse engineer). The high-income economies protect IPRs very strongly, for obvious reasons. The middle-income countries offer the least protection for IPRs.

However, three important events change the shape of the debate.

1. Investment flows are seeking global destinations and the ability of TNCs to protect their knowledge assets becomes a more important determinant in choosing the destination. The regime dictating the appropriability of the returns to their knowledge assets can make the difference between using

it to position themselves as leaders or losing out to the lowest cost imitator. The willingness to offer strong protection works as a signalling device for FDI flows.

2. All members of the WTO who are signatories to the TRIPS agreement have now agreed to reform their IPR regimes by 2004. This new 'rule of the game' is now set and, regardless of its effects on particular host economies, provides the level playing field for globalization that all countries have to accept.
3. Many developing countries are becoming, or will soon become, innovators in their own right. Some are also becoming R&D bases for TNCs. The Asian NIEs are now important holders of patents in the US (NSF, 1998). For these countries, stronger IPRs are necessary for promoting innovation and R&D-based inward FDI. For countries further down the technological scale, stronger IPRs may also be desirable to promote the development of a technology culture.

The industrial property regime in Kenya is embodied in an Act of 1989 and is administered by the Kenyan Industrial Property Office (KIPO), set up in 1990. The main aims of the Act were to promote indigenous technology, protect foreign patents, and encourage the acquisition and diffusion of technology. KIPO registers patents, trademarks, industrial designs, utility models and service marks. However, it does not register and administer issues relating to copyrights; this is carried out by the Attorney General's Office. The Kenyan law on patents conforms to the UK law, with some features of the European and US systems. Patents are granted for 17 years, but will be raised to 20 years in conformance with the TRIPS agreement at the WTO.

KIPO earlier used to register technology transfer agreements to ensure that royalties and fees did not exceed the stipulated 3–5 per cent of the turnover of local firm. The registration was necessary to get Central Bank permission to remit royalties and fees. Since 1992, this registration has become redundant since fees can be remitted freely. Thus, now almost no firms come to KIPO for this function.

Since 1990 patents have been registered through KIPO, African Regional Industrial Property Office (ARIPO, located in Zimbabwe) and the Patent Cooperation Treaties (PCT). Patents registered with both KIPO and ARIPO are accepted in 14 member countries. The largest number of licences are granted in agrochemicals, pharmaceuticals, mechanical, electrical, electronics, machinery and equipment. However, according to KIPO, most local applications are from individuals and research institutions: *not a single Kenyan manufacturing firm has yet applied for a patent.* This is another reflection of the weak state of local technological activity, discussed below. Table 3.1 shows the numbers of patents registered since 1990.

Table 3.1 Kenya, number of patents registered

Year	KIPO	ARIPO	PCT
1990	10	-	6
1991	28	-	22
1992	34	-	33
1993	50	-	52
1994	35	-	41
1995	15	4	42
1996	27	24	117
1997	32	30	237
1998	31	28	194
1999	24	13	N/A
Total	286	99	747

Source: KIPO.

KIPO handles disputes related to patent infringements. These are placed before a tribunal, with further recourse to the High Court if necessary. The tribunal consists of a chairman and four members appointed by the minister; two members are qualified lawyers and entitled to practice as advocates, while the other two have experience in industrial, scientific and technological fields. The chairman is a person who has been a judge or is qualified to be appointed a judge of the High Court. Most disputes are on trademark infringements, though given the small size and low growth of the local market there is relatively little piracy. There are no qualified patent attorneys in Kenya; the nearest ones are in South Africa. This can become a disincentive to the development of an effective and modern IPR regime in Kenya. The legal processes involved in patent cases appear to be slow and cumbersome.

KIPO has a data centre for collection, classification and dissemination of technological information. It earns about 300 million Kenya shillings per year from registration, renewal and maintenance fees for patents. However, its earnings go directly to the Treasury, which authorizes all its expenditures separately. This lack of autonomy on its budget is seen as constraining. KIPO has over the years focused its awareness promotion activities on micro and small-scale industries, the R&D fraternity in universities and public research institutions. This has been carried out through seminars/conferences in the capital city and provincial towns, fairs and shows, and it could be easily expanded.

KIPO provides training and information to local institutions, industry and

SMEs on patenting. It also gives assistance to applicants. However, staffing and skill shortages mean that the institution is unable to meet these training and advisory functions adequately. In addition, it faces conflicts of interest in advising applicants and examining patent applications: the two functions have to be clearly separated or placed in different institutions.

In general, KIPO is a relatively passive organization, and lacks the technical skills to play the role expected of a modern intellectual property office under the new WTO. Given the widespread lack of innovative activity in Kenyan industry, *its role in technology promotion is minimal.* The lack of legal skills in patent law in the country may however be a gap that needs to be addressed in the future. In addition, there is a *need for a stronger competition policy* regime to offset the stronger intellectual property rights granted to TNCs. This falls outside the direct scope of technology policies, but it is clear that effective domestic competition policy is a necessary part of the framework for stimulating the use and creation of technology.

TECHNOLOGY IMPORTS AND TECHNOLOGICAL ACTIVITY

Table 3.2 shows recent values of FDI (and its share in total investment in Kenya), capital goods imports and technical payments abroad in Kenyan shillings. The value of technology imports in all these forms is very low; for instance, total technical payments came to less than $2 million in 1998. What accounts for such low levels, when the Kenyan economy is being subjected to intense import competition and needs to upgrade technologies rapidly?

The policy framework for technology imports is now liberal. There are no controls on capital goods imports or licensing. Tariffs on machinery are uniformly low, around 5–10 per cent. Earlier controls on foreign exchange remittances are virtually gone. Unlike many import-substituting countries, Kenya never had legislation for regulating the transfer of technology (apart

Table 3.2 Technology inflows into Kenya (K sh. million)

	1996	1997	1998
FDI	37.8	51.5	34.5
FDI % Total investment	2.2	4.8	2.0
Capital goods imports	2073.2	2335.0	2530.5
Royalties, technical fees	77.7	114.2	120.5

Source: Central Bureau of Statistics, Nairobi (1999).

from the 3–5 per cent limit monitored by KIPO, mentioned above). The government did not intervene in contract negotiations between domestic and foreign companies. The policy regime does not therefore constitute a constraint to manufacturing enterprises seeking to upgrade technology.

Another reason mentioned in the past for the tepid technological response of the industrial sector was the uncertainty and lack of credibility of the liberalization process. However, this has diminished over time as it has become more widely accepted by industry that liberalization is irreversible and will only accelerate. The real reasons therefore lie in *structural* problems of technology upgrading: lack of information on sources of technology, cost of upgrading technology (reflecting the distance between existing technologies and the frontier), lack of managerial and technical skills and financial constraints. Many of these can be reduced by technology support and skill formation policies. A few Kenyan firms *are* paying attention to technology upgrading. While they are not technologically advanced or innovative by NIE standards, they are doing a creditable job in the new liberal environment. See Box 3.1 for an example.

BOX 3.1 TECHNOLOGICAL UPGRADING BY POWER TECHNICS, KENYA

Power Technics started in 1982 as an electrical engineering firm. It manufactures lighting equipment and fixtures under licence from Groupe Schneider (France) and Thorn Electrical (UK); and it provides electrical cabling lighting systems for buildings. Its total employment of 180 people includes 14 engineers – these have been extensively trained in-house to overcome the poor quality of training given in universities. It has developed considerable expertise in sheet metal work, for which it uses computer numerically controlled (CNC) machine tools, one of the few firms in the region to do so. Its own engineers are able to maintain the CNC tools after relatively brief (10 days each for two engineers) training with the suppliers in Europe. The firm imported powder-coating technology from India; having mastered this technology, it improved upon the original technology and obtained more advanced equipment from Germany. It persuaded Schneider to grant it a licence to make a new switchboard, the only non-affiliate to be given this licence throughout the world. Schneider now sources components from Power Technics for various projects in the region. The firm plans to obtain ISO 9000 certification in 2000. It started exporting on its own to the region about four years ago, and its exports now account for around 15-18 per cent of sales.

The firm invests heavily in training its employees. However, the government provides no incentive or tax deduction for in-house training to Kenyan firms, despite repeated representations. It provides external training financed by the training levy, but Power Technics finds such training irrelevant to its needs. The MD has also proposed to improve the quality of university training by getting firms to sponsor students and providing practical experience of industry; the government should meet part of the costs involved. India has such a scheme and it is considered very successful.

Its major competitive problems include import tariffs (15 per cent) on major components like circuit breakers (which are too sophisticated and scale intensive to make locally): these tariffs are set at the same level as on final products. It cannot obtain tariff rebates on imported components for export and so suffers a cost disadvantage (import content is around 50 per cent). The inability to obtain tariff drawbacks on exports by firms that sell mainly to the domestic market may be a significant constraint to future export development and diversification.

Infrastructure is expensive and unreliable. It took the firm one and half years to get a telephone connection. It has its own water supply and generator, both raising costs. Security is very expensive. Otherwise labour costs are low: the firm pays $73 per month for unskilled workers and $200 for experienced skilled workers. Fresh graduate engineers receive $333 and engineers with five years' experience $670. These salaries compare well with countries like India and are well below salaries in South East Asia.

In spite of these problems, the firm has built up substantial sheet metal working and electrical system design capabilities. Its positive attitudes to technology and training mark it apart from the bulk of local manufacturing firms.

Source: Interview with Mr. Naresh Mehta, Managing Director and founder of Power Technics, Nairobi, 1999.

These exceptions apart, there is surprisingly little technological activity in Kenyan enterprises. The tradition has long been to passively import (relatively simple) technologies and use them at relatively low levels of technical efficiency with the help of expatriate skills. Capital goods and design engineering are almost all foreign. These weaknesses mean that technological learning and diffusion are limited. Formal R&D in industry is confined to a very few large enterprises, but even here it is fairly marginal. The employment of trained engineers is very low, and in-house training is limited to creating the basic skills needed to operate the equipment. While liberalization has induced firms to upgrade their capabilities, the effort remains inadequate. The government does not offer any fiscal incentives for enterprise R&D; such expenditures are not even allowable as legitimate tax deductible expenses.

A recent study of technology in Kenya notes,

> High and indiscriminate import protection [in Kenya] shut out competitive pressures and induced the acquisition of industrial capabilities for home market production, including those to substitute local raw materials for imports, to stretch and maintain equipment, and to introduce simple products. Production technologies became obsolete as most forms of technology import were restricted by foreign exchange controls ... (Now) there is a high propensity to start with used equipment and most firms have machinery over ten years old ... weaknesses remain in several aspects of skill formation. The employment of engineers is quite limited and highly concentrated in the largest firms. There is little emphasis on in-house or external training ... However, there is too little resort to foreign technology contracts and most firms purchase technology embodied in used equipment. Few firms have systems for continuous inventory control. The capacity to develop new products is weak and none of the firms carry out formal R&D. Industrial engineering as a separate function is notably absent. Linkages with other firms or technology institutions are rare. (Wignaraja and Ikiara, 1999, pp. 79, 92)

The bulk of R&D in Kenya is conducted in the public research institutions and universities. Within R&D institutes funding is overwhelmingly public. Generally the government's contribution is 90 per cent and the private sector's contribution around 10 per cent. Public research is biased towards agriculture and away from industrial research (Table 3.3). Most research institutions face serious budgetary problems, with 81 per cent of recurrent expenditure devoted to personnel costs and very little going into technological work. In addition, budgeted operational funds are not always disbursed, with the average disbursement to approved expenditure ratios ranging between 20 and 80 per cent for development expenditures. The effects of such serious underfunding of operations are that scientists are unable to conduct research efficiently. Though much effort has been directed in the past to staff training and recruitment and to constructing modern facilities, these efforts are wasted without sufficient operational funds to perform research tasks.

Table 3.3 Sectoral shares of R&D expenditure in public research institutions 1996-97 (percentages)

Sector	Recurrent	Development
Industry	6	4
Agriculture	45	82
Medical	24	3
Forestry	14	1
Marine/Fisheries	11	10

Source: National Development Plan, Republic of Kenya (1977).

INWARD FDI

Kenyan policies towards foreign direct investment have been relatively unwelcoming for a long time. The World Bank's 1986 report described FDI policies as follows:

> The Government's attitude has been ambivalent, desiring the inflow of funds and associated skills and entrepreneurship, but at the same time, wanting Kenyanisation by participation in ownership and management. At the moment there are five major impediments to new inflows of direct foreign investment. First, repatriation of the initial capital is limited to the original Kenya shilling equivalent of the foreign investment, regardless of intervening inflation and exchange rate movements; any capital gain may be repatriated only after a five-year waiting period during which it must be placed in a blocked capital account earning a low interest rate. Second, dividends may be repatriated up to an amount equal to 10 per cent per annum of the original investment, though this limit has been applied with flexibility. Third, there are restrictions, graduated by extent of foreign ownership, on the amount of domestic borrowing, thereby limiting expansion. Fourth, majority foreign owned firms are subject to a higher rate of income tax at (52.5 per cent) than domestic firms (45 per cent). Fifth, permission to employ expatriate personnel has become increasing difficult to obtain. (para. 3-34)

The government improved the FDI regime in the 1990s (Wignaraja and Ikiara, 1999). The 1990-91 budget lowered the corporate tax rate from 42.5 to 40.0 per cent. An Export Processing Zone (EPZ) was established in 1990 to attract export-oriented investors. It offered them 10-year tax holidays for export activity, exemption from withholding tax on dividends for 10 years, VAT exemption, duty free access to inputs, the right to establish foreign currency accounts and work permits for expatriate employees. The Kenya Investment Promotion Centre was established in 1985 to provide a one-stop facility for foreign investors. Foreign investments were guaranteed against nationalization and all after-tax profits were repatriable under the Foreign

Investment Protection Act. There are now no legal restrictions in manufacturing on activity or ownership shares. A new Investment Code is under consideration to further improve the investment climate.

However, these improvements have not resulted in sustained increases in FDI inflows. It seems that several bureaucratic impediments remain. A large number of specific licences are needed before a foreign investor can set up; some, like land title transfer and registration, can take from 6 months to 8 years (TSG, 1998). The Kenyan government still presses investors to increase Kenyan ownership shares. The granting of investment incentives is variable, with discretionary, case-by-case operations that give rise to delays and non-transparent procedures. It is still difficult and cumbersome to obtain expatriate permits, an increasingly important determinant of FDI location as technical change makes it imperative to move skilled personnel quickly. Kenya has a negative image because of corruption and rent-seeking, with rising violence and security problems exacerbating the situation. While these are not specifically associated with FDI, they strongly colour investor perceptions. A survey of business executives by the World Economic Forum (1998) for its *Africa Competitiveness Report* identifies corruption, crime and political instability along with weak infrastructure as the main constraints to competitiveness (and FDI) in Kenya.

KIPC (which has just been moved to the Ministry of Tourism, Trade and Industry from the Ministry of Finance) offers facilitation and registration services. However registration is not compulsory, nor is it necessary to obtain incentives. Many investors of Asian origin or traditional European investors use their own sources of information and assistance. Other investors come to the KIPC to get (free) help with legal formalities, licences and permits. However, KIPC has no direct influence over other ministries and so is relatively ineffective in speeding up the bureaucratic process. Thus, its one-stop centre function remains largely on paper. The new Investment Code may help: every concerned ministry will have to respond to KIPC requests within 14 days.

The KIPC does not practise investor targeting. It lacks the skills and capabilities to evaluate investors and does not have a strategy to assign investment or investor priorities. Its budget is also too small to permit it to mount effective investment promotion, even to travel abroad (in 2000 its total budget was under US$1 million). By comparison, the Singapore Economic Development Board has an annual budget of $34.2 million and the Malaysian Industrial Development Authority a budget of $11 million. Even the Mauritius Export Development and Investment Authority has an annual budget of $3.1 million.

The KIPC staff of 65 contains only 14 officers, mostly economists and marketing specialists. Salary scales are tied to the rest of the government, and may prevent the KIPC from attracting private sector people with the necessary skills and orientation. The information base on potential investors at the country or company level is very weak.

The KIPC works on a short planning cycle closely linked to its annual budgets rather than to a long-term national investment promotion plan. International experience suggests that a one-year planning cycle is inadequate for formulating and implementing a strategic programme, particularly to attract FDI in new industrial and service activities. The lack of coordination with other ministries and the absence of any authority over their actions mean that any strategic plan will in any case be difficult to implement. For instance, the KIPC cannot ensure that investors' skill, infrastructure, procedures or supply support needs can be addressed. Yet, such coordination is a critical part of investment targeting and upgrading in many countries, particularly NIEs like Singapore.

KIPC promotion does not have sufficient private sector participation or representation, beyond the presence of private entrepreneurs on the occasional foreign mission. The agency does not do enough 'homework' on prospective investors to be able to target and attract promising firms. It has not been successful in changing the poor image of Kenya in the investment community at large. The information provided to prospective investors does not match that offered by leading investment promotion agencies in Southeast Asia. While there is data (much of it over 3 years old) on economic aggregates, there is nothing on the costs that are relevant to making a preliminary investment evaluation, and nothing compared to what other similar agencies offer elsewhere.

Local businessmen - as sources of information, potential partners, suppliers or buyers - are not helped to deal with the business needs of potential joint venture partners or foreign customers. Their financial, managerial, marketing, technological and other capabilities are often not up to the demands of international investors, and KIPC does little or nothing to help them develop these capabilities.

EXPORT PROCESSING ZONES

EPZs can, apart from their primary role of promoting industrial competitiveness, be a source of technology transfer, upgrading and diffusion. Once export-oriented enterprises strike roots, they can raise the capital-intensity of their operations, transfer more advanced technological functions and strike greater local linkages (for example with the electronics industry in Malaysia). However, EPZs in Kenya are not serving these functions.

The Kenya EPZ authority was launched in 1990 but started its activities in

1993. By end 1999, there were eight operational EPZs in Kenya, of which five were privately run. In contrast to many Asian countries, where EPZs have reached very significant proportions, these EPZs together had only 22 active exporters (of which under one-third were wholly foreign owned and another 50 per cent were joint ventures) by 1999. The total value of their exports was only about $30 million in 1998. Of this, around three-quarters was in garments, a very weak performance considering that the minimum wage was only $1.50 per day.[4] Total employment came to 3860 employees, of which 60 per cent were females. The main obstacles identified were infrastructure such as power, roads and telecommunications, and bureaucratic procedures.

TECHNOLOGY INFRASTRUCTURE AND UNIVERSITIES

The two main institutions that provide technology support to the manufacturing sector are the Kenya Bureau of Standards and the Kenya Industrial Research and Development Institute.

Kenya Bureau of Standards (KEBS)[5]

The standards and metrology system provides essential infrastructure services for technology and industry in any country. Standards are the basic technical 'language' that allows firms to communicate specifications to each other and achieve economies of scale. In a developing country, the spread of standardization can encourage technology diffusion and raise the use of local inputs that meet the relevant standards. Metrology services (calibrating measuring and control instruments) are essential for maintaining quality; their international traceability allows products to be accepted for quality in export markets. Testing services are essential for quality control and certification in local and foreign markets. Quality management standards like the International Standards Organization (ISO) 9000 and 14000 series are becoming important assets in international competitiveness. In the absence of strong local standards institutions, industry has to use imported services at high cost and can lag in quality control. The active promotion of standards to SMEs can be an important tool of technology diffusion.

KEBS was set up in 1974 to develop standards, provide testing and metrological services and help the industrial sector with quality management and standardization. By end 1999 it had developed (by a number of technical committees) around 2000 standards. It was also the repository for a variety (over 150 000) of international and foreign standards. It operates a product certification scheme and can provide a 'Diamond Mark of Quality' as well as a 'Quality System Certification Mark', a 'Calibration Mark' and a 'Safety

Mark'. It has seven lead assessors able to provide ISO 9000 certification and has so far certified 10 companies with this standard. Its quality control laboratories provide testing facilities, with capabilities in a range of areas relevant to Kenyan needs (but rather limited in terms of new technologies). Its Metrology Division maintains national measurement standards, and serves industry in Kenya as well as other countries with calibration services. The calibration standards are traceable to Germany and South Africa. Two KEBS laboratories (Volume and Flow Laboratory and AC/Direct Current Laboratories) have been accredited by the German calibration services. KEBS also carries out repair and maintenance of measuring instruments for industry.

KEBS is funded by a standards levy on all manufacturers (0.2 per cent of ex-factory sales up to a ceiling of US$4000 per annum), imports quality inspection fees, annual government grants and services sold to industry. In addition, it provides a range of training courses for industry.

On the basis of the field interviews carried out (in 1999) by the authors, it appeared that a relatively small proportion of Kenyan firms demand KEBS services or interact with it in other ways. There is a low level of awareness among enterprises (particularly SMEs) of the importance of product quality. Firms that tried to use KEBS services some years ago complained of long delays (Wignaraja and Ikiara, 1999). The paucity of testing centres in the regions meant that industry, and especially food processing, outside major urban areas faced difficulties. Additional problems acknowledged by KEBS relate to the skill scarcity and to the weak quality culture in industry. An internal training scheme has been started, with people sent also to Japan and Sweden for further training. A further problem is related to the flight of trained employees into private industry, where they enjoy substantial salary differentials.

Kenya Industrial Research and Development Institute (KIRDI)

KIRDI, the main industrial R&D institution in Kenya, is one of eight R&D institutes established in 1979 after the break up of the East African Community (though it is a descendant of the Kenya Industrial Management Board set up in 1942). Its mission was 'to enhance the national industrial innovation process through the development of a sufficient national capacity in disembodied and embodied industrial technologies for the attainment of a self-sustaining industrialisation process' (KIRDI, 1999a, p. 2). Its main focus until the mid-1990s was food processing and chemicals. However, it admits that this work had little impact on industrial technologies in use: large industrial companies relied on foreign sources of technology while SMEs had little to do with KIRDI despite their urgent technological needs. A study by Bwisa and Gacuhi (1997) confirms the lack of links between research institutes/universities and industry in Kenya.

In 1994, a team from the UK examined the R&D institutions in Kenya and its findings led the government to reorient them to meet industrial needs. KIRDI was placed under a new director, who redefined its work to move from R&D to *industrial technology support* and thoroughly reorganized the institution. Since then KIRDI has become strongly *market oriented*, with all work funded by projects. Around 50 per cent of its work is contracted by the government, the remainder by aid donors and industry. The reorganization involved substantive retrenchment, from 700 to 289, with almost all the shedding confined to support staff rather than technical personnel. Productivity indicators were put in place, based on impact on industry rather than research publications. These indicators show a ten-fold increase in productivity. In general, therefore, there are some very positive signs in terms of the management of KIRDI and its growing links with industry.

There are six centres in KIRDI. The Engineering Development and Services Centre makes dies, tools, jigs, spares and prototypes for industry. The Leather Development Centre offers training services to industry and demonstration of leather processing techniques. The National Industrial Information Centre offers various types of search and library services. The Laboratory Services Centre provides analytical and quality control laboratory services. The Industrial Plant and Machinery Unit conducts economic feasibility and appraisal studies, and has links with sources of finance for new projects (in 1998 it successfully 'sold' 12 industrial projects). The Traditional Food Development Centre promotes traditional food processing technologies.

All divisions offer consultancy services, and are allowed to retain all their earnings except for costs and a 15 per cent overhead. Each staff member is assigned work targets, with salary increases tied to achievement. The average achievement rate is around 60 per cent; staff members unable to meet 30 per cent of targets are fired. Advisors are taken on on a part-time basis from private industry, apparently a very successful strategy. With this reorganization, industrial demand for KIRDI services has increased significantly to the extent that there is a waiting list for its services (October 1999), and KIRDI has outsourced some of the projects to the university. The main demand has been from SMEs but recently large firms have also started to approach KIRDI for help with energy and environmental audits and waste management.

Its main internal constraints are the lack of trained personnel, often due to poor salaries (KIRDI, 1999a, p. 7). Its training efforts are being intensified, and ISO 9000 certification for its various divisions has been proposed. New attempts to package technologies (based on importing and adapting foreign technologies) into suitable packages for use by enterprises have been recorded.

In sum, the reorganization and reorientation of KIRDI under a dynamic new director has transformed the institution and made it much more useful to industry. However, the concentration on industrial support services has meant that there is no institution in the country conducting R&D. This may not be very important at this stage of Kenya's industrial development but will become significant when the industrial sector deepens and grows more competitive. However, the relative lack of interest by large firms in terms of their core technologies and products suggests that KIRDI does not offer very much in terms of modern technical competence. In particular, it is likely to be very weak in modern electronics and IT based technologies.

A negative signal of KIRDI's scientific and technological standing is its inability to arouse any technological interest (apart from testing) in MNC affiliates in Kenya. These rely on internal and parent company resources for all their technological needs, that are relatively simple in any case. The lack of a strong local capital goods industry is a major constraint on 'real' technology development, which needs the capability to manufacture and adapt equipment. In general, however, the lack of technological innovation in private industry represents a major constraint on the provision of technology support by R&D institutions. Without a more dynamic 'technology culture' in private industry, an institution like KIRDI cannot provide much more than mundane technical services. There is no attempt to link the research institutions with industry, though the Indian, and other countries' experience suggest that such an attempt can be very productive.

Universities and Colleges

The Kenyan post-secondary educational institutions are largely oriented to general art and science, with technical and engineering enrolments constituting a small part of the total (Wignaraja and Ikiara, 1999). The three premier institutions for technical manpower are Kenya Polytechnic, and the departments of engineering of the University of Nairobi and the Jomo Kenyatta University of Agriculture and Technology (JKUAT). Both universities have a small number of engineering graduates. Before 1990, JKUAT was producing diploma holders. Kenya Polytechnic specializes in training middle-level technical manpower, producing diploma-holders in mechanical, electrical, automobile, aeronautical, telecommunication, building and civil engineering fields.

Apart from training, most of these technical institutes provide little or no research or technical services to industry. A recent survey revealed that the proportion of R&D in total university budgets has declined from an average of 1 per cent in the 1980s to around 0.5 per cent in the 1990s. The institutions directly involved with technology development are poorly funded. Their administrative structures and facilities do not encourage the staff to work on industrial technological problems or interact with firms, and laboratory facilities are poor. Low salaries make it difficult to recruit or retain good staff and no funds are available to commercialize research findings (Bwisa and Gacuhi, 1997). In turn, firms do not consider that academic institutions have anything to offer them in technological terms. These credibility, information and cultural gaps prevent potentially fruitful interactions. As with research institutions, the absence of a 'technology culture' in industry means that firms do not seriously look for technical information and support.

The Kenyan situation has much in common with other university systems in Africa, which have failed to provide information, consultancy and technological support to productive enterprises. In a study for the IDRC, Ayiku (1991) notes a number of deterrents to *linkage formation between universities and firms*. From the university side, these are:

- Lack of multidisciplinary departments in African universities that can meet the complex problems of productive enterprises.
- Lack of understanding of enterprise business practices, time pressures, commercialization and confidentiality by university staff.
- Lack of flexibility within universities in appointing, promoting and remunerating staff to make it attractive to establish links with industry.
- Lack of recognition of value of industry linkages in universities.
- Clash between academic freedom of publication and needs of industry.

On the part of industry, the constraints include:

- Inability of firms to understand and define their technological problems clearly enough to seek academic assistance.
- Unwillingness of enterprises to finance university collaborations or contracts.
- Mistrust of domestic technology compared to imported technology.
- Lack of appreciation of what universities can offer by way of technology support.
- Weak in-house technological capabilities within firms, making it difficult for them to seek external assistance.

Assessing the Technology Infrastructure

Kenya's technology infrastructure is advanced by most African countries' standards, although small in comparison with other developing, and especially Asian, countries. It does not perform much technology generation for Kenyan industry, nor does it assist firms in accessing, adapting and improving foreign technologies. Apart from essential testing functions performed by the KEBS, it traditionally has little direct relations with the productive sector.

KEBS seems reasonably competent in the limited range of functions it undertakes, but it is difficult to evaluate whether it would be able to provide testing and calibration services to a more complex industrial sector. Ideally, its testing functions should be placed in a separate institution or assigned to private testing laboratories, with KEBS providing an accreditation and monitoring function. Moreover, it should strengthen its research function into standards development to the extent necessary for specific Kenyan needs. The government should remedy the skill shortages that affect its recruitment and training. As the industrial sector develops, the government should also consider setting up a separate metrology institution with much broader capabilities.

KIRDI has done much to reorient itself to meet the technical needs of industry, in particular of SMEs. Its reorganization and downsizing seem to be working, with growing demand for its services. However, these services aim at relatively mundane problems unrelated to its original R&D function. This may be desirable at this time, before private providers of such services have come into being; however, in the longer term the government must revive more substantive technological effort. The industrial focus of KIRDI is also fairly limited, and there appears to be a conspicuous gap in the area of electronics and IT technologies.

Universities in Kenya at this time are essentially irrelevant to industrial technology development. They lack the ability, and perhaps the incentive and flexibility, to seek out and address the needs of firms. Firms in turn find little to gain in interacting with university engineers, and also complain of the relevance of the training provided by universities.

Much of the difficulty in conducting research *for* industry lies in the weak technological capabilities of enterprises themselves. Firms are able to identify their specific technological needs and absorb inputs if they conduct technological activity in-house. They are willing to spend on contract research and to devote personnel time to external interactions. Where such capabilities are lacking, as they are in Kenya, even good technology institutions can do little. However, technology institutions in Kenya are products of the same culture and capabilities, and also need considerable strengthening. They are conscious of this need, but are not guided by a coherent overall technological strategy.

CONCLUSIONS ON TECHNOLOGICAL CAPABILITIES AND SOME POLICY IMPLICATIONS

The general level of technological capabilities in Kenyan industry is low relative to industrializing countries in Asia or Latin America, though it is advanced by the standards of its close neighbours. The recent liberalization has stimulated some upgrading of capabilities (Wignaraja and Ikiara, 1999), but such a positive response has been confined to a few larger firms. Many other firms, threatened by import competition, have died out or moved to other activities. Few have mounted technological strategies to take raise their capabilities and take their technologies to world frontiers. Even technologically 'good' firms show no evidence of the sustained and systematic search for improved productivity and quality, efforts to raise the capacities of equipment or substitute materials and processes, or improve worker skills, that mark the successful firms in the NIEs (Lall, 1999c). As a result, manufacturing growth is mainly taking place in activities that do not face direct world competition; apart from resource-based products, manufactured export growth is confined to niche markets in the neighbourhood. This would not matter if this were a prelude to more substantive and broad-based technological development that would stimulate competitive industrial growth - however, the signs of this are not promising. All indicators of technological activity and institutional support point to a 'low level equilibrium' rather than a shift to dynamic growth.

Thus, the post-liberalization period shows little noticeable rise in technology imports or technological effort. Formal R&D remains minuscule. The positive technological response, where present, is narrow, based on a few firms using new equipment and introducing better quality management and process engineering. It seems insufficient to dynamise the industrial sector or to develop new areas of competitiveness. The employment of technically qualified personnel remains low by international standards. While on-the-job training is given by many firms, this tends to be the minimum needed to transmit basic operational skills from existing to new operatives. More formal in-house training is carried out by relatively few enterprises. This is not compensated for by external technical training, which tends to be modest,[6] exacerbated by a lack of local institutions able to provide training relevant to industrial needs.

It is imperative to tackle the whole range of problems - in a careful and phased manner - if Kenya is to make technological progress, as it must if it is to industrialize at all. The liberalization process, which has been prolonged, hesitant and uncertain, has to be made credible, transparent and time-bound. It has to be supported by a coherent strategy to develop the capabilities needed to cope with import competition. There should be an effort to gauge the technological status and needs of Kenyan enterprises. In the advanced industrial and newly industrializing countries, technology development strategies use enterprise skill and technology audits, benchmarking of technical performance against international levels and concerted efforts to inform firms of the challenges facing them. These are backed up by policies to provide the necessary training, technology upgrading, quality certification, finance and reduction of transaction costs. There is much that Kenya can learn from them.

Links with technology institutions are confined to necessary, rather basic, activities like mandatory certification of products or material testing. There is very little research contracting or using institutions to search for and adapt new foreign technologies. In fact, firms seem generally unaware of the technological services or capabilities available in government institutions, or regard them as irrelevant or inefficient. Their view is not entirely unjustified: the institutions offer little, since they suffer from similar technological weaknesses. The technology infrastructure and the productive sector are isolated from each other. The adjustment process has reduced institutional funding and may have further isolated the institutions from the productive sector. The lack of institutional support for technology development is unfortunate, since firms face market failures in identifying their technological problems, obtaining relevant technical information and financing and mounting the necessary technological effort.

The better firms, while having reasonable degrees of competence in the technologies they operate, are still at the lower ends of the technological spectrum in their respective activities, and need to considerably enhance their physical and human capital and technological effort in order to grow and diversify under liberalized trade. FDI could play a major role in injecting new technologies and skills and raising capabilities to conduct local technological activity. However, FDI in general has been low and unresponsive to policy reform, and in technology-intensive manufacturing activities it is practically absent. In some part, low FDI is itself a reflection of local capabilities, though political, rent-seeking and security factors, combined with bureaucratic impediments, are probably larger deterrents to international investors.

The policy implications of this analysis are manifold, and the following issues are especially relevant to Kenya.

Technology strategy formulation

There is no institutional mechanism in Kenya for comprehensively evaluating and setting S&T priorities for the country. There is no well-developed science and technology plan, and the responsibility for relevant policies is spread over a large number of uncoordinated ministries and institutions. This setting is not conducive to supporting technology upgrading in Kenya.

In contrast, the strongly market and export-oriented Asian Tigers (Hong Kong excluded) have long had elaborate technology plans to identify and act upon strategic technologies for future development, and most developed countries have driven the process by defence and what has been termed 'mission oriented' objectives. Thus, the Kenyan government should review and improve its strategy making capabilities, and entrust one body with analysing technology needs at the broad economic level and designing and implementing strategies that cut across many ministerial and departmental lines. This body should include high level representatives from all the ministries and institutions concerned (universities, research institutions, standards and so on) and the private sector. It should report to top levels of the government to ensure that cross-cutting policies can be undertaken effectively, and this should occur within a context of a general sense of urgency and commitment to policies for technology upgrading.

Improving human capital and skills

Kenyan industry needs a larger stock of qualified technical and managerial personnel to cope with the competitive demands of the current technological revolution. A better trained workforce may contribute to a country's ability to respond flexibly to rapid economic and technological change, to produce higher quality products, to adopt and improve upon new production processes and technologies and to develop new skills as the structure of jobs evolves. Over the past decade, concerns regarding the supply of skilled workers have become acute not only in developing but also in developed countries. International comparisons suggest that the base of technical skills in Kenya is weak and its relevance to emerging technological needs limited. This may not constitute an immediate constraint to upgrading technology, but in the longer term it will certainly hold back a move into more advanced technologies.

The quality of education in Kenya seems to have declined, and has affected the system at all levels. Dropout and failure rates are high. Vocational training is held in low regard by employers, and fails to meet emerging industrial needs. Though there are ample technical colleges, their equipment tends to be poor and staff weak. Industry generally employs low levels of formally trained people. In-house training by industrial enterprises is used to compensate for the deficiencies of the formal system, and is fairly good by regional standards. However, such training is concentrated in large (particularly foreign) enterprises, and is aimed at providing basic operational skills rather than upgrading them.

In view of all this, a number of policy recommendations can be made:

- Comprehensive surveys of skill needs should be conducted on a regular basis, using techniques such as international benchmarking. This can serve as the basis for prioritizing training needs at all levels; the government should target new skills that are likely to be critical for future competitiveness, in particular in food-processing, capital-intensive process industries, and electrical and electronics engineering.
- The government must ensure effective interaction between employers and training institutions on a continuous basis.
- New types of training institutions more directly linked with, and in

some cases managed by, industry may be launched, involving also industry associations.

- Firm-level training must be encouraged by information and persuasion and, where desirable, by incentives and the setting up of institutions and programmes.
- SMEs have to be targeted by special information and incentive programmes to recruit better trained labour and to invest in formal training.
- Other skill weaknesses should be addressed - such as the shortage of the legal skills needed to operate a modern intellectual property regime, the standards and metrology skills, and the deficient training in applied R&D.

Stimulating and improving technology imports

Kenyan industry imports surprisingly little new technology, a clear sign of how poorly it is coping with the new liberal environment. There are no longer any obvious policy impediments to technology import. The IPR regime is improving though its implementation appears to be slow and cumbersome; however, this does not seem to be a significant constraint to the transfer of technology. The market is too small and local competition too underdeveloped for weak IPR implementation to hold TNCs back from transferring technology.

The main focus of technology transfer policy has to be on information provision to enterprises, particularly SMEs, on sources, costs and appropriateness of foreign technologies, backed by the provision of technical extension services to help them absorb new technologies. In fact, it is impossible to separate technology support measures from measures to facilitate technology imports.

Productivity centres are a well-tried and effective means of raising the quality and impact of technology transfer to industry. Kenya might set up such centres, starting with major industries like food processing and metalworking. Another means of improving productivity, especially of SMEs, is through the use of benchmarking exercises, similar to those carried out elsewhere (for example by the Department of Trade and Industry in the UK).

Improving the R&D climate

There is little awareness in industry of the importance of in-firm technological effort. Most firms tend to import technology and use it passively, often at well below international best practice levels. When the technology changes, they resort to further imports but again do little to master it. The required 'technology culture' does not exist in Kenya - and many other developing countries - and the government does not make any efforts to stimulate it. For instance, there are no fiscal incentives for enterprise R&D, which is not even allowable as a tax-deductible expense.[7]

A first step would be to accept R&D spending as a tax-deductible expense. Further measures may include granting a modest subsidy to R&D (say by providing matching grants to enterprises) or setting up a technology development fund to support R&D in critical areas. However, tax incentives are unlikely by themselves to stimulate much technology upgrading. To this end, concerted information and persuasion campaigns, backed by prizes and targeted measures to ensure that technology consciousness diffuses could be launched.

Strengthening the technology infrastructure and institutions

KEBS seems to be a well-run and competent institution within its sphere of activity, but it is doubtful whether it could provide the testing and metrology facilities suited to new technological needs. KEBS can develop itself into a stronger national and regional centre for metrology, standards, testing and quality (MSTQ) services if it enhances its range and skills. To this end, it is essential that the government undertake a strategic review of KEBS capabilities, investment needs and salaries and take appropriate measures to establish Kenya as a regional hub for MSTQ activities.

KIRDI has made great efforts to reform its operations and link itself to its industrial clients, especially to SMEs. However, the main constraint it faces now is a lack of trained personnel, in turn due to low salaries. The government should help remedy this, by raising remuneration to market levels. In the longer term, however, it is necessary for KIRDI to conduct more R&D work for industry rather than simply providing technical services. KIRDI should therefore have a strategic plan to help develop the private provision of routine technical services and itself move into more difficult and complex areas of technology work, potentially relevant to more advanced manufacturing activities.

FDI attraction

While Kenya has greatly improved its FDI regime, several bureaucratic impediments remain. A large number of specific licences are needed before a foreign investor can set up. The granting of investment incentives is variable, with discretionary, case-by-case operations. Moreover, it is still difficult and cumbersome to obtain expatriate permits, and Kenya has a negative image because of corruption and rent-seeking, with rising violence and security problems. It is vital for KIPC to bring its investor services to modern and competitive levels. It has to become a real 'one-stop shop', with an increased speed of services, bearing in mind that 'best practice' in FDI approval is less than one day in countries like Singapore. This needs considerable improvements in skills in the KIPC and a more substantial budget for undertaking effective promotion, guided by investor tracking and targeting strategies.

More important, FDI policies have to be based upon an understanding of the new determinants of investment location today. It is likely that FDI will be the main avenue for technology transfer and upgrading in Kenya, and that foreign affiliates will be the major performers of technological activity locally. Therefore the government must do everything in its power to raise its attraction to TNCs.

Strengthening intellectual property rights

The Kenyan government has to improve its capabilities for drafting competition policy, price regulation, targeted subsidies or other transfer mechanisms that would help mitigate the potential negative effects of stronger ownership rights on intellectual property. As far as IPRs are directly concerned, the lack of qualified patent lawyers in Kenya is a handicap that has to be remedied. Moreover, there is substantial need to expand awareness in provincial towns, fairs and shows to raise consciousness of the importance of IPRs.

Having a strong legal regime is no use, however, if implementation is slow, cumbersome and non-transparent. Kenya needs not just qualified patent lawyers and judges but an efficient system which acts quickly and fairly, and is seen to be doing so. As noted, however, the potentially anti-competitive effects of strong IPRs have to be offset by effective competition policy. This is itself a very demanding and skill-intensive task, which no developing country today can afford to neglect.

To end, it is vital for Kenyan development to raise technological levels in industry if it is to prosper in the new international environment. Its record so far is not impressive, and it is falling behind fast-moving competitors. However, there are signs that awareness of the issues is growing. What is now needed is for this awareness to be transformed into a coherent strategy, with a strong commitment to its implementation.

NOTES

1. For instance, a severe drought caused water and electricity shortages, prompting the introduction of energy conservation measures in 1992. Access to imports was constricted because of a suspension of foreign aid in 1991. Coupled with weak export growth, this reduced capacity utilization in manufacturing significantly. See Wignaraja and Ikiara (1999).
2. *Kenya Gazette Supplement* No. 33: 1999. Nairobi, Government Printer, 1999. However, effective duties on textile and clothing products are lower because of smuggling of used (*mitumba*) products without duty.
3. The research institutions set up were the Forest Department in 1902, Agricultural

Laboratories in 1903, Coffee Research Services in 1910, the Njoro Plant Breeding Station in 1927 and the Tea Research Foundation in 1951.
4. Mauritius had over $1.5 billion of clothing exports in that year with much higher wages.
5. The KEBS website (http://www.kebs.org) provides background information on this institution.
6. A World Bank study (Biggs et al., 1995) also notes the low levels of internal and external training efforts, and their limited scope and sporadic nature, among African manufacturing firms in their samples. In Kenya, it is only the best garment-exporting firm that has been able to draw upon its relationship with foreign buyers to improve training.
7. In 'latecomer' Asian Tigers like Malaysia and Thailand, where the government is desperately trying to develop a 'technology culture', R&D is given 150–200 per cent tax subsidies.

4. Tanzania

INTRODUCTION

At independence, Tanzania inherited a small and simple industrial base. The base expanded over time, but its progress was halting and slow, and was reversed in the early 1980s as output and capacity utilization fell. The decline was stopped in the late 1990s. Earlier strategies of inward-looking import substitution were dropped and manufacturing was exposed to fairly rapid trade and domestic liberalization. However, the industrial sector remains rudimentary, dominated by simple activities. Competitive responses to market forces have been weak, with little sign of sustained technological or export dynamism. The economy remains heavily dependent on agriculture and other natural resources, without the structural transformation that long-term development requires. One of the critical challenges facing Tanzanian policy-makers, having opened the economy to global market forces, is to catalyse technological upgrading in industry and start this transformation.

The government has shown a growing awareness of the need for such technological upgrading. As the Ministry of Science, Technology and Higher Education (MSTHE) (1996, pp. 3–5) says,

> The vital role of science and technology in socio-economic development is acknowledged the world over, by all nations, both developed and developing. It is therefore imperative for developing countries like Tanzania to embrace science and technology as a vital tool for accelerating their social economic development. It is becoming increasingly clear that developments in science and technology are not only important determinants of a country's level of development but also enhance its international competitiveness and its position in the world economy ... A realistic Science and Technology Policy for Tanzania should therefore guide government ministries and parastatal organisations, including universities and other research and training institutions as well as the private sector and non-governmental organisations in the choice, assessment, transfer and adaptation of technologies.

The government launched an S&T Plan in 1996. The plan had ambitious targets, including, among others, one that R&D in Tanzania reach 1 per cent of GDP by 2000. It also proposed that foreign technology inflows are monitored and additional high level research and technical manpower created. Within manufacturing specifically, the plan proposed the development of export-oriented activities based on local resources, improvements in productivity and technology, raising capacity utilization and strengthening of SMEs. The strategies to achieve this included enhancing design and engineering capacity and encouraging regional and international cooperation in R&D activities. They encompassed improving access to technology imports, strengthening R&D links with enterprises to raise the production of modern capital goods, and setting up engineering workshops for the maintenance, manufacture and repair of machinery. The plan also envisaged a greater use of intellectual property rights to encourage innovative activity.

A later government publication (COSTECH, 1998) amplified on industrial R&D objectives. Among others, it mentioned chemical engineering, clean production, IT, biotechnology, new materials, metal resources, and high quality spares. A new S&T Plan was on the drawing board at the end of 1999.

None of these ambitious objectives seem to have been realized. The plan remains largely on paper, while technological activity in Tanzania languishes. There is very little dynamism in private industry, while technology support institutions are passive and largely de-linked from productive activity. Total R&D is 0.35 per cent of GDP, down from around 0.5 per cent in 1984. More importantly, R&D is conducted almost entirely in the public sector and largely devoted to non-industrial activities. Research institutions for industry are poorly funded, staffed and motivated; they have weak links with industry and contribute little or nothing to operational technologies. In the meantime, liberalization has affected manufacturing severely, more so than in neighbouring Kenya and raised the need for technological strengthening to restart industrial development.

INDUSTRIAL BACKGROUND

Tanzania launched its industrial strategy, as did most other developing countries, with import substitution. Its initial industrial base was, as noted, small and rudimentary. There were less than 400 manufacturing establishments in 1961, largely involved in primary processing and simple consumer products. To deepen this base and promote self-reliance, the government adopted a 'Basic Industrial Strategy' in the 1970s, involving the promotion of consumer as well as intermediate and capital goods (Wangwe, 2000). The latter part of the strategy largely failed; simple consumer products continued to dominate manufacturing activity. After an initial spurt in output, growth rates declined, inefficiency grew and capacity utilization fell to very low levels.

Tanzanian GDP grew at 3.9 per cent per year in real terms during 1966–75, with manufacturing growing at 4.8 per cent. The export orientation of manufacturing declined steadily after the 1960s, the share of exports in output falling from 12.4 per cent in 1970–75 to 9 per cent in 1976–80 (Deraniyagala and Semboja, 1999). In 1981–85, severe trade restrictions were imposed. GDP growth fell to 0.7 per cent per annum and manufacturing output declined at an annual rate of 5 per cent. The share of manufacturing in GDP fell from 12.9 per cent in 1976 to 8.1 per cent in 1988, and the share of exports in manufacturing output to 4.6 per cent in 1981–85.

The government started to liberalize trade during 1985–88, with currency devaluation and the opening up of selected imports. 'Serious' liberalization, however, was launched after 1988, when most import restrictions were dismantled, tariffs reduced and the tariff structure rationalized. Thus, the 18 tariff categories in 1980, with dispersions rating from 0 to 200 per cent, were reduced by 1992 to 5 categories with rates of between 0 and 40 per cent (Deraniyagala and Semboja, 1999). Effective rates of protection declined and quantitative restrictions on imports were virtually scrapped. Between the fiscal years 1993/94 and 1997/98, the trade-weighted average tariff rate fell from 25 per cent to 20 per cent. By the early 1990s, Tanzania was one of the leading countries in Africa in the consistency and spread of liberalization.

While the post-liberalization period showed improved performance, GDP growth rates were still low (at 3 per cent per annum), below the population growth rate. The decline in manufacturing growth was reversed, with growth rates averaging around 3.5 per cent per annum in 1986–94. However, its performance lagged that of the agricultural and service sectors, with growth rates of 5 and 4.2 per cent respectively. Investment increased sharply, with the ratio of fixed capital formation to GDP rising to 32 per cent in 1986–92; this was largely the result of increased external financing consequent on structural adjustment rather than higher domestic savings. This increased investment was mainly directed at agriculture, with the share of manufacturing falling from 24 per cent in 1981–85 to 13 per cent in 1986–92.

Export growth improved, averaging 9 per cent per annum between 1987 and 1992 and reversing its decline during 1980–86. There was also diversification in export composition: the share of non-traditional in total exports increased from 24 per cent in 1985 to 41 per cent in 1989. Manufactured exports constituted a major part of this diversification, with the share of manufactured in total exports increasing from 13 per cent in 1980–85 to 21 per cent in 1986–91. However, these growth rates must be placed in context: the values involved are tiny, with total manufactured exports only reaching $99 million in 1996/97 and growing at a rate of 3.6 per cent since the early 1980s (see Chapter 2).

In recent years, manufacturing performance has been very erratic, and average capacity utilization still has not recovered to levels achieved around

Table 4.1 Recent manufacturing performance in Tanzania

Year	MVA growth rate	MVA (%GDP)	Manufactured export growth rate	Share in total exports (%)	Capacity utilization (%)
1992	−4.1	8.2	−8.7	16.0	38
1993	0.6	8.2	−19.0	11.8	50
1994	0.2	8.1	48.0	14.8	46
1995	1.6	7.9	41.9	16.0	–
1996	4.8	8.0	1.4	14.6	48
1997	5.0	8.1	−5.7	14.5	–
1998	8.0	8.4	−31.0	10.7	55
Average	2.3	8.1	3.8	14.1	47

Source: Wanga (2000). The definition of 'manufactured exports' differs from that used in Chapter 2.

two decades ago (Table 4.1). Labour productivity in 1990 was 21 per cent lower than in 1965, primarily because of poor parastatal performance. Average labour productivity in Tanzania in 1989 was only 3.7 per cent of that in US manufacturing - a rough indicator of technological levels after discounting for differences in capital intensity of manufacturing (Szirmai et al., 2000).

The contribution of MVA to national income is stagnating at around 8 per cent (around the same as in 1985) and the share of manufactured exports in total exports has declined over 1992–98. Of manufactured exports, nearly 80 per cent comes from resource-based activities. Within manufacturing, labour-intensive activities like clothing exposed to intense import competition have suffered massive declines in output. Despite low wages and quota free access to EU markets, there are only two export-oriented garment firms, both doing very low-value work for the US market. While less exposed activities like engineering have invested in upgrading their equipment, technological competence remains low and the intensity of the response is very muted (Deraniyagala and Semboja, 1999). While the overall picture is similar to that of Kenya, the level of industrial development and vigour of response to liberalization are much lower.

SCIENCE AND TECHNOLOGY POLICIES

Policy background

The Tanzania National Scientific Research Council (TNSRC) was established in 1969 to manage science and technology development. In 1985, the government published the National Science and Technology Policy document, reflecting its socialist philosophy. Following this publication, it set up the Commission for Science and Technology (COSTECH) in place of TNSRC, giving it a wider and clearer mandate of coordinating and promoting S&T policies. It also provided for the establishment of a Centre for the Development and Transfer of Technology (CDTT); the National Fund for the Advancement of Science and Technology (NFAST) and the Tanzania Award for Science and Technological Achievement (TASTA). The government reviewed S&T policies in 1996 to take into account structural reforms that shifted the emphasis from state-led and planned development to a market-oriented, private sector-led economy. As noted, the 1996 document of the MSTHE set broad and ambitious objectives, which have been enhanced in the 1998 COSTECH document.

These documents, however, are optimistic ‘wish lists’ by the science ministry rather than realistic government strategies for upgrading Tanzanian science and technology. They are not based on serious analyses of the technology status or problems of Tanzanian industry (Mlawa, 1999, p. 55). They are not even a coordinated amalgam of the views of different government ministries. The strategies required to implement them are not spelled out. They fail to take account of institutional structures and weaknesses and of the resource constraints to R&D activities. They ignore the skill constraints that bedevil capability development in Tanzania, and the negative response of industry to liberalization.

Institutions

After the dissolution of the East African Community in 1977, which led to the loss of regional R&D institutions, the Tanzanian government set up national institutions to fill the gap (Wangwe, 2001). The Tanzanian Industrial Research and Development Organization (TIRDO) was set up in 1979 as the main body to promote technology development for manufacturing. The Tanzanian Engineering and Manufacturing Design Organization (TEMDO) was established in 1980 to promote engineering services and provide technical training to enterprises. The Institute of Production Innovation (IPI) started in 1981 at the University of Dar es Salaam to carry out product innovation and transfer this to industry, and to provide technical consultancy for enterprises. In addition to these R&D related institutions, the Small Industries Development Organization (SIDO) was set up in 1973 to provide extension services and marketing support to SMEs.

Many of these institutions suffered during the adjustment and liberalization process. Their financial resources declined. Those heavily dependent on donor financing – the majority – were more affected as funding was cut or switched to other uses. In the 1990s there was increased fragmentation of R&D institutions as costs mounted, staff morale declined and fixed assets had to be sold in some instances to finance current expenses (Wangwe, 2001). Industry showed even less interest in local technologies after liberalization, despite increased efforts by the institutions to market their wares to the private sector. We return to some specific cases below.

Intellectual property rights

The Patent Act (1987) provides the legal framework for IPRs in Tanzania. Based on the UK patent system, it was initially geared more to the needs of foreign companies that wanted protection in Tanzania rather than to those of domestic innovators and inventors. Since the patent system started operating in Tanzania only six patents have been issued to Tanzanian nationals (companies or individuals). However, this may reflect more the paucity of domestic technological activity than problems with the patent system. The technological value of the locally filed patents is not known, but in view of the evidence on local technological activity (below) it is likely that they were filed by individuals and not exploited commercially.

The Patent Office also has weaknesses. It lacks facilities for online search of patent information, so that it only serves as a re-registration office for patents registered abroad. It also lacks the resources to employ the skilled legal and technical personnel needed in a modern patent office, and in any case, many of these skills do not exist within the country. It does little to promote awareness of IPRs in industry. A strong and well-administered IPR system would be desirable in the long term to promote both the transfer of new technologies to Tanzania and to stimulate local technological activity. However, at this time the weaknesses of the institutional system are not very relevant to technology development in Tanzania - although they reflect other, underlying structural deficiencies that deter technology import, FDI and indigenous technological effort. It is only when these are remedied that the IPR system would become an independent constraint to technology development.

TECHNOLOGICAL IMPORTS AND ACTIVITY

The paucity of both technology import and generation by Tanzanian industry has been noted in Chapter 2, which showed how low capital goods imports were. The available Central Bank data on royalties and technical fees paid abroad show that in 1996 there were no recorded payments. In 1997 payments were \$0.3 million, in 1998 \$4.7 million and in 1999 \$3.8 million. While this suggests an encouraging trend, it is not clear whether the payments were for manufacturing technology or for management and technical fees in recently privatized utilities.[1]

Tanzanian industry does very little or no formal R&D. Though some firms claim to conduct R&D,[2] it is likely that they are including other technical functions (like quality testing, simple design adaptation and so on) under this heading. Recent studies of Tanzania (see Lall, 1999c; Semboja and Kweka, 2000; and Biggs and Ratauri, 1997) suggest that informal technological activity and learning - while they exist - are also relatively weak, and smaller than in other African countries (see Table 2.18). The low level of capabilities in Tanzanian industry is a vital constraint on its ability to respond positively to liberalization.

In the garment industry, as noted, this lack of capabilities has led to devastation. Many manufacturers have closed down and few have emerged to take advantage of low wages and liberal trade rules in world markets. Only two garment firms in the country are export-oriented. In response to liberalization, Tanzanian garment firms suffered an average 70 per cent decline in employment, and capacity utilization for firms that stayed in production fell from 60 per cent to 30–50 per cent in the 1990s. A survey showed that only 5 per cent of garment firms were even aware of ISO 9000 standards. Liberalization led firms to reduce their maintenance and product design personnel. Garment production is further affected by the very low labour productivity in the upstream textile industry: the time in man-hours needed for weaving a given length of cloth was 4.5 times higher than in Kenya, 5.2 times higher than India and 11.4 times higher than Turkey (Wangwe, 2001).

This suggests that even in the simple activities where Tanzania should be building new competitive advantages after liberalization, the base of capabilities remains too low to provide a positive response. As Wangwe (2001) puts it,

> although changes in the macroeconomic environment have introduced competitive pressures among manufacturers (for example, injecting a sense of quality consideration), many of the earlier weaknesses in technological development have not been resolved. Changes in macroeconomic policy and enterprise level rehabilitation programmes are not enough for industrial restructuring to be realised.

There are some signs of technological improvement, however, mainly in resource-based industries taken over from the government by foreign companies. For instance, the Tanzania Cigarette Company was taken over by RJ Reynolds, which then introduced modern technology and work practices, significantly raising productivity (Box 4.1). Another example is Tanzania Breweries, taken over from the government by a South African firm (Wangwe et al., 1997).

BOX 4.1 TANZANIA CIGARETTE COMPANY AND UPGRADING VIA FOREIGN DIRECT INVESTMENT

RJ Reynolds (USA) took over the Tanzania Cigarette Company (TCC) from the government in 1995. While the company had a virtual monopoly of the protected domestic cigarette market, it had been showing losses and was losing out to smuggled products from Kenya. It suffered from over-employment and weak technological and management capabilities. Waste rates were high, product quality low and work incentives inappropriate. There was no use of information technology in the firm.

After the takeover, the firm recruited new managers, mostly Tanzanians trained in foreign universities (local universities bred the 'wrong attitudes'); it used the Internet to track down possible recruits. Redundant workers were fired, and the workforce reduced from 1300 (750 on the shopfloor) to 800 (300) over four years. Productivity per employee rose by 300 per cent and total output by 35 per cent. The waste rate declined and product quality rose to international levels. Inventory was cut significantly. The firm is now considering putting in for ISO 9000 certification. Around 10–15 per cent of output is now exported through the parent company network. The firm has catalysed a lot of new investment in tobacco growers who supply the raw materials.

The firm undertook substantial amounts of training for its employees. it changed supervisors and gave performance related incentives, with far greater transparency on pay and benefits. It raised quality control efforts, and generally provided a much more congenial and clean work environment. Foreign technicians were brought in to raise production standards, and new equipment was imported to raise productivity and quality.

The main constraint to further improvement is the lack of skills, especially at the technical and managerial levels. The educational system is weak and the curriculum and teaching methods are obsolete. There is great emphasis on rote learning rather than problem solving. The firm has no interaction with local technology institutions, and finds that they have little or nothing to offer that it would find useful.

Sources: Interview with Mr. N. Gotecha, MD of the Tanzania Cigarette Company; *Financial Times* (1999).

INWARD FDI

Tanzania has undertaken several measures to improve its FDI regime and inflows have increased recently as a result. However, the amounts are still very low by developing country standards and most inflows have gone into privatized public utilities or resource-based manufacturing enterprises aimed at domestic markets. There is relatively little inflow into export-oriented or non-resource-based manufacturing.

The agency in charge of promoting and facilitating FDI is the Tanzania Investment Centre (TIC), formerly the Investment Promotion Centre (IPC), established in 1991 under the National Investment Promotion and Protection Act of 1990. In 1997 reforms were undertaken to make TIC a single point for efficient promotion of private investment. One indicator of the government's commitment to improving the FDI regime has been its response to an 'Investor Roadmap' exercise undertaken in 1996 (TSG, 1997). This exercise 'painted an intimidating picture of a red-tape ridden, bureaucratically dominated economy. This study ... forced the TIC to rethink its strategy, to streamline its procedures and to shift focus from a screening agency that inhibits decisions to a facilitative agency that promotes investment (*Financial Times*, 1999).

Tax rates were brought down, with corporate taxes now at 30 per cent, down from 35 per cent. Import duties have been lowered and rationalized. At the time of the field visits, there was a new Bonded Warehouse Scheme for exporters, which granted five-year tax holidays and duty free access to imported inputs.[3] No EPZ was in operation but one was under consideration, with possible World Bank funding. Low labour costs are attractive, with the minimum wage in Tanzania set at US$45 per month; a fresh graduate is paid US$120 per month and an engineer US$220. However, expensive and low quality infrastructure represents a major disincentive for FDI (WEF, 1998).

By March 1999, TIC had approved 1250 projects worth Tshs. 2779 billion. Of these, 598 projects (47.8 per cent) were put forward by local investors, 249 projects (19.9 per cent) by foreign investors, and 403 projects (32.3 per cent) by joint ventures. Of all projects, 627 (50 per cent) were in industry and 182 (14.6 per cent) in tourism. However, about 50 per cent of all projects had not been implemented.

Despite these improvements, however, the investment climate still faces problems. The TIC is not a real 'one-stop shop', though it claims to be (TIC, 1998, p. 11). It tries to assist investors to go through the bureaucratic hoops in the various ministries but has no effective voice in these matters. Its own approval takes only 3–14 days but subsequent approvals can take much longer. Its promotion is weak and it lacks the financial and human resources for undertaking effective promotion. It is unable to effectively coordinate the various agencies involved, say by gearing local infrastructure, skills and institutions to the needs of investors. Obtaining expatriate work permits can still be a long and difficult procedure. In 1999, the same consultants undertook another 'Investor Roadmap' exercise in Tanzania. Box 4.2 summarizes the findings.

BOX 4.2 NEW TANZANIA INVESTOR ROADMAP, 1999

An Investor Roadmap for Tanzania was completed in 1999 for USAID by The Services Group in consultation with TIC. The report noted a number of serious policy and procedural deficiencies that added to investor costs and could deter FDI inflows. The 1999 Roadmap was an update of a similar effort in 1996, and was intended to analyse improvements in the regime in four areas: employment, location, reporting and operating. The report finds a mixed picture since 1996: significant improvements as well as no change or even some regression. Taking each major process:

- *Employment* While the situation has improved and most investors would not be deterred by red tape on employment issues, 'the country's labour laws remain woefully inadequate to support a modern private sector economy'. The use of expatriate staff has improved. The hiring of labour is not a problem, but labour laws are outdated and biased in favour of workers. Terminating employment is difficult and complicated, the cost of worker benefits is high, and skilled labour is scarce, particularly in management.
- *Location* Earlier complex and inefficient land acquisition processes have improved, but securing a title remains time-consuming and complex. There are many authorities involved with no means of coordinating them. Thus, receiving a land title can take several months to years, and non-Tanzanians have limited land ownership rights. Developing land for industrial purposes can be cumbersome and expensive, with multiple approvals needed and rent-seeking behaviour. Infrastructure services such as for example power and water, remain poor and costly.
- *Reporting* There are considerable improvements in reporting and registering requirements. The most important of these is shift in emphasis of the TIC from approving and regulating to facilitating FDI. Several incentives are now

automatic and the list of incentives has expanded. However, the TIC is still not a one-stop shop. The number and incidence of taxes remain high. Tax collection procedures are onerous. The number of licences and overlapping regulatory mandates, without proper coordination among government agencies is a deterrent to private investors.

- *Operating* Despite improvements, regulations and procedures still impose high transaction costs on investors in Tanzania. Import and export procedures are cumbersome and complex in spite of a significant shortening of clearance times. On the other hand, the liberalization of exchange and financial markets has largely eliminated problems in acquiring and remitting foreign exchange.

These procedural problems are compounded by a number of economic (infrastructure, human capital, currency fluctuations and so on) and legal problems that deter FDI that were not addressed in the Roadmap. On infrastructure, for instance, the Roadmap noted that there was a backlog of some 50 000 applicants in Dar for telephone installation, in spite of the very poor telephone service, with a mere 45 per cent call completion ratio in the metropolitan area.

The legal system poses significant problems that are summarized thus: 'Many laws are outdated and several acts contradict one another, creating considerable confusion for investors. Further, the integrity of the Tanzanian justice system has been widely questioned and few legal reforms have borne fruit. In general, the courts are seen to be slow, inefficient and, especially at the lower levels, easily corruptible. Companies are loath to settle contractual and labour disputes in the Tanzanian court system for fear of being embroiled in lengthy and often corruptible court cases ... The inadequacies of the commercial court system and lack of a functioning small claims court or binding arbitration mechanism makes some companies feel vulnerable while doing business in Tanzania' (p. vi).

In conclusion, the regulatory and administrative environment for new investors in Tanzania 'has improved in recent years, [but] it still falls short of what many investors have come to expect, and of what will facilitate high levels of foreign and local private investment ... Tanzania's procedural barriers are still enough to make some investors look elsewhere, especially when comparisons are made with other countries ... Many regulations and procedures significantly increase the cost of conducting business in Tanzania and these are compounded by the enduring problems with corruption, conflicting and confusing regulations, low skill availability and high production costs. This makes Tanzania less attractive a destination of FDI than many developing countries' (p. 118)

Source: Based on TSG (1999).

TECHNOLOGY INFRASTRUCTURE

Wangwe et al. (1997, p. 23) summarize the situation on technological activity and support in Tanzania:

> The manufacturing sector is still immature, thus little or no R&D activities are carried out within industries. Links among the industrial R&D institutions are seemingly weak, and where these do exist, they are usually driven by necessity and often dictated by the prevailing circumstances. There is also a weak link between these technology parks, institutions and the manufacturing sector. No formal R&D is done in most firms. There are few instances of major improvements to process technology or the introduction of new processes based on local efforts.

The following section considers the problems facing the main industrial technology institutions in the country.

Tanzania Commission for Science and Technology (COSTECH)

COSTECH (under the Ministry of Science, Technology and Higher Education) was formed in 1986 from the Tanzania National Scientific Research Council (which was started in 1972). Its mission was to manage S&T in the country, advise the government on S&T policies and sponsor research. In practice its main focus is science rather than technology (Mlawa, 1999). Its staff of 80 includes 20 scientists. Its main functions are as follows:

- COSTECH manages the National Fund for the Advancement of Science and Technology, set up in 1995 to support research. In 1998–99 it disbursed about US$265 000 (from the government and foreign donors) under this fund.
- It gives the Tanzanian Award for Scientific and Technological Achievement for worthy advances, holds annual scientific seminars, and issues permits to foreign researchers to conduct work in Tanzania.
- It grants research funding to scientists, based on peer review of

> proposals and rigorous vetting; almost all the applicants are academic scientists rather than industrial researchers. Nine technical committees drawn from various disciplines advise it.

Before liberalization it used to intervene in technology transfer contracts to promote 'appropriate' technology, but this function was dropped after 1994.

When COSTECH conducted an internal study of industrial R&D, it found that there was almost none in the country. Enterprises have often proved very unwilling to respond to COSTECH promotion efforts. When asked by the UNCTAD mission, it *could not identify a single firm* in Tanzania conducting real R&D. It also tried to patent two of its research findings but was unsuccessful.

COSTECH is entirely funded by the government and foreign donors and does not raise resources independently. As sources of funding get tighter, it is finding it increasingly difficult to continue its research funding operations. One problem in promoting R&D in Tanzania is that different research institutes are under different ministries and are not answerable to COSTECH. This makes it very difficult to have a coherent strategy and to coordinate research efforts. It tried to convince the government to centralize the research function but failed. COSTECH also finds it difficult to interact with R&D in higher education institutions, to the extent that this exists. There is no strategy for the creation of technical and research manpower in these institutions, though this would be very desirable, and sometimes graduates stay unemployed because of a serious skill mismatch.

In principle, COSTECH could be a pivotal institution for technology development in Tanzania, but it is not yet fulfilling this role. It has not been able to coordinate research in the various institutions that conduct it, and lead them to carry out research valuable for the industrial sector. However, with better funding, management, motivation and remuneration COSTECH could fulfil its mandate much better.

Tanzania Bureau of Standards (TBS)

TBS started in 1976 under the Ministry of Industry and Commerce to manage standards, testing, metrology and quality functions (MSTQ) in Tanzania. It currently has a staff of 135, which includes 80 scientists and engineers. It operates a Certification Scheme with a TBS mark and provides testing facilities for this purpose and for use by industry. Its metrology section is the custodian of primary calibration for temperature, mass, energy, volume, pressure and weight; its measures are internationally traceable. TBS provides training facilities in standards and quality assurance, and runs an awareness campaign for quality. To 1999 it had written around 700 standards.

However, quality consciousness is low in Tanzania. Only two firms (a soft drinks firm and a battery manufacturer) have been awarded ISO 9000 certification. Most SMEs are not even aware that such certification exists. However, liberalization and privatization have helped raise awareness; there are now 270 products certified with the TSB mark as compared to 80 in 1996.

TBS laboratories are not internationally accredited and the Bureau lacks the capability to accredit independent testing laboratories. The lack of international accreditation means that exporters cannot use its tests for export purposes. This can add significantly to their costs in activities where such tests are required and can constitute a barrier to manufactured export growth. TBS claims to be trying to upgrade its food and chemical laboratories to reach the levels needed for accreditation in the near future, but needs international team tests, new equipment, facilities and staff training. The lack of resources is constraining this upgrading.

TBS earns about 70 per cent of its budget from testing services, with the remainder coming from the government. Its testing facilities are not adequate to the needs of industry and many tests have to be performed in other countries, such as Kenya and South Africa. In the long term, testing should become a private service activity and ideally the government should fund standard setting activities. TBS should also be provided with the resources and incentives to undertake a more aggressive quality campaign, particularly to reach SMEs that are far behind in quality management and standardization. There are apparently no private consultants available on quality management in Tanzania - a major gap that needs to be addressed if industrial technology is to make any progress. There are also no university courses available in standardization and quality management in Tanzania (many go to India for training). Capabilities are also limited in metrology, particularly in the energy field.

In general, therefore, the TBS is *underfunded and technologically lagging*. While it has a large stock of trained and motivated technical personnel, its equipment and specialized capabilities are not able to serve existing, let alone future Tanzanian needs. Its passive approach to promoting quality awareness and in reaching out to SMEs should be radically changed.

Tanzania Industrial Research and Development Organization (TIRDO)

TIRDO was started in 1979 to conduct industrial research and offer consultancy services to industry. It derived from the decentralization of the research activities of the East African Community, initially conducted in Nairobi, after the breakdown of the Community (see Chapters 3 and 5). By end 1999, it had around 75 staff, of whom 35 were scientists and engineers. According to the TIRDO leaflet,

> the core of our operation is to promote technology utilisation in economic ventures ... The organisation is mainly involved in carrying out industrial research for the purpose of developing products and processes suitable for the Tanzanian industrial environment. In this regard, the emphasis is to promote the use of indigenous raw materials that can be processed using equipment fabricated largely by local workshops. Based on the technology developed, entrepreneurs are consequently invited to spin off and establish production plants following a two-years field trial.

In addition, TIRDO offers the following services:

- The instrumentation centre provides maintenance and repair services for instruments.
- The chemical laboratory offers a range of analytical services.
- The energy management centre offers advice on the efficient use of energy.
- The materials laboratory offers a range of mobile non-destructive tests as well as physical tests on various materials.
- The mechanical workshop offers a range of fabrication, welding and regrinding services.
- The furniture workshop is able to undertake manufacturing jobs.
- The National Cleaner Production Centre (part of a UNIDO/UNEP project) provides policy advice on environmental management, demonstrating clean technologies, training industry personnel and providing technical information.
- The industrial information centre responds to technical enquiries on industrial matters, and collects technical information from around the world by publications and the Internet.

Moreover, TIRDO offers trouble-shooting and advisory services on technology selection, product diversification and process control and optimization.

The objectives with which TIRDO were set up were fairly modest – using local raw materials, developing simple appropriate technologies and providing support and information services to local industry (mainly SMEs). They were well suited to a country at Tanzania's level of industrial development. However, how well have these objectives been met?

There is little interaction between TIRDO and the private sector; where this takes place it is mainly with large firms using specific technical services. Some 58 per cent of the TIRDO budget came from services sold to industry in the 1999 financial year, with the remainder coming from the government budget. Due to financial pressures (there is an unfinished building on the site for administration, abandoned because government money ran out), there is *almost no money left for R&D activity*.

Most of TIRDO's activities are thus industrial services, for which it charges full cost at rates based on the use of staff and equipment. The biggest earner is the sale of non-destructive testing services to the public sector petrochemical industry. Other earners are (state-owned) power stations seeking the analysis of fuel characteristics.

TIRDO has never taken out any patents. It has developed process know-how for such products as caustic soda, chalk and chipboard manufacturing, largely using mature technologies from other developing countries. It can get the simpler components manufactured locally, but all complex parts have to be imported because of the weaknesses of local engineering. There is no electronics engineer in TIRDO, greatly restricting its ability to work in modern technologies.

TIRDO salaries are tied to government scales, reducing its attractiveness to young graduates or to ambitious qualified people generally. While employees are allowed to keep 30 per cent of the value of services sold to industry, this does not provide sufficient incentive to go out and seek work or help SMEs solve technical problems. It certainly does not stimulate any genuine technological activity.

Hardly any of the technologies developed by TIRDO have been used by industry, and liberalization has not stimulated any new demand for its services. The larger firms and foreign affiliates that have upgraded technology have looked overseas rather than at TIRDO, presumably because it is unable to offer real assistance. Its 'image' with industry is poor, and its capabilities lack credibility. Most of the laboratory equipment was given by donors, and with their loss of interest has suffered from obsolescence. In fact, some of it cannot be used because it is no longer possible to get spares (particularly electronics) for old models. SMEs rarely use TIRDO technical services. Hardly any technology development projects have been commisioned by industry; one exception that was mentioned was the development of particleboard based on rice husk, undertaken by a MSc student at the University of Dar es Salaam using TIRDO facilities, and did not involve research staff.

A detailed study of TIRDO (Bongenaar and Szirmai, 1999) looked at 12 of the 25 technology projects undertaken during 1979–96 (the small number of projects over the 27 years is itself noteworthy). The authors found that most projects were undertaken at the initiative of TIRDI staff rather than at the request of industry. 'This lack of involvement of productive enterprises is characteristic of all activities of TIRDO in the development of new technologies' (Bongenaar and Szirmai, 1999). Project evaluation was entirely in-house and did not look in depth at technical or economic desirability or the environmental aspects of projects. The original technology was imported and generally simple – and mostly over five years old. The main objective was to use local materials and as much as possible of local equipment. Success was defined by the technical objectives of the staff rather than application by industry or commercial success. There was no attempt to relate technological efforts to industrial competitiveness. Once developed, marketing of the technologies to potential users was weak - very few projects reached the stage where TIRDO looked for entrepreneurs to implement them. According to Bongenaar and Szirmai, *not one* reached the stage of technology transfer from TIRDO to private industry.

This suggests that TIRDO is a largely dormant institution. Despite its potential role in supporting, stimulating and producing industrial technology efforts, it so far has not been able to link itself to industry, identify real industrial needs or provide new technologies. It has not met even its modest ambitions of promoting the use of simple technologies by industry. It is surviving by providing low-level services that would normally be sold by small firms. Its staff is poorly paid and seems demoralized. There is little sign of managerial initiative to improve its functioning; this contrasts with the recent experience of its Kenyan counterpart KIRDI (Chapter 3).

TIRDO's situation is not unusual for a public industrial technology institution. Its lack of credibility and dynamism reflects not just its internal constraints, but also general technological apathy in local industry. If enterprises are not technologically active and aware, it is difficult for support institutions to provide them with assistance (Rush et al., 1996). The lack of industrial technological capabilities, in other words, limits the innovativeness of support institutions. It is not surprising, therefore, that the main response to technological challenges during liberalization has been withdrawal (Lall, 1999c).

Small Industries Development Organization (SIDO)

SIDO was set up in 1973 to help SMEs and handicraft producers by setting up industrial estates and by giving consultancy, credit, training and marketing. It has 25 regional offices throughout Tanzania (but not in Zanzibar). It has set up 14 industrial estates with an average of 10 rentable premises each, and 3 training-cum-production centres. It operates a consultancy and technical assistance scheme. Its main functions are thus credit delivery, training and consultancy.

SIDO has managed the 'Sister Industrial Programme' funded by the Swedish government, supporting the transfer of equipment and technology from Sweden. This programme was later transformed to 'Triangular Cooperation', where Swedish funds were used to source technology and equipment from other developing countries (mainly India and the Philippines). The programme ended with the exhaustion of Swedish funds. As with many aid-dependent activities in Tanzania, SIDO suffered downsizing in recent years. From a peak of 800 at the end of the 1980s, its employment by late 1999 was 240, of which some 70 were in the headquarters in Dar. The Tanzanian government also reduced its budget over time, and SIDO was unable to earn much from industry.

To some extent the inability to recoup full costs is inherent to SME support agencies. SMEs the world over have severe financial constraints; in developing countries they are often unable to define their problems or spare the time and effort to seek institutional assistance. However, the problems of SIDO appear to reflect both the weak state of SMEs in Tanzania and deficiencies in the institution. These weaknesses, in terms of staff, salaries, equipment or morale, seem to be even greater than for TIRDO.

In general, SIDO appears to be doing little effective work to upgrade technology and productivity in SMEs. It is rather passive in reaching out to enterprises, and does not have the ability to meet firms' needs for packages combining finance, technology, skills and marketing. The staff is poorly paid and even more poorly motivated. Its facilities and equipment appear to be quite inadequate to the task of upgrading and modernizing SMEs to cope with modern technologies and management methods. While SIDO claims to be putting a lot of effort into SME export promotion, its effectiveness has been low, and SME exports from Tanzania remain tiny.

The institution is, however, trying to revive itself. It has appointed a new Board and is seeking further foreign assistance. The government has no explicit strategy for assisting SMEs, though it is trying to develop one with UNIDO assistance. However, the persistent tradition of relying on foreign inputs and expertise is disturbing; there is no indication that SIDO is planning to change its approach, staff and capabilities to serve SMEs better. Industrial estates can be easily managed and operated by private entrepreneurs. The real emphasis of SIDO should be to reach out to SMEs with aggressive and coherent programmes of technology, training and marketing assistance. This requires much greater skills, dedication and resources than the institution now has or is likely to get under current policies. Yet SMEs are likely to be a vital element in Tanzania's industrial development strategy and the government has to formulate much better support strategies (for examples from other countries, see Lall, 1996; and Guerrieri et al., 2001).

This is not to argue that foreign assistance is undesirable. However, aid dependency coupled with domestic lack of capabilities does nothing to ensure that the process is effective or sustainable. Aid must be used by local institutions able to package and deliver the assistance effectively, and be backed by government commitment to continue the programme.

Institute of Production Innovation (IPI)

IPI was set up in 1981 in the University of Dar es Salaam, initially as a department within the Faculty of Engineering, and later as an autonomous institute within the university. Its objective was to develop product prototypes and transfer technology to industry, provide consultancy services and provide curriculum advice to the engineering department (Wangwe and Diyamett, 1998). The German government financed the physical facilities and trained the staff, while the Tanzanian government provided some minor financial support, less than it had promised. The idea of linking university to industry was a promising one, and the initiative marks something of an innovation in the African setting. However, the link failed to work and the engineering faculty established another link to industry, the Bureau for Industrial Cooperation. Both institutions compete for the same clients, with similar degrees of success or lack thereof (Wangwe and Diyamett, 1998).

IPI specializes in making simple machines (for sugar milling, oil processing, grain milling, solar heating) and structures (telecommunication towers) for sale on the market. In 1998 its sales were around US$267 000. The technology is copied from existing designs abroad, and there is no long-term R&D activity in the institute. No patent has been applied for.

In essence, IPI has become a small manufacturing unit rather than a technology development centre. As may be expected, its record of technology transfer to the private sector has been abysmal. According to Wangwe and Diyamett (1998), its approach till 1994 was a supply-driven one, where engineers conceived the research problem and developed prototypes for sale to industry. The feasibility and competitiveness of the technology was not evaluated and there was little effort to market technologies to industry. Not surprisingly, there was no demand from industry for the technology and not a single prototype was sold for commercial use. IPI's manufacturing activities made firms regard it as a competitor rather than a technology transfer agency. As a consequence, the institute had a poor image with industry, and most SMEs in the country were not even aware of its existence.

In 1994 IPI shifted to a more market-driven model. It tried to ensure via market analysis and dialogue with potential users and other agencies, that proposed products were in demand in industry. The new approach led to more visits to industry and by industry to IPI. In 1996, there was one technology transfer to an SME (Wangwe and Diyamett, 1998). The main activity continues to be small-scale manufacturing for direct sales to the market. Despite this, the institute is failing to earn its keep.

Summing up on the Technology Infrastructure

The overall picture of the leading technology infrastructure institutions in Tanzania is not very encouraging. The infrastructure is small and largely ineffective, poorly funded and motivated, and has weak or no links with industry. Its ability to develop, adapt and disseminate industrial technologies is inadequate. It seems to have little awareness of the competitive needs of Tanzanian industry, even less of how new technologies can be introduced to potential users. There are some attempts to reform and improve the main institutions, but in the absence of government support, the culture of dependence on external aid and the lack of involvement by the private sector are important handicaps.

Technology policy formulation is uncoordinated and the main institution in charge of S&T policy making, COSTECH, is weak and unable to influence the agencies in the government that conduct R&D. Much of the R&D is in any case irrelevant to industrial needs. The Standards Bureau is well staffed and motivated, but lags in technological terms and is underfunded. None of its laboratories are internationally accredited, and it is unable to meet many industrial needs. TIRDO does not produce any significant technological benefits for industry, though it performs some useful technical functions. It tends to lack credibility with private firms, and does too little to reach out to them. SIDO is even weaker. IPI has turned into a manufacturing rather than technology development institution. This infrastructure is clearly unable to help an industrial sector with weak technological capabilities facing a growing international competitive threat. The gap between local institutions and world best practice is very large and growing with time.

Part of the problem of any technology infrastructure institution in a country like Tanzania is the technological backwardness of private industry. The same lack of technical skills and information that afflicts industry also afflicts the institutions, despite their access to international sources. Public ownership, low salaries, inefficient management and lack of incentives make a bad situation worse. At the same time, in the absence of private technological activity, there is a greater burden of responsibility on the public institutions to undertake more technological effort and ensure its effective delivery.

CONCLUSIONS

Technological weaknesses in Tanzanian industry are emerging as an important constraint not only to manufacturing growth and competitiveness but also to the structural transformation of the whole economy. Without such transformation, and in a setting of liberal trade and investment flows, Tanzania cannot hope to enjoy the sustained growth in incomes, employment and exports that it needs in the future. There are a few pockets of 'good practice' in technology, mainly concentrated in recently privatized enterprises taken over by foreign companies. However, their ability to raise productivity shows how the injection of new capabilities and work practices can significantly raise technological levels. The lessons for the rest of Tanzanian industry are clear, but they are not being adopted. Technology imports, which should be rising rapidly, remain very low, technological effort even more so. There are few other signs that adjustment or liberalization is leading to dynamic upgrading and competitiveness in industry. The skill base is small and has shown little improvement in recent years. Hence, it is difficult for industrial enterprises to realize the value of new technology and skills, and to try and achieve the upgrading necessary.

Yet the window of opportunity for Tanzanian industry to upgrade is narrow, given the time it has to survive until the time granted for full liberalization runs out (in the next few years). The competitive environment for Tanzania is changing very rapidly, affecting even the primary producing and processing activities that constitute its current comparative advantage. There is a need to pay special attention to industrial capabilities, and to the development of local skills. Enhancing capabilities will also entail much larger inflows of foreign technology and skills in the form of FDI and licensing. The SMEs that form the core of the indigenous manufacturing sector will have to be helped to use modern technology and management more effectively.

At this time, the institutional technology infrastructure and strategy making are completely inadequate to the task. While their deficiencies reflect the larger problems of capability building in Tanzania, there is a particularly acute need for strong institutions to provide the necessary public goods of technology development. The current strategy of industrial and technological development in Tanzania is not even addressing the right issues (Mlawa, 1999). It consists largely of statements of good intent and ambitious plans, with a very weak institutional base that is unable to implement them. There is therefore a need to re-examine the basic strategy of technology development and all the institutional structures that support it.

POLICY RECOMMENDATIONS

The Tanzanian government is aware of the need for rapid technology upgrading and for a systematic and coherent technology strategy. It is clearly committed to full liberalization and privatization of the economy, and to joining the globalization process. However, none of these processes will yield sustained growth and development benefits to the economy unless it raises its competitive abilities. Insofar as manufacturing is expected to play an important role in structural transformation, as it must if the experience of other developing countries has any lessons, it is *vital to invest in upgrading industrial technology*. Only then can it hope to compete effectively in the simple activities in which Tanzania currently has a comparative advantage, and over time move into more advanced activities that hold the best prospects for growth and learning spillovers.

The need for technological upgrading will not be met by encouraging Tanzania to 'innovate' or pick winners in high-tech activities. Tanzania must use its existing resources more efficiently and change its competitive advantages in line with changing technologies and rising wages. Technology development in Tanzania should thus first focus on strengthening existing activities like processing local resources and making simple consumer goods and metal products. These should be made as internationally competitive as possible and assisted to move into export markets, using FDI as much as possible to help overcome technology, skill and marketing gaps. Tanzania has low wages but also very low levels of skills (Chapter 2); an immediate priority must be to raise skill levels to use this vital resource. As a competitive base is established in simple activities, the government should create the endowments and institutions needed to move into more advanced activities. Simple as this sounds, this requires a coherent and coordinated policy approach. Few countries have been able to carry it through successfully.

Technology strategy formulation

COSTECH has the vital task of masterminding S&T policies within the MSTHE. In order to do this effectively, it should enhance its capabilities and its ability to implement strategy. Enhancing the capabilities of COSTECH needs actions on many fronts. The basic S&T strategy, as expressed in the 1996 Technology Plan, was overambitious and general. It was a 'supply push' strategy, with little attention paid to the demand for technology from the industrial sector. Moreover, it lumped together science and technology, when the economic priority in Tanzania lies clearly in the latter, and seemed to ignore the fact that most technological activity in any economy takes place within the productive sector, not in R&D institutions isolated from production activity.

In addition, it is important for the government to raise the skills and resources available to COSTECH. Finally, if technology policy is to be effective, it must be *coordinated across all the agencies* that play a role – education, finance, FDI, industry, agriculture, education, infrastructure and so on – give a prominent role to the private industrial sector, and make explicit the fundamental link between competitiveness and technological effort.

Improving human capital and skills

The human capital base in Tanzania is small and is lagging relative to regional industrial powers like Kenya and Zimbabwe. The low output of skills is exacerbated by the poor quality and low relevance to industrial needs of the training imparted. Enterprises invest very little in employee training. The government should attach absolute priority to the launching of a new skill strategy aimed at creating competitive skills for industry. Not only raising formal skill levels is important, but also the skill composition of new employment generation is shifting rapidly in response to technical change and liberalization, and specific industrial skills for the most important industrial activities in Tanzania should be targeted. The stimulation of *in-firm* training is another key area of policy intervention that needs to be undertaken in the short to medium term.

Stimulating and improving technology imports

Tanzanian industry imports very little new technology, in spite of the relatively limited policy impediments. A strong focus of policy should be on information provision to enterprises, particularly SMEs, on sources, costs and appropriateness of foreign technologies, backed by the provision of technical extension and financial support to help them absorb new technologies. In fact, it is impossible to separate technology support measures from measures to facilitate technology imports. Several means and strategies exist to this aim, including *Productivity Centres* adopting a proactive approach, with qualified teams visiting enterprises, offering free diagnoses and putting together *packages* of technology, training and finance. The Hong Kong experience offers remarkably useful insights in this regard (Lall, 1996).

Stimulating technological activity by enterprises

Tanzanian industry does not have full awareness of the importance of in-firm technological effort. Most firms import technology and use it passively, often at well below international best practice levels. A 'technology culture' does not exist in Tanzania, and the government should act to create such a new attitude. Among the possible alternatives is to accept enterprise R&D as a tax-deductible expense (no fiscal incentives for enterprise R&D existed in Tanzania at the time of writing). However, to persuade enterprises to utilize such provisions requires concerted information and persuasion campaigns, for example selecting leading technology performers as technology models for the rest of industry, showing best practice of technology imports, mastery and improvements.

The stimulation of technological effort in fact requires governments to act on a range of interlinked fronts: infrastructure, supply chains, skills, finance, technological support and so on. Hence, it is necessary to prioritize and select components that are relevant to important industrial activities on the basis of well designed, thorough and continuous technology audits of Tanzanian enterprises.

Strengthening the technology infrastructure and institutions

The laboratories of the *Tanzania Bureau of Standards* need to be internationally accredited and the Bureau has to develop the capability to accredit independent testing laboratories and so help a private technology services market to develop. Efficient, modern and internationally accepted standards are essential for technology development, and the government should attach priority to this investment. TBS should consider encouraging testing to become a private service activity and focusing on its core standard setting activities. It should also be provided with the resources and incentives to undertake a more aggressive quality campaign, particularly to reach SMEs that lag badly in quality management and standardization. At the same time, private consultants on quality management in Tanzania need to be encouraged.

TIRDO has become a passive and rather demoralized body, with low salaries and minimal technological development activity. Its revival would require a thorough overhaul of its organization, management, staff and skills, and should be based on a comprehensive strategic plan developed in consultation with the private sector. The focus of the organization should shift to providing services in demand by firms, with appropriate incentives to staff to reach out and discover what is needed. The reform of its Kenyan counterpart, KIRDI, may offer useful lessons (Chapter 3).

SIDO was in an even worse state than TIRDO. Its regeneration needs a strategic plan that looks at its approach, staff and capabilities. SIDO should not be in charge of operating industrial estates, as these can be easily owned and managed by private entrepreneurs. Its strategic role should focus on reaching SMEs with programmes of technology, marketing, training and marketing assistance. This requires much greater skills, dedication and resources but promises far greater effectiveness. The promotion of subcontracting (between large firms and SME suppliers) and the strengthening of SME clusters should also be considered as possible policy alternatives.

Attracting FDI

While Tanzania has greatly improved its FDI regime and the TIC is a much more active institution than before, several bureaucratic impediments remain and the procedural barriers may drive investors to look elsewhere. Many regulations and procedures significantly increase the cost of conducting business in Tanzania, and problems with corruption, conflicting and confusing regulations and the long management time spent in negotiating with government officials (Figure 4.1) negatively affect investors' assessment of Tanzania as an investment destination. In view of all this, promotion has to be all the more effective, to offset (to the extent possible) the handicaps the above issues involve and the poor image they create. An important role may be played by TIC insofar as it manages to bring its investor services and targeting to modern and competitive levels. It has to become a real 'one-stop shop' able to obtain all the necessary permits and agreements investors need.

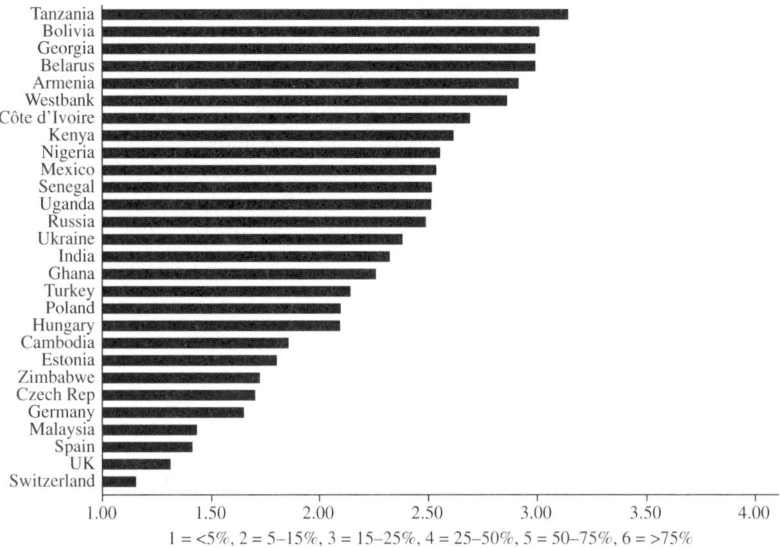

Figure 4.1 Senior management time spent negotiating with officials on regulations

Intellectual property regime

The policy implications here are very similar to those for Kenya and readers are referred to the previous chapter on this issue.

IN SUM

The Tanzanian government is conscious of the importance of technology and of the need for policies to support technology development. The rapid pace of technical change is, however, threatening to leave it behind, stranded on a stagnant base of low-skill, low-value activities. Liberalization has not catalysed an adequate technological response from its industrial sector, and the evidence on its skill and institutional base suggests that there will be no change in the foreseeable future unless there is a significant shift in policy. The current policy and institutional structure are clearly inadequate to the task facing Tanzania in terms of transferring, mastering and using technology.

Most of the policy challenges facing the Tanzanian government are of a medium to long-term nature. The trade and macroeconomic environment has undergone considerable reform and there do not seem to be many immediate problems as far as technology is concerned. The main exception is the level of business transaction costs, which are still unacceptably high and can be addressed by short-term measures. The long-term issues are more serious – and more difficult to tackle. The low base of skills is perhaps the most important, and underlies many of the other institutional and capability deficiencies. However, the lack of real government interest in technology is a major handicap to institutional improvement. Technology institutions are decaying for lack of resources and the absence of strategic thinking. The strong commitment needed by the leadership to technology development is conspicuous by its absence in Tanzania. Progress has therefore to start at the top levels of decision making.

NOTES

1. Comparable payments by Kenya are lower (below $2 million in 1998), suggesting that the Tanzanian data reflect sporadic activity rather than sustained technology upgrading in manufacturing.
2. See the survey by Semboja and Kweka (2000).
3. At the end of 1999, two units had been attracted into this scheme, for cosmetics and medicines, and aiming at regional markets.

5. Uganda

INTRODUCTION

Uganda is one of the poorest countries in the world. In spite of the stabilization and growth recorded since 1986, when the current government came to power, its 1997 per capita GNP was US$324, compared to the average for Sub-Saharan Africa of US$533 (World Bank, 1999). Life expectancy at birth had fallen from 46.4 years in 1970–75 to 41.9 in 1995–2000, compared to the average of 48.8 for the whole of Sub-Saharan Africa (UNDP, 2001). A series of military governments, civil wars and political upheavals in the 1970s and early 1980s left the economy in an appalling state (Harvey and Robinson, 1995; DFID, 1999). By 1986, much of the economic infrastructure was destroyed, and income per head was almost 40 per cent below its 1976 level. Macroeconomic imbalances were extreme. Inflation was running at above 150 per cent per annum. The exchange rate was grossly overvalued, with the black market rate running at a premium of over 600 per cent. The Central Bank had to finance most of government spending, about 6 per cent of GDP (Harvey and Robinson, 1995).

INDUSTRIAL BACKGROUND

The situation has improved since 1986, but the country remains highly dependent on agriculture, which accounts for most of GDP, employment, and exports. The non-monetary sector of the economy, essentially subsistence agriculture, represented 23.6 per cent of GDP in 1997 (Ministry of Finance, 1998). Manufacturing accounts for a small, though rising, share of GDP: 9 per cent in 1997, up from 5.3 per cent in 1988 (Table 5.1). Most industry has been state-owned for a long time, and divestiture was undertaken only recently. Most enterprises use simple technologies and are oriented to the local market. Only a few have been able to reach export markets, and there is no major manufacturing exporter. The bulk of exports still come from such agricultural products as coffee and tea.

Manufacturing production has grown rapidly in recent years (Table 5.2), largely as the result of using existing excess capacity to meet local market

Table 5.1 Uganda: structure of the economy, 1987-97

	% of GDP (at constant 1991 prices)		
	Agriculture	Manufacturing	Other*
1988	54.5	5.3	40.2
1989	54.1	5.5	40.4
1990	53.5	5.5	41.0
1991	52.1	5.9	42.0
1992	51.2	6.1	42.7
1993	50.5	6.4	43.1
1994	48.8	6.9	44.3
1995	46.6	7.5	45.9
1996	44.7	8.2	47.1
1997	42.4	9.0	48.6

Note: * includes mining and quarrying, electricity/water, construction and other services.

Source: Ministry of Finance, Planning & Economic Development, 1998, calculated from GDP at constant (1991) prices.

needs. The most intense revival was in 1994–95; growth slowed down thereafter. Food processing and textiles/garments dominate the structure of manufacturing. Chemicals also represent a large share, but other complex activities are minimal. In general, the technological needs of manufacturing are very limited. The low exposure to foreign competition in export and local markets (there is considerable 'natural' protection in the domestic market, due to poor infrastructure and low incomes) has probably accentuated technological lags over time.

Following macroeconomic reforms, private investment (in constant prices) grew from 7.8 per cent of GDP in the years 1986–89 to 12 per cent in 1996–97 and 13.5 per cent in 1997–98. Public investment showed the opposite trend, falling from about 10 per cent of GDP in the late 1980s to 5.9 per cent in 1997–98. However, investment in machinery and vehicles was only 4.8 per cent of GDP in 1997–98. A recent study suggests that investment at the firm level may have been even lower (Reinikka and Svensson, 1999a).[1] For comparison, in the fast growing East Asian economies the share of investment was around 30 per cent of GDP for many years.

While investment rates in Uganda are in line with the (low) African average, its average reported profit rates are much lower, about one-half of those for a pooled African sample (Bigsten et al., 1999).[2] This is attributed to the Ugandan firms' higher confidence in the economy than their counterparts

Table 5.2 Uganda: index of industrial production (1987 = 100)

Sector	Weight	1990	1991	1992	1993	1994	1995	1996	1997
Food processing	20.7	174.9	227.4	245.6	245.8	309.7	361.8	411.0	423.6
Textiles & clothing	16.3	116.3	110.9	111.9	92.7	68.1	62.7	47.9	113.5
Leather & footwear	2.3	75.3	60.1	79.5	68.4	97.1	164.4	287.9	158.9
Timber, paper, printing	9.0	183.6	198.2	220.5	251.1	299.8	383.1	552.6	468.6
Chemicals	12.3	183.5	192.9	252.0	339.5	383.0	512.7	510.3	776.4
Steel and steel prod.	5.3	107.7	149.3	190.7	259.0	389.9	490.5	480.7	451.5
Others	3.7	181.3	251.2	272.3	381.0	487.3	598.6	627.9	577.3
All industries	100.0	155.5	178.2	191.2	215.6	260.3	330.9	384.4	441.3
Annual % change	-	7.1	14.6	7.3	12.8	20.7	27.1	16.2	14.8

Note: Weights were set according to the value added of 110 establishments covered in a survey conducted in 1988 by UNIDO.

Source: Statistics Dept.

elsewhere: thus, Ugandan firms invest more at a given profit rate. According to a recent (1998) survey (Reinikka and Svensson, 1999a, 1999b), the major constraint to investment in Uganda is the high price and low quality of utility services (electricity, telephones, water, waste disposal). Poor public capital, erratic infrastructure and utility services, and high transport costs, raise costs and reduce productive investment by firms.[3]

Table 5.3 shows the low values of Ugandan manufactured exports and its specialization in simple products like textile yarn and fabric (nearly 40 per cent of manufactured exports). Medium and high-technology exports seem to include re-exports of products like transport equipment, iron and steel or special machinery that are not manufactured in Uganda. There are very low exports of other labour-intensive manufactures like garments, footwear or travel goods. This suggests that textile exports are primarily resource-based rather than driven by low-wage cost and labour efficiency.

POLICY FRAMEWORK FOR TECHNOLOGY DEVELOPMENT

Strategic Policy Statements and Objectives

The Government of Uganda (GOU) attaches great importance to S&T and advanced industrial development in its public statements (Republic of Uganda, 1999). However, its technology policy design and technological efforts do not consider the relevant needs of the productive sector. The institutional infrastructure needed to provide basic services and inputs into enterprise technological activity is weak. S&T policy has low priority, with much more emphasis on primary education, health, poverty eradication and subsistence agriculture. Most of the expressed intentions to promote S&T for the country's industrial development remain on paper; they have not been translated into concrete policy measures, and implementation has generally lagged.

After years of structural adjustment, the presence of the state in industry is still widespread, although in 1994 it had been officially declared that the private sector should be at the centre of industrialization.[4]

> The involvement of the private sector in the articulation of these policies and the industrialisation framework is in line with the current trend in which the private sector is poised to play the lead role. The role of Government will be a facilitating one geared to the provision of the necessary infrastructure, the formulation of appropriate macro-economic policies and generally ensuring that a conducive environment for investment and doing profitable business is maintained. (Foreword to MOTI, 1994, by Hon. Kaijuka, Minister of Trade and Industry)

Table 5.3 Uganda: manufactured exports, 1993-97 (US$ million)

	1993	1994	1995	1996	1997
Total exports	222.6	463.5	576.5	702.3	605.1
Total manufactured exports	4.7	8.0	19.7	42.4	29.4
Manuf. as % of total exports	2.1	1.7	3.4	6.0	4.9
Leather manufactures	0.05	0.03	0.10	0.43	0.12
Rubber manufactures	0.05	0.03	0.28	0.03	0.27
Cork-wood manufactures	0.02	0.03	0.04	0.02	0.10
Paper and pulp	0.45	0.25	0.33	0.40	0.12
Textile yarn and fabrics	0.30	0.44	0.00	3.19	11.61
Apparel & clothing accessories	0.13	0.02	0.29	0.09	0.08
Footwear	0.09	0.26	0.10	0.40	0.04
Travel goods	0.00	0.09	0.05	0.06	0.00
Non-metallic minerals	0.28	0.17	0.16	6.70	1.51
Iron & steel	0.02	0.03	2.46	14.25	1.36
Non-ferrous metals	0.01	0.11	1.79	0.27	0.13
Metal manufactures nes	0.66	1.63	0.33	2.40	0.90
Power gen. machinery & equip.	0.00	0.01	0.17	0.07	0.26
Machinery for special industries	0.87	0.26	0.28	3.64	2.00
Metalworking machinery	0.02	0.00	0.23	0.00	0.03
General industrial machinery	0.31	0.29	0.14	3.28	0.51
Office machines	0.01	0.01	0.04	0.01	0.02
Telecommunications equipment	0.03	0.93	0.48	0.08	0.46
Electrical machinery	0.05	0.14	0.46	0.05	0.00
Road vehicles	1.01	0.99	4.30	4.16	4.93
Other transport equipment	0.01	0.21	0.49	0.22	0.00
Misc. manufactured goods	0.58	0.00	0.00	0.00	0.00
Prefabricated buildings	0.04	0.04	0.14	0.08	0.00
Furniture & parts	0.06	0.22	0.46	0.32	0.05
Scientific instruments	0.02	0.10	0.03	0.41	0.15
Photographic & optical goods	0.00	0.86	0.09	0.00	0.00
Other manufactures	0.25	0.82	1.45	1.87	2.96

Source: Uganda Revenue Authority, Bank of Uganda, and other local sources

The Ministry of Trade and Industry (MOTI) in its 1994 paper, *Industrialisation Policy and Framework 1994-99*, acknowledged the existence of constraints to industrialization. Two of the seven constraints were in the S&T area (MOTI, 1994, p. 6), namely:

- Shortage of skilled personnel (especially technical and management);
- Lack of standards and quality consciousness.

The government seeks to concentrate on:

- Establishing a National Industrial Research Organization (NIRO);
- Encouraging enterprises to undertake R&D by tax exemptions;
- Strengthening the National Council for Science and Technology, the Department of Technology and the Industrial and Technological Information Unit in the MOTI, and other training institutions;
- Introducing an industrial training levy;
- Providing adequate finance for R&D.

Unfortunately, few of these objectives have been translated into policies. They essentially remain a wish list, not based on detailed analyses of the needs of industry. The S&T focus that sometimes emerges out of official documents appears casual and not rooted in a clear diagnosis and awareness of the role of innovation and technological capabilities for industrial development. As shown below, technological activity remains minimal and the support institutions remain largely dormant.

Policy Framework and the Private Sector

Uganda has managed its macroeconomic policies relatively well in the 1990s, and has been praised by donors and the international financial community (Dijkstra and Van Donge, 2001). The relationship between Uganda and the donor community has been depicted as smooth (Holmgren et al., 1999). Liberalization has been pursued on several fronts: exchange rates are now market determined and inflation rates are low; trade liberalization has been extensive, including a complete removal of quantitative restrictions, and reduction of import duties gradually over time (World Bank, 1996a). As a result, Uganda's import tariffs are now among the lowest in Africa, the highest official rate being 15 per cent on consumer goods. Raw materials carry a rate of 7 per cent, and capital goods are zero-rated. Regional tariffs are even lower. Accordingly, Uganda is the first country to benefit from the new Highly Indebted Poor Country (HIPC) initiative of 1998 (McPherson, 1998).

Within this context, institutional reforms have been undertaken to encourage the private sector. Investment laws and procedures have been streamlined to attract domestic and foreign investors. A new Investment Code (1991) has replaced the Foreign Investment Act (1977) and Industrial Licensing Act (1969). The new Code is a restrictive and control-oriented regime for FDI (UNCTAD, 2000), that, if implemented to the letter, could seriously deter FDI. However, in practice Uganda has taken a much more welcoming stance towards foreign investors, and since 1991 there has been substantial improvement in the general legislative and policy climate for investment. It is being debated how to modernize the Investment Code, but as of late 1999 the Code of 1991 remained in force.

The Income Tax Act of 1997 streamlined the system of tax incentives and broadened the tax base. This reduced the unpredictability of tax incentive policies observed during the 1980s and the early 1990s (Obwona, 1998). The reform was preceded by the introduction of duty free treatment of imported capital goods for all firms. Among the major changes introduced were the deductibility from companies' income of 50 per cent of plant and machinery investments (75 per cent outside Kampala, Jinja and Entebbe, Uganda's major cities), and of 100 per cent of research and training expenditures. In principle, these measures should have encouraged enterprises to invest in technology and skill upgrading.

However, such tax incentives are not likely to be effective when there is no *culture of technological activity* in industry. Enterprises are largely unaware of their technological or skill needs or, when they are, of how to go about meeting them. There is no source of finance for innovative activities or even for long-term industrial investments.[5] The main sources of technology lie abroad, and as noted for Kenya and Tanzania there is little effort to master and improve the technology in use. R&D in the sense understood in developed countries is totally absent.

Private sector interests are represented by a few institutions. The most prominent one is the Uganda Manufacturers Association (UMA). Over the years UMA has developed a strong partnership with the government in designing policy, and regularly presents studies and recommendations on policy issues. However, it is not clear how influential UMA would be if major differences with the government emerged (Holmgren et al., 1999). The Uganda Manufacturers Association Consultancy and Information Services (UMACIS) is a registered company that provides consultancy and other services to UMA members. It is largely funded by donor agencies (USAID, UNDP, and the German government among others) although it earns an increasing share of income from services rendered. It is demand-driven and close to the interests of the private sector. UMACIS is also active in raising quality awareness in the country, through a project co-financing the consultancy costs of local enterprises to achieve ISO 9000 certification. Some interesting, though small, contributions to technology transfer have come from a scheme to attract nationals under the Transfer of Knowledge through Expert Nationals (TOKTEN) scheme, and the TIPS programme to foster South-South enterprise cooperation. UNDP is funding both programmes.

The association representing the small-scale sector, the Uganda Small-Scale

Industry Association (USSIA) is a non-governmental organization that was created in 1979. Since then, it has aimed at becoming a national forum for discussion on issues related to SMEs, promoting and encouraging their development and efficiency, and providing policy advocacy to voice SMEs' requests to the government. According to the only available and relatively comprehensive survey, the small-scale industries (SSI) sector is a significant one in the country. In 1993 it employed 14 per cent of the workforce and contributed 20 per cent of GDP and 80 per cent of manufacturing output (APT-USSIA, 1993). One of the authors visited the USSIA Secretariat in Kampala during an UNCTAD mission, and obtained the impression of a weak organization, lacking funds and clarity of direction. Seven people work with the Secretariat (not all full time), and the organization provides training to some of its 1000 members, and it is almost completely donor-funded. Only 1 per cent of the yearly budget comes from membership fees. They have brand-new facilities (funded by Austrian aid) to house an exhibition hall, but few activities to carry out there. In principle, SMEs deserve support and advice, especially in their start-up phase, but USSIA appears uninfluential and passive in this respect.

Other private sector actors are the Uganda Exporters' Association (UEA), the Uganda National Chamber of Commerce and Industry (UNCCI), and the Private Sector Foundation (PSF). The last one was created in 1996, largely funded by USAID and the World Bank/IDA to provide policy advice and management training services. The most interesting project being operated by PSF since 1996 is the Business Uganda Development Scheme (BUDS) a cost-sharing grant scheme to subsidize 50 per cent of enterprises' consulting service expenditures, up to a maximum of US$50 000 per firm. The design and rationale of this instrument are appropriate and could contribute to facilitate enterprises' efforts to acquire and improve management and technical skills. Among the services co-financed is the training received by nine firms to certify for ISO 9002, under the guidance of a local consulting firm, an offshoot of a Norwegian company.[6] However, during the period October 1996–March 1999 the scheme has reimbursed only a total of US$915 000 (US$30 000 per month). The slow implementation of the scheme appears to be due to the difficulties in convincing firms to pay for a service, and to its slow financing by the funding agency. Although this appears a missed opportunity so far, this scheme is well conceived and designed, and reflects the right kind of approach to foster industrial development, especially of SMEs, in an emerging economy like Uganda.

Intellectual Property Regime

The Uganda Patent Law was approved in 1991, and is administered by the

Uganda Registration Services Bureau (URSB). Prior to this all patents were registered in the UK and then stamped and re-registered in Uganda. Thus the system served the needs of foreign companies wanting protection on the local market more than those of Ugandan innovators and inventors. The URSB is presently a department of the Ministry of Justice, and a member of the Africa Regional Intellectual Property Organization (ARIPO) in Harare as well as of the World Intellectual Property Organization (WIPO). It is in charge of copyrights (for which no legal provision exists to date) and patents, industrial designs and trademarks (for which the law exists). Under the TRIPS agreement, all pending intellectual property activities will be retrospectively enforceable.

There are proposals to restructure URSB as an autonomous unit with a larger range of services, thereby attaching greater importance to its functions than in the past, but although the relevant law was passed in 1997, it is not yet operational and lacks funding. At the moment the Bureau has only eight lawyers and three clerks, and all technical examinations continue to be undertaken by ARIPO in Zimbabwe. The Bureau is presently too weak to actively protect innovation and ensure effective enforcement of its decisions. If it is to play an important role in intellectual property protection in Uganda it should be strengthened, especially in its enforcement function, and its funding increased. However, patenting remains a marginal activity of the Bureau, as foreigners have registered practically all patents utilized in the country. The bulk of its operations concerns trademarks, of which there were nearly 23000 by September 1999.[7] However, at this stage of industrial development, the nature of the institutional system for intellectual property protection appears irrelevant to technology development. It simply reflects the structural fragility of the technology system, and the lack of incentives to attract technology transfer and to foster indigenous technological efforts. Only in a long-term perspective should the URBS be substantially strengthened and given a strategic role, once the country reaches a higher level of industrial and technological development. At present, it may suffice to have a system protecting foreign firms in the local market and relying on regional institutions, such as ARIPO, for the more complex and technical cases.

A TRIPS-compatible system of intellectual property protection was due to be in place by end 1999. Least developed countries, however, have some latitude, and have 2005 to bring their legislation into conformance with the provisions of the agreement. This is going to prove a significant challenge to Uganda in terms of incorporating the laws, reforming institutions and establishing the relevant procedures. The need for such reforms does not appear to be felt strongly yet, due to the limited level of local technological and innovative capabilities.

TECHNOLOGY TRANSFER TO UGANDA

Capital Goods Imports

Imports of machinery and equipment by Uganda have fluctuated widely during the 1990s. Though capital goods can be brought duty free, they account for small and declining shares of total imports, from 11.5 per cent in 1993 to 4.7 per cent in 1997 (Table 5.4). The introduction of tax deductibility (50 per cent to 75 per cent) of plant and machinery investments in 1997 has not stimulated machinery imports. The poor and costly communication and transport system that raise the cost of importing equipment may partly explain this (see Reinikka and Svensson, 1999a, 1999b), but the main reason seems to be technological apathy.

According to the available central bank data on royalties and technical fees paid abroad, there have been *no* recorded payments in these years.

FDI

Investor confidence in Uganda has increased in recent years. UNCTAD (1998b) described Uganda as a 'front-runner' among African countries in

Table 5.4 Ugandan imports of capital goods, 1993-97 (US$ millions)

	1993	1994	1995	1996	1997 prov.
Power generating machinery	3.1	7.8	10.4	10.1	14.5
Machinery for special industries	23.5	24.3	53.1	34.1	25.8
Metalworking machinery	2.5	2.2	4.5	3.2	1.7
General industrial machinery	17.3	20.5	29.6	31.2	18.0
Office machines, ADP machines	6.2	19.5	11.9	11.5	5.0
Telecommunications, sound apparatus	10.1	13.7	26.2	19.5	10.6
Electrical machinery, apparatus	22.4	28.8	39.6	36.5	22.9
Road vehicles	57.6	95.0	149.1	124.0	109.9
Other transport equipment	1.0	7.3	3.1	3.5	1.0
Total imports	402.5	715.6	970.9	1341.9	1285.0
Industrial machinery imports	46.4	54.8	97.6	78.5	60.0
Percentage of total imports	11.5	7.7	10.1	5.9	4.7

Source: Uganda Revenue Authority and Bank of Uganda, The Statistical Abstract 1998, Ministry of Finance, Planning and Economic Development, The Republic of Uganda.

attracting FDI in 1992–96, and this is confirmed by the recent figures on FDI inflows (Chapter 2). As measured by the *Institutional Investor*, Uganda's investor confidence index increased from 8.4 in September 1993 to 20.3 (out of 100) in March 1999.[8] In 1988 this index had hit a bottom value of 5.2 (Atkinson, 1999). However, in September 1998 the situation worsened slightly (19.9) because of the regional security situation. The main threat in the future is political uncertainty related to the move to a formal multi-party system (a referendum is due in 2001) and the civil unrest in Northern Uganda and in the Great Lakes region (McPherson, 1998).

The Uganda Investment Authority (UIA) was created in 1991 to administer the Investment Code and act as a one-stop centre for investors. Under the Investment Code the UIA has five main functions:

- Regulation of foreign investment and registration of agreements for transfer of foreign technology or expertise
- Administration of incentives
- Foreign investment promotion
- Investor facilitation
- Policy advocacy

Recently, UIA has also been given the responsibility of promoting the development of the Namanve Industrial Park. Over time, its emphasis has shifted from 'authorizing' to 'attracting, promoting and facilitating' investors (UIA, 1999). Under the Investment Code no foreign investor may undertake business in Uganda unless a licence is obtained. UIA licenses all foreign investments over a minimum of US$100 000, provided that the application is in accordance with the code and the activity is not unlawful, contrary to the national interests or environmentally damaging. In principle this provision could be used to block any new FDI if the government were so inclined. However, it is understood in practice that this does not occur. The threshold for domestic investors is lower (US$50 000). It has been rightly argued that this may discriminate against SMEs, whose investments may fall below this limit. However, it is not clear to what extent SMEs' investments are being discouraged by this limit rather than by other factors.

UNCTAD *Investment Policy Review of Uganda* (UNCTAD, 2000) spells out in detail the specific standards of treatment that apply to foreign investors. There is no general assurance of 'national treatment' to foreign investors given in the Investment Code, and in some instances, they may be provided with lesser entitlements than national investors. Anyway, these provisions appear to remain on paper in most cases. Applications are supposed to be processed quickly (2–5 days), but in fact procedures tend to be cumbersome and slow (Lall, 2000a).

In fact, obtaining an investment licence is not as great an impediment to foreign entry as obtaining the licences needed to operate a business, contracts with the utility companies and access to serviced land (Obwona, 1998).[9] UIA carries little weight with other ministries and agencies. Although it aims at becoming a one-stop shop, empowered to grant all licences needed for operation, it is still far from being an effective institution facilitating and promoting foreign investor interests in Uganda.

Several proposals have been put forward to improve the functioning of the UIA (UNCTAD, 2000). In particular, it has been recommended that UIA adopt a more proactive strategy, promoting foreign investments, and targeting them by activity within a consistent industrial policy framework. It is also recommended that it help national investors to establish links with foreign partners, and become an effective advocate in policy design. Only within such renewed approach can it contribute fully to Uganda's acquisition of foreign technology.

What sectors have attracted FDI recently? According to UIA (Table 5.5), 47 per cent of approved investments has gone to manufacturing. However, this

Table 5.5 Investment approvals by sector by Uganda Investment Authority, 1991-98

Sector	No. of projects	Investment (US$ thousands)	%
Agriculture, forestry & fishing	127	77 268.9	5.4
Construction	73	26 094	1.8
Financial services	43	38 644	2.7
Manufacturing	1 031	677 658	47.4
Mining & quarrying	30	49 195	3.4
Social services	99	17 492	1.2
Tourism	113	95 711	6.7
Trade & restaurants	30	21 610	1.5
Transportation, comm., storage	191	99 630	7.0
Real estate	153	30 173	2.1
Water, energy	7	95 825	6.7
Other services	124	201 030	14.1
Total	2 021	1 430 329	100

Note: The figures include both foreign and domestic investment approvals as recorded by UIA.

Source: UIA.

needs to be qualified. The data include domestic as well as foreign investments, and are based on applications rather than realizations. Much of the manufacturing investment has come from Asians returning to revive operations abandoned earlier. The activities are likely to be in very simple technologies oriented to the domestic market. Technological effort by foreign investors is very limited and not considered important (UNCTAD, 1998b). The largest foreign investors in the country source their technology abroad and have few links with the local S&T system, although sometimes contribute with substantial training of managers and staff (Box 5.1)

BOX 5.1 TRAINING AND SKILL DEVELOPMENT BY TNCS - UNILEVER UGANDA

Unilever Uganda Ltd is one of the leading foreign investors in Uganda, specializing in the manufacture and distribution of foods, detergents, soaps and related products. In 1997 the company had sales of US$15 million, and was expected to grow to US$20 million in 1998. It is part of the global Unilever group, and has strong linkages with Unilever subsidiaries in Kenya, India, the UK and South Africa. The company has a long history in the country, dating back to 1960 as a subsidiary of East African Industries Ltd based in Kenya. Later it was partly nationalized under the Obote government, and became a distribution outlet for its mother company in Kenya. In February 1996 Unilever bought 100 per cent of the shares and now the company reports independently to London.

The major sources of benefits to Uganda's transfer of technology and skill development depend on the relationship Unilever Uganda entertains with the parent company. Unilever is a world leader in personnel development. Rigorous reviews for management staff are carried out every year, to identify existing capabilities, their possible lack, and measures to fill these skill gaps. Under the Management Trainee Programme, selected young graduates are sent on a six-months' training programme to prepare them for managerial posts within the group. Within the programme of internationalization of managers, Ugandan managers and management trainees are seconded for international postings, and overseas managers are sent to the local operations. Through these measures, local managers and staff are exposed to modern management techniques developed by any subsidiary of the global Unilever Group. Technology is sourced from the parent company, and almost no research and technological efforts are carried out locally. Practically no use of local S&T and training institutions is made and relationships are only occasional.

Sourcing of intermediate inputs from local firms still occurs to a limited extent, essentially of packaging materials, calcium carbonate (key material for the Vim detergent), and a few others. Major bottlenecks mentioned are the high cost and unreliability of power and telecommunications services, smuggling, and the incentive regime, that has been defined as unstable and unpredictable by the local staff.

Source: UNCTAD (1998b, company profile pp. 60-4).

While foreign affiliates have struck some local linkages, the percentage of inputs sourced locally is still low. Only 40 per cent of the firms obtained more than 50 per cent of their inputs (mostly primary) locally during 1997 (UNCTAD, 1998b). Field interviews with foreign firms revealed that many local suppliers are high cost and unable to assure regular and consistent supply of quality goods. According to UNCTAD, foreign investors undertake substantial training, often by seconding an expatriate senior manager to work in Uganda during the initial years of the project. Ugandan staff replaces foreign experts in due course. However, this is more often the case with larger affiliates, while in smaller companies expatriates tend to remain.[10]

HUMAN CAPITAL

Human capital, in particular technical skills, are a major weakness of most Sub-Saharan African countries, and even more so in Uganda (Chapter 2). A 1998 report on skills and technologies suggests that Ugandan enterprises employ few technically skilled personnel; its findings for a sample of 121 enterprises are shown in Table 5.6 (UIA, 1998). Part of the skill shortage is met by employing foreigners; half the firms providing information were using expatriates. Mechanical engineers topped the list of foreign technical experts, possibly because local engineering schools do not offer training in sugar, cement and machinery sub-sectors. Local engineers were used in light electrical industries.

The report suggests, naively in our view, that there is no shortage of local engineers: 'Uganda currently has about 1300 engineers distributed as 550, 400, and 350 civil, electrical and mechanical engineers respectively. Hence,

Table 5.6 Technical skills in 121 Ugandan enterprises, 1998

Mechanical engineers	60
Electrical engineers	33
Civil engineers	5
Industrial engineers	15
Chemical engineers	2
Total engineers	115
Chemists	28
Food technologists	17
Mechanical technicians	120
Electrical technicians	72
Science technicians	48
Total technicians	240

Note: Total respondents 121 firms.

Source: UIA (1998).

there should be no scarcity of mechanical and electrical engineers' (UIA, 1998, p. 27). The comparative data presented in Chapter 2 shows how poorly Uganda fares in educating technical manpower in relation to its economic size.

In-firm training is very low in Ugandan industry. The Vocational Training Centres that should provide technical training for shop-floor workers lack financial resources, and enterprises do not regard their graduates highly. Similarly, the body in charge of developing curricula and instruction material for primary and secondary schools, the National Curriculum Development Centre (NCDC) appears to be underfunded and isolated from the industrial sector. NCDC was set up by decree of 1973, and develops curricula and instructional material for primary, secondary and teacher education colleges. Since 1986, it has reviewed primary and secondary programmes in English, mathematics, science and social studies, and is now addressing other subjects including technology. It intends to introduce the teaching of business and entrepreneurial skills in primary schools. Similar changes are envisaged at the secondary school level, with greater emphasis on business and technical education. However, the main stumbling block to any radical modification appears the financing of the necessary infrastructure and teacher retraining, and its distance from and lack of credibility with the private sector.

There are three vocational training schools in Uganda, in Lugogo for building and metal machining, in Nakawa and in Jinja for mechanical fabrication, electrical and automotive. The Nakawa School, created in 1971, was closed for many years, and reopened in 1997 thanks to substantial Chinese aid. In 1999 it offered short and long-term courses to 365 trainees (including part-timers and short-term trainees). The courses offered include electronics, electrical installation and fitting, automotive repair and maintenance, carpentry and joinery, sheet metal and plumbing, welding and fabrication. Some of the qualifications offered are highly regarded by industry, but courses are not sufficiently demand driven. The technical teaching staff (42) are poorly paid even by local standards, and the number of technicians produced is very small in relation to industrial needs.

The Management Training and Advisory Centre (MTAC) has the mandate of 'management development, entrepreneurship and productivity improvement in Uganda'. This institute was established in 1969 and operates under the Ministry of Tourism, Trade and Industry. It currently carries out consultancy to private and public institutions and firms; training in strategic management, human resources management, finance and accounting, project planning and management, production and engineering management, marketing and sales management, supervisory and administrative management, and computer skills. In 1998 almost 1200 workers were trained in programmes ranging from two days to two weeks, a larger number than in the past. It had a professional staff of 11, with four holding Masters' degrees. The government contributes 20 per cent of its revenues through a monthly grant of US$1500. Some 54 per cent of revenues come from fees, and 30 per cent from renting out buildings. Established initially as an ILO-UNDP project, it has also been supported by the World Bank and, recently, the Austrian Government.

Being under the ministry, MTAC should have strong linkages with institutions such as UNBS, UIRI, and the Vocational Training Centres at Nakawa and Lugogo. However, such linkages are neither strong nor continuous, although they would be extremely useful to provide effective training geared to the specific needs of Uganda's industry. The technical staff is not well paid. There is little effort to market services or to reach out to local firms, and there was no explicit targeting of SMEs. Overall it is too small, underfunded, and unrelated to other technology institutions in the country to play a strategic role. It does not appear to have a significant impact on management skills in the country.

The main university, Makerere University (MU), was founded in 1922 as one of the three East African Constituent Colleges of the University of East Africa, has one of longest histories and is one of the most highly regarded in the continent. MU is autonomous but still remains under Government of Uganda jurisdiction. It is largely a teaching university, and does relatively little research. It offers a wide variety of courses, but its orientation towards the humanities is stronger than towards technical subjects. Only around 20 per cent of students are enrolled in science degrees (Table 5.7). Overall, the

Table 5.7 Makerere University enrolment and graduates by discipline, 1991–97

	Enrolment				Graduates			
Area of study/course	1991	1995	1996	1997*	1991	1995	1996	1997*
BSc Engineering	191	312	252	67	45	46	57	66
BSc Science	880	963	1057	1020	283	173	254	256
BSc Agriculture	271	327	340	342	97	79	79	76
BSc Forestry	98	126	132	149	33	33	31	32
B Food S&T	42	83	95	119	N/A	22	18	17
Total sciences (incl. Agric.)	1482	1811	1876	1697	458	353	439	447
As % of total university enrolments	23.8	23.1	18.5	19.7	26.7	18.5	21.2	18.5
B Commerce	267	297	316	332	75	150	90	201
BA Social sciences	1166	1230	2130	2342	369	403	422	473
Total	6229	7826	10165	8600	1716	1903	2074	2420

Note: * The smaller total for 1997 is due to data on some special schools not yet available.

numbers of science graduates - even including commerce and social sciences - are minuscule for a country wishing to develop and strengthen its manufacturing sector, as Uganda is. Until recently, MU was a nearly fully residential university with the vast majority of Ugandan students given government scholarships. Recently however, government funding has fallen drastically. Additional funding is from research sponsorship, largely from external sources and foreign aid.

Industry–university linkages are very low. However, some collaboration has been growing with the Faculties of Technology and Science for material testing, biochemistry and industrial chemistry. The Science Faculty collaborates with the National Agricultural Research Organization, and exchanges of research staff are frequent. However, there is almost nothing by way of R&D work for industry, and no technologies are developed and transferred from university to enterprises.

An interesting incipient initiative in this area is through the Uganda Gatsby Trust, established in 1994 with UK funding. This provides some research funding, helps in the preparation of business plans and provides extension and training services to small and micro enterprises. In 1998 it served about 1000 clients and managed a loan portfolio of US$140 000. Gatsby Trusts also exist in Cameroon, Kenya and Tanzania, but the one in Uganda appears to specialize more on the provision of technology services. In Kenya, in 1998 it had over 5000 clients and focused on providing organizational and accounting support to NGOs. In Tanzania, with around 1000 clients and a smaller size of operations, the Trust fostered its borrowers access to local and international markets.

SCIENCE AND TECHNOLOGY INFRASTRUCTURE

Introduction

Ugandan S&T institutions, with the exception of the strongly donor-supported National Agricultural Research Organization (NARO), are generally small, understaffed and poorly funded. In most cases linkages with industry are low or ineffective. The system is organized under the planning and supervision of the Uganda National Council for Science and Technology (UNCST). The government created UNCST in 1990 under the Ministry of Planning and Economic Development as an umbrella organization, replacing the National Research Council established in 1970. Its functions are to integrate science and technology into socio-economic development, manage S&T policies, advise the government on S&T policy, coordinate S&T development and provide S&T leadership and guidance.

UNCST operates on a US$250 000 recurrent budget paid by the government, of which more than 80 per cent goes into personnel salaries. This budget is supplemented for specific projects by donor funding from IDRC (on transfer of telecommunications technologies to rural areas), UNEP (on biosafety in biotechnology in Uganda), International Health Policy Programme, the International Foundation for Science, the Council on Health Research for Development, CIDA of Canada, the Commonwealth Science Council, WHO and others. Further, it is in the process of setting up a Consultancy and Advisory Services Unit to generate income to supplement government financing. It currently employs 10 senior and 10 junior staff (three hold PhDs and one an MSc), and has several research associates working in other bodies and institutions. The organ responsible for the institution's policies is the Council, composed of eminent individuals, and activities are executed by Specialized Committees on Agriculture and Allied Sciences, Medical and Veterinary Sciences, Industrial and Engineering Sciences, Natural Sciences, Physical Sciences, and Social Sciences and Humanities.

While the institution is important for technology development, as it stands it lacks the financial and human resources to meet its mandate to 'co-ordinate all scientific and technological activities geared to national needs, and promote, develop and integrate S&T in the national development process' (from UNCST 1999 brochure). This is an ambitious objective, whose fulfilment requires it to have strong influence over all the agencies involved in S&T and industrial development. At present, the UNCST lacks such influence, and there is little coherence or coordination across the national technology system in Uganda. As noted for the other countries in this study, its technological output is of very little use to the industrial sector.

Standards and Quality

The Uganda National Bureau of Standards (UNBS) is in charge of developing standards and providing metrology, laboratory testing and quality assurance services to Ugandan industry. It is a statutory organization under MTTI, established in 1983 and in operation from 1989. It is a member of the International Organization for Standardization (ISO) and also of the Africa Regional Organization for Standardization (ARSO). UNBS is the national contact point for FAO/WHO *Codex Alimentarius* Commission that is responsible for the World-Wide Food Standards Programme. It is also the enquiry point for the World Trade Organization on the Agreements on Technical Barriers to Trade and on Application of Sanitary and Phyto-Sanitary measures. In conjunction with the Kenyan and Tanzanian standards bureaux UNBS is also involved in the elaboration of East African harmonized standards within the framework of East African Cooperation.

The official mandate of UNBS is to formulate and promote national standards, and to develop quality control and assurance systems to enhance consumer protection, public health and safety, industrial and commercial development and international trade. Its functions include:

- Standards development and promulgation;
- Industrial and legal metrology and calibration services;
- Product testing and certification;
- Shipment inspection for exporters;
- Provision of technical information and documentation.

Strengthening the UNBS had been a priority for MOTI for the period 1994–99, 'to prepare the necessary standards, to develop policy directives on standardisation, to ensure the application of these standards and to create a quality and standardisation awareness in all sectors of the economy, will be a key priority in implementing industrialisation and export promotion policies' (MOTI, 1994).

However, this target is far from being accomplished. There is little awareness of quality among Ugandan entrepreneurs, and the UNBS is not undertaking effective action to raise it. While it is difficult to evaluate UNBS's technical skills, it appears that few Ugandan firms demand its services, except for some compulsory testing of imported items. The Bureau had granted the Uganda Standard Certification Mark to only seven companies by end 1998 (UNBS, *Catalogue of Uganda Standards and Services*, 1998). It is starting to raise ISO 9000 awareness among firms through seminars and the provision of documentation. At the time of the authors' visit (September 1999), only one Ugandan firm had been awarded ISO 9000 certification, though this did not appear yet in the ISO statistics. A dozen others were undertaking the training to qualify.

The private sector, under the Uganda Manufacturers' Association with German cooperation, and under the PSF with US and World Bank funding (see above), is subsidizing the consulting costs of local companies being helped by foreign experts achieve ISO 9000 certification.

Ninety per cent of the UNBS resources come from the government, which has committed about US$1 million per year (though not more than 70 per cent of this is actually paid). Its operations have been helped by the ITC and by UNDP with a 2.5-year capacity building and technical assistance project expiring at end 1999. The bureau is beginning to generate resources by selling services, essentially metrology and calibration, that are charged at market prices, while other fees are set by the government. UNBS has a staff of almost 80, with 30 technicians and 20 scientists with university degrees (2 of which are PhDs and 5 are MScs).

UNBS laboratories are not internationally accredited, nor does the bureau have the capability to accredit independent private laboratories. This represents a serious drawback for Ugandan industry, and especially for exporters, who need to have their goods tested abroad, at high costs. One strategic target that has been expressed by the management of the institution is to qualify for ISO 9000 certification within two years. However, this objective appears unrealistic: there are few indications that requisite skills and resources are available.

Summing up, the institution suffers from mutually reinforcing difficulties such as:

- Limited awareness of quality in the country;
- Poor funding and insufficient personnel to perform the role assigned;
- Lack of international accreditation of measuring and testing laboratories.

In the emerging trading environment, with increasing stress on industrial standards, the weaknesses of the UNBS represent a serious competitive disadvantage for local industry. In general, the UNBS appears underfunded, lacking the necessary physical facilities and human technical skills. Hopefully international cooperation (currently by UNDP) will help relieve the latter constraint. Its technical staff is smaller than the Tanzanian equivalent (not to mention Kenya or other more advanced emerging countries) and salaries are insufficient to attract young graduates. It is too passive in promoting quality awareness among firms and especially SMEs, and the private sector (UMA and PSF) appears much more active in this respect.

In the short run, its financing should be increased, subject to stringent requirements in terms of productivity and quality achievements. It needs to carry out an intense national campaign to raise quality awareness within the private sector and induce it to invest in quality improvements and techniques. In the longer run, the role of the UNBS should be reassessed, especially its relations with the private sector and with the other institutions in the country's S&T system. Thus, in the future the bureau could focus on certifying private laboratories rather than carrying out testing in-house. Moreover, it should necessarily be part of a comprehensive and consistent strategy to improve Uganda's competitiveness, involving the private sector in its design and implementation on a continuous and interactive basis.

R&D Institutions

The largest and most active research institution in Uganda, the National Agricultural Research Organization (NARO), was established in November

1991 as a semi-autonomous institution under the Ministry of Agriculture, Animal Industry and Fisheries. Its prominence reflects the agricultural nature of the Ugandan economy. Its main aim is to coordinate and undertake adaptive research in crop, livestock, fisheries, forestry and related production systems, ranging from agricultural engineering and food science to natural resources management. It also plays an important role in the transfer and dissemination of technology to small-scale farmers.

The World Bank has largely funded NARO, initially for five years (beginning in 1992) for over US$20 million, then for a six-year second phase with US$26 million. Additional funding has come from DANIDA, FAO, the Rockefeller Foundation and others. In recent years, NARO's annual budget has been around US$10 million, and GOU has contributed 30 per cent. It employs 210 scientists and over 600 support staff, and the financing from the private sector has increased. Strong links exist with the Faculties of Agriculture, Science and Veterinary Medicine of Makerere University. Research collaboration also extends to other institutions in Kenya and in East Africa. Innovativeness and academic achievements appear to matter and contribute to the promotion of employees. The technical and scientific capabilities of NARO, the effectiveness of its technology transfer, and the effects on the agricultural sector's productivity could not be assessed in all details. However, judging from the resources available, the number of projects implemented, the range of technical skills available, and linkages with the Ministry of Agriculture and other R&D institutions, NARO enjoys a priority among S&T institutions and performs a useful function in promoting adaptive research and technology diffusion.

The situation in the manufacturing sector stands in sharp contrast. The industrial sector is supposed to be served by the Uganda Industrial Research Institute (UIRI), which is supposed 'to undertake applied industrial research and to develop and acquire appropriate technology in order to create a strong, effective and competitive industrial sector for the rapid industrialisation of Uganda' (UIRI leaflets). The East African Community (EAC) conceived UIRI in the 1970s as one of the regional centres to promote research in industry. During the early days of the EAC, most industrial research was conducted by the East African Industrial Research Organization based in Nairobi. However, in 1974–75 the Research Council of the EAC decided to decentralize industrial research in Uganda, Kenya and Tanzania on the basis of local resources. Kenya set up the Kenya Industrial Research and Development Institute (KIRDI) while Tanzania established the Tanzania Industrial Research and Development Organization (TIRDO). The Research Council of the EAC recommended and approved the setting up of a *Food Technology and Industrial Ceramics Research Institute* in Kampala.

When the EAC broke up in 1977, each individual partner state took over the financing and management of local R&D. Due to the extended political and economic problems of Uganda, the establishment of an R&D institute in Uganda was postponed till 1994. The government then obtained an interest-free loan of US$6 million from China, along with a grant of US$3.6 million for laboratory and office equipment, workshops, generators, and technical assistance. This allowed the setting up of facilities in the Nakawa industrial area, where the UIRI is presently located. The Institute was turned into an autonomous body in 1999 under the UNCST umbrella. The Government of Uganda funds recurrent activities, amounting to US$250 000 in 1998–99.

Until recently UIRI mainly provided training and product development services in the food and ceramics sectors. However, it now appears to be increasingly engaged in repair and maintenance of equipment for other industries, and in training and the provision of business services. The main operational projects include: the Value Added Meat Products to improve meat processing capabilities of Ugandan firms, and funded by FAO and GTZ from 1997 to 1999 (US$1.4 million); the Fermented African Dairy Products Project, essentially a training project funded by DANIDA and the World Association of Industrial and Technological Research Organizations from 1997 to 1999 (€140 000). UIRI currently employs 35 people, with 2 holding Masters' and 16 undergraduate degrees.

The institution finds it difficult to recruit good scientists at the low salaries offered. Most of the Institute's budget is used to pay salaries (35 per cent), and materials, utilities, buildings and equipment (over 50 per cent). Only 10 per cent of the institution's resources go to R&D, which consists essentially of low-level adaptive work rather than innovative work. The number of clients (essentially urban SMEs) is small but has grown from 50 in 1998 to almost 100 in 1999. Most services provided by UIRI are for relatively simple testing and trouble-shooting rather than research or development. The staff could not provide any instances of UIRI technologies being used in commercial production by private enterprises. The Institute's activities appear supply-driven, with the output of little use to most industries. As virtually no original research is carried out, any capability to market research results is also absent. The inability to identify the problems of their clients, especially smaller ones (the majority), was acknowledged by the staff. Nor does UIRI provide assistance to enterprises in identifying and importing foreign technologies.

UIRI is a largely dormant institution. Its history as a food and ceramics support institution still casts a shadow, and its activities have spread to other sectors and firms only to a very limited extent. The difficulties are compounded by the lack of demand from industry, with its poor capital base and deficient technological capabilities. Nevertheless, in the present situation, the public goods that industry needs to operate efficiently are not met in Uganda.

While perhaps not as starved of resources as TIRDO in Tanzania, the Ugandan R&D institution is not apparently any more effective in terms of stimulating local technological effort. Again, this is not surprising in view of the low technological level and lack of dynamism of local industry. This is a frequent problem in SSA, as shown in Box 5.2 below. The poor technological level of local industry breeds even poorer technology institutions that cannot, in turn, contribute to local industrial capabilities.

BOX 5.2 WEAK ENTERPRISE-TECHNOLOGY INSTITUTION RELATIONSHIPS CONSTRAIN INDUSTRY IN SUB-SAHARAN AFRICA

The relationships between enterprises and technology institutions are especially weak in Sub-Saharan Africa, and this represents a major area of inadequacy of the industry support system in the region.

A recent study reports some evidence on the extent and characteristics of the relationships that firms have with institutions providing technical support in three Sub-Saharan countries (Biggs et al., 1995, pp.105–8). The study notes that, compared with other parts of the world, such as Asia and Latin America, the number of collective services in Africa is rather meagre. In SSA, collective service provision is largely centralized, with government, often supported by foreign donors, as the largest provider. Business associations and other types of industry-specific organizations, while they exist, deliver virtually no technology services to their members (nor do local governments deliver any business services as one might find in parts of Asia in specialized industry districts).

One way of assessing the quality and coverage of these service institutions is to observe the actual usage of the services by potential clients. The conclusion is straightforward: collective technical support systems are used to a minimal extent in all three countries. The only service which is consistently utilized is the Bureau of Standards, mostly by food processing and metalworking firms. The second most-used services are those involved in training. On the whole, however, these figures clearly indicate the low-intensity utilization of external collective support mechanisms in the three countries studied. Institutional linkages are also weak in Zimbabwean manufacturing. The vast majority of companies in a recently-investigated sample have no links with any research or S&T institutions (Latsch and Robinson, 1999). These are very passive, and firms regard their abilities poorly and expect little from them. There is no contracting of industrial research to technology institutions, and the few companies that have links at all use mostly testing facilities. A similar picture emerges from a recent analysis on Kenya, where the recent increase in institutional linkages is mainly due to the links with the Kenya Bureau of Standards. Moreover, according to the sample enterprises, the average ranking of the quality of service provided by different technology institutions show that none of them was rated by the sample firms as 'good' or 'very good' (Wignaraja and Ikiara, 1999).

Among the many explanations offered, one is centred on the notion of centralization, isolation and lack of contact with the productive sector: 'the fact that most collective technical support services in Africa are provided by the centralised institutions of government is important in analysing their low quantitative and qualitative impact on manufacturing activities in the economy. Even in East Asia, where government's track record in industrial policy is often praised, the record of centralised government provision of collective technical services is, at best, uneven. The reason for this is that there is a vital need for institutions delivering broad based or high intensity collective technical support to be close to and familiar with the needs of client groups. Centralised providers of all kinds of services, particularly in Africa, have a history of being disconnected from clients and lacking familiarity with their needs' (Biggs et al., 1995, pp.107-8). Another possible explanation focuses on the inadequate government civil service pay scales in Africa, that make it almost impossible to staff centralized government institutions with the type of skills and competence required to organize and deliver such services. This is also related to the differences in background, attitudes and 'technological languages' often encountered between firms and technology institutions. An additional problem may be the lack of cooperation between public and private providers of support services.

Sources: Biggs et al. (1995); Latsch and Robinson (1999); Wignaraja and Ikiara (1999); Wangwe and Diyamett (1998).

CONCLUSIONS

Uganda has a short tradition in manufacturing. The small industrial sector stagnated for many years under various regimes until 1986. The industrial structure comprises rudimentary and low value added activities, using simple technologies at low levels of efficiency. Local industry lacks any culture of R&D, quality and technological effort. Although it is difficult to measure the general level of technological capability in Ugandan industry, casual observation and comparisons with other countries suggest that it is rather low even by regional standards.

The Ugandan economy has been growing well since 1986 largely because of rehabilitation and use of existing capacity. It is unlikely, however, that these growth rates can be sustained in industry without higher investment and technical improvements (Reinikka and Svensson, 1999a). There are various constraints on the technological front. Uganda has a poor endowment of skills and has invested little to improve it. Imports of foreign technology into the country are low and are not rising in response to liberalization. Capital goods imports have been minimal for several years, fluctuating widely during the 1990s and declining in their share of total imports. The introduction of tax deductibility for plant and machinery investments in 1997 has not reversed this trend, possibly due to poor and costly communication and transport. Local firms pay virtually no royalties or technical fees abroad. While FDI has increased recently, much of it is explained by privatization and by the return of investors expelled in the 1970s and 1980s. While a sign of confidence in the new business environment, much of these inflows go into services rather than industry. Prospects for increasing manufacturing FDI, particularly in export activities, are not very promising.

Technological efforts to adopt, improve and adapt foreign technology are very limited at the firm level. Awareness of the need for technological effort is lacking. Skill development still occurs in the form of on-the-job training, with the notable exceptions of some TNCs that invest in formal skill upgrading programmes. A culture of quality and efficiency in manufacturing is beginning to emerge, but it is still confined to few enterprises. Policies and institutions do not help in this regard.

The macroeconomic framework is now favourable to business. Major improvements include the liberalization of foreign trade, the privatization of several state-owned enterprises, and the removal of restrictions to private entry. However, all this does not address the need to foster Uganda's industrial and technological development. The science and technology system is weak, with underfunded and de-linked institutions. Most do not have a clear idea of their mandate and do not cooperate among themselves. A notable example is non-traditional rose exports from Uganda, that are suffering from such a gap, and from the absence of a *technology system* in the country (Box 5.3). In sum, the Ugandan government lacks a strategy for technology development, in the sense of a coherent set of policies to remedy market failures and encourage the business sector to undertake the effort needed.

BOX 5.3 EMERGING EXPORTS AND THE LACK OF A *TECHNOLOGY SYSTEM*: ROSE EXPORTS FROM UGANDA

Cut flowers are a 'non-traditional' commodity for Uganda, and their exports have notably increased since 1993. However, like all new industries, the flower industry in Uganda is suffering from several difficulties related to the absence of all the public goods that are provided within a developed *technology system*. The lack of technology and marketing support institutions hindered the emergence of innovating entrepreneurs, and may threaten the consolidation and sustainability of the initial success by worsening the effects of market failures and imperfections.

Let us briefly review the history of this industry in the country. In 1993 and 1994 five farms perceived the profit potential and began investing. A loan obtained from the Africa Project Development Facility (APDF) helped to hire a foreign consultant to carry out a feasibility study of a rose farm. The warm climate and the abundant rainfall and water near Lake Victoria appeared very favourable factors to rose farming. These growers mainly opted for the highest grade of roses (hybrid teas, the long-stemmed big flower heads variety) that make the highest prices in the Dutch auctions in Amsterdam. However, as temperatures never fall below 16°C near Lake Victoria, the roses tended to ripen earlier than elsewhere, and never reached the length and head size of the competing roses from Northern Kenya and Arusha (Tanzania). Thus, they had to be sold at a discount and would have needed a different marketing strategy. No expert or farmer could have forecast it, and the industry pioneers were forced to learn at a high price. Now Ugandan production is more diversified, with several varieties farmed on 75 hectares, and with the hybrid teas and the sweetheart short-stemmed, smaller head varieties each accounting for half of total production. According to some experts, the latter may be more suitable to Uganda's conditions, allowing more abundant but lower quality production than elsewhere. In the following years, other farms followed: six in 1996-97 to reach a total of 18 by September 1999.

Exports of Roses from Uganda

Years	1992	1993	1994	1995	1996	1997
Thousand US$	–	158	531	34	2 809	1 114

Source: Uganda Revenue Authority.

In the early stages of the life-cycle of the industry in Uganda, the inexperienced entrepreneurs obtained their technology mainly from foreign experts (for feasibility studies) often from neighbouring Kenya, and from utensils suppliers offering advice and appliances (for example, cold stores, steel greenhouses) at very high prices.

All essential technical inputs still have to be acquired abroad. The soil sample testing needs to be made in foreign laboratories (for example, in Holland). NARO provided no technical knowledge, as the industry was totally new to the country. The inefficient cold storage facilities at the airport further damaged flowers' quality. Moreover, the country suffered from the lack of the marketing skills to sell in distant European markets. Detailed knowledge of the characteristics of this market and of the roses that could be produced locally was absent, no conscious effort was made to acquire it, and local institutions could not help. Similarly, the idea of what pricing strategy to adopt is very vague, as the world increase in flower production is making it a high-volume low-margin activity. All the Ugandan farmers targeted the demanding Dutch auction, which charges a 25 per cent commission on gross sales and requires very high quality. Only after years of experience, has it been realized that Uganda's climatic conditions and the country's weak technology support system only allow low quality roses. For the last three years average prices of Uganda's hybrid tea and sweetheart varieties have been lowest when compared with those from other neighbouring countries, like Kenya, Tanzania, Zambia, and from India and Israel. In turn, this should require a different marketing strategy targeting retail shops and supermarkets in Europe, where demand looks very promising, and the quality concerns are less stringent. Recent concerns have emerged, as the Amsterdam auction classified Ugandan flower exports as second grade, and the European Union is imposing increasingly strict environmental rules. Local institutions could not help enterprises to address these difficulties, and no strategic and comprehensive response has been designed or implemented.

In sum, the industry clearly has potential, as shown by the export growth figures, but little is being done to make this process sustainable by helping firms to upgrade quality and devise a consistent marketing strategy. The absence of a *technology system* may hamper the consolidation of this initial success, and its diffusion to new enterprises.

Source: Pietrobelli (2001); based on interviews with staff from Uganda Flowers Exporters Association (UEFA), September 1999.

Several policy recommendations may be proposed, both long and short term.

Long-Term Strategic Policies

The government of Uganda needs to review and improve its strategic capabilities. Some institution must be able to analyse technology needs and design and implement strategies that cut across ministerial and departmental lines. At present, many institutions in the country deal with science, technology, education, technical and management training, curricula design and assessment, intellectual property protection, standards design and implementation, but little coordination exists among them. Their mandates are not specific and often overlap. Linkages with the private business sector are weak. The ability to mount a coordinated strategic effort, often with inputs from the private sector and in some cases transnational investors, is the basis of success in all emerging countries. At present, Uganda lacks a body with the mandate, the competence and the political strength to perform this role. This should be remedied within the context of a comprehensive restructuring of the S&T system. Although the promotion of S&T appears in all policy statements and strategy papers, good intentions are not followed up by the design and implementation of specific policies.

Like most countries in Africa, Uganda lacks a *culture of technology and innovation*. There is little understanding of what 'innovation' is, why it is useful for business and how it can be carried out. Changing these attitudes is difficult and time-consuming, involving a gradual shift in primary and secondary education focus and priorities, national campaigns and promotion.

The national base of human capital and skills needs to be improved. A major constraint to Ugandan industry is the inadequate supply of skilled manpower, technical personnel, and qualified managers. This requires both a long-term commitment to basic as well as advanced technical education. The government has prioritized primary education for donor support, especially in the countryside to reduce poverty (DFID, 1999). However, to develop industry and enhance technology transfer and innovation, technical skills need to be developed much more. It is also vital to provide support to training institutions and activities that can help skill formation at the firm level.

Although the insufficient protection of intellectual property does not appear relevant to Uganda's technology development at this stage, URSB must be strengthened over the longer term, both to provide a suitable environment for technology transfer and to encourage incipient local innovation.

Short-Term Actions

The macroeconomic framework for business activities has improved, but specific industrial issues need to be addressed. A true 'one-stop shop' for foreign investors does not exist in Uganda. UIA has substantially gained in efficiency, but it is not empowered to grant all licences needed for operation, and still carries very little weight with other ministries and utility companies (Obwona, 1998). Its role should be re-analysed within the framework of a renewed set-up to improve the government's strategy making capability (see above among the strategic priorities).

The NCST has the mandate to 'integrate science and technology into socio-economic development, manage S&T policies, advise the government on S&T policy, coordinate S&T development efforts and provide S&T leadership and guidance'. However, this broad mandate is not coupled with sufficient funding and influence over other institutions. The institution is far removed from industry and is unable to formulate or implement technology strategy.

The government does little to foster R&D in private as well as public institutions. Only donors finance R&D in the university and often in other public bodies. Tax deductibility of R&D and training expenditures has been introduced, but such incentives are inadequate to stimulating a technology 'culture' in the Ugandan environment.

Industry–university linkages are very low. There is almost nothing in universities by way of R&D work for industry, and no technologies are developed and transferred from university to enterprises. The universities should be helped to carry out basic research, but they should also be encouraged to collaborate with the productive sector.

Regrettably, education at the secondary level has little relevance to employment needs in industry. The National Curriculum Development Centre is in charge of designing education curricula. It is underfunded and its distance from and lack of credibility with the private sector should be addressed and remedied, through, for example, involving the private sector in the design of curricula and in the development of specialized education and training modules.

Management training is inadequate and needs to be substantially increased and improved. MTAC should have strong linkages with the other research, technology and training institutions (such as UNBS, UIRI, and the Vocational Training Centres). The diffusion of a culture of quality and efficiency should be promoted by national campaigns, revision of training modules in all public training institutions, and subsidies to expenditures on management consulting.

The weaknesses of UNBS represent a serious competitive disadvantage for local industry. In general, UNBS is underfunded and lacking in the necessary physical facilities and technical skills. It is too passive in promoting quality awareness among firms and especially SMEs. In the short run, its financing should be increased, subject to stringent requirements in terms of productivity and quality achievements. This should be carried out together with an intense national campaign to raise private sector's quality concerns, and induce it to make new efforts geared to quality improvements. In the longer run, the role of the UNBS should be reassessed, especially its relations with the private sector and with the other institutions in the country's S&T system. Thus, in the future the bureau could become a body in charge of certifying private laboratories, rather than carrying out all the testing in-house. Moreover, it should necessarily be part of a comprehensive and consistent strategy to improve Uganda's competitiveness, involving the private sector in its design and implementation on a continuous (interactive) basis (see above).

UIRI activities are supply driven, with their output of little use to most industries. As virtually no original research is carried out, the capability to market research results is also absent. The difficulties faced by this institution are compounded by the poor capital base of Ugandan industry, its low awareness of the role of R&D and its deficient level of technological capabilities. The institute should be re-funded and radically alter its priorities to move closer to the needs of industry. Ways to cooperate with the private sector on a continuous basis should be investigated; the strengthening of its technical staff and equipment is an essential starting step.

NOTES

1. On average the investment rate is slightly over 10 per cent, while at the median firm it is below 1 per cent (Reinikka and Svensson, 1999a). Thus, in spite of the economic reforms, investment rates are still very low.
2. This applies also after controlling for additional explanations of the investment rate such as size and foreign ownership.
3. According to this same survey, 89 operating days are lost in a year due to power cuts. As a consequence, 77 per cent of large firms, 44 per cent of medium-sized firms, and 16 per cent

of small firms own their own power generators. In terms of cost, this expenditure represents 16 per cent of the value of total investment and 25 per cent of the value of investment in equipment and machinery in 1997. Similar conclusions apply to transport and import-related costs, that on average double the cost of imported inputs compared to the cost in the country of origin (Reinikka and Svensson, 1999a, 1999b).

4. Privatization has been pursued on a sustained basis since 1993, following Uganda's Public Enterprises Reform and Divestiture (PERD) Statute No. 9, implemented by the PERD Secretariat.
5. To remedy this, the PSF (see below) launched in 1997 a 'Uganda Equity Financing' Project. However, this never really started operations. The risk-evaluation capacity in the country was very poor and one of the important causes of the failure (authors' interviews, Kampala, September 1999).
6. In 1998 Uganda Batteries Ltd. became the first company in the country to receive the ISO 9000 certification.
7. Trademarks application fees stand at USh.2000 and US$150, and on approval, USh.4000 and US$250 for local and foreign applications respectively, although the disparity is contentious under the TRIPS agreement and may need to be eliminated.
8. The *Institutional Investor* regularly develops country credit ratings based on the information provided by leading international banks, money management firms and economists. Each country is graded on a scale from zero to 100, with 100 representing those with the least chance of default. Factors considered range from short-term capital flows, to current account changes, to sovereign risk. For the sake of comparisons, in March 1999 the credit ratings of other African countries were the following: Botswana 53.5, South Africa 45.8, Ghana 29.5, Zimbabwe 26.5, Kenya 24.1, Tanzania 18.3, Ethiopia 16.2, and Congo, the last in the global rank, 6.1
9. See for an example the case of Metro Cash and Carry (U) Ltd., that took more than two years to identify an appropriate site for the store, then had to negotiate with a handful of wealthy landlords who wanted a premium for their plots. Because of the delay in opening up, the company was caught up in the changes of the incentive regime: while it had been initially attracted by the favourable tax holidays on investments, this regime was removed before the company could start (UNCTAD, 1998b, p. 74).
10. Interview with South Korean investor in the fishing industry that recently diversified into EPS insulated sandwich panels. At the time of writing, the company was employing fifteen Koreans in managerial and engineering positions, and the linkages with local manufacturers were marginal (all materials and machinery were imported from South Korea). UNCTAD field visit, September 1999.

6. Ghana

INTRODUCTION

For the first 25 years after independence in 1957, Ghana pursued a strong import substitution strategy to promote industry, with a large role for state-owned enterprises. These policies failed to promote growth, and the economy went into a prolonged period of decline. By the 1970s there were signs of collapse everywhere (Chand and van Til, 1988); in 1982 the situation was greatly aggravated by a severe drought and the influx of over a million Ghanaians expelled from Nigeria. The government turned to foreign assistance and a macroeconomic programme was agreed with the IMF and the World Bank in April 1983. The agreement took the form of a structural adjustment programme (known as the 'Economic Recovery Programme', ERP). This aimed to stabilize the economy and reform economic policies.[1] The main features of the ERP were as follows:

- Unification and successive devaluations of the exchange rate;
- Liberalization of international trade;
- Dismantling most price and distribution controls and eliminating many subsidies;
- Broadening the tax base and improving tax collection;
- Increasing reliance on foreign development assistance, to bridge the gap between domestic savings and investments through access to external savings.

Ghana used to be cited as an outstanding example of the success of structural adjustment (World Bank, 1993): GDP and consumption per capita grew in spite of deteriorating terms of trade. However, the outcome is more mixed and needs to be carefully interpreted. From a long-run perspective Ghana's economic performance is not notable. GDP fell by 0.1 per cent per year in the period 1970–80, then grew 3.0 per cent in 1980–90 and 4.3 per cent in 1990–97 (Table 6.1). However, GDP per capita virtually stagnated, falling in the 1970s and growing only moderately thereafter. In other words, recent growth is a rather weak response to earlier stagnation: 'Ghana's performance (in the 1980s and early 1990s) largely reflects the depth of economic decline before the reform' (Leechor, 1994, p. 155).

Table 6.1 Ghana (1970–98) selected growth indicators

	Real GDP	GNP pc*	MVA	
1970–80	−0.1	−3.0	6.5	(1965–73)
			−6.9	(1973–84)
1980–90	3.0	−0.1	4.0	
1990–97	4.3	0.5	2.7	

Note: *1970–83 for 1970–80, 1980–92 for 1980–90 and 1996–97 for 1990–97.

INDUSTRIAL BACKGROUND

After independence in 1957 Ghana adopted

> a 'fast track' strategy of industrialisation, founded on the notion that rapid economic development was feasible, provided that the State assumed the entrepreneurial function... The Government embarked on an accelerated programme of establishing a large number of state-owned import substitution industries producing a wide range of previously imported consumer goods for the domestic market. By 1970, Ghana had one of the most diverse and dynamic manufacturing sector in SSA. (MIST, 1992, p. 1)

However, manufacturing remained highly protected and import-dependent, failing significantly to become competitive in world markets. After an initial period of expansion in investment and output, performance deteriorated and by 1984 manufacturing output was only 39 per cent of the level reached in 1977. After the launch of the ERP in 1983, the performance of manufacturing industry improved sharply, but largely as the result of the availability of imported inputs and of higher domestic demand fuelled by better cocoa prices and aid inflows rather than because of improved technical efficiency.

Not surprisingly, rapid industrial growth was not sustained. MVA growth rates fell significantly and by 1992 manufacturing had not yet regained the level of 11.3 per cent of GDP that it had reached in 1971. In 1996 MVA was only 9 per cent of GDP (Table 6.2). In a comparative perspective, in 1996 total MVA in Ghana was at around 70 per cent of Kenya's, 47 per cent of Zimbabwe's, and 2 per cent of Malaysia's (Chapter 2). In per capita terms, MVA grew only at 0.3 per cent per annum in 1980–96.

The modern industrial sector is concentrated in food processing and intermediate industries, largely owned by foreign companies (Pietrobelli, 1994a). The equipment industry is very backward. The vast majority of manufacturing enterprises operate at small scales, use simple machinery, are

Table 6.2 Manufacturing production and growth rates, Ghana, 1986-97 (index numbers 1977 = 100)

	1986	1987	1988	1989	1990	1991	1992	1993	1994	1995	1996	1997*
Food	40.6	50.5	53.6	48.0	57.5	59.3	62.8	90.3	90.8	99.6	102 5	109.3
Beverages	75.1	85.2	89.0	98.0	94.0	93.0	112.2	105.5	109.4	109.0	116.2	123.9
Tobacco	57.6	54.9	58.0	51.0	57.1	49.6	47.1	52.2	53.0	52.0	53.1	53.1
Textile, garments	22.9	26.1	28.7	24.0	37.7	39.1	23.7	60.2	48.0	54.8	56.1	55.5
Sawmill, wood	79.5	79.3	98.3	80.0	74.2	133.6	120.2	91.9	98.2	100.2	105.3	105.0
Paper, printing	70.5	59.7	52.8	48.0	53.5	49.3	54.6	33.7	47.1	45.1	49.3	54.1
Petroleum ref.	76.6	62.7	67.7	87.2	70.5	92.2	65.0	65.8	94.4	101.4	103.5	7.3
Chemical	38.0	51.9	67.5	62.0	57.6	44.7	56.7	38.4	129.8	140.0	148.2	159.8
Cement	47.4	49.7	73.4	100.0	117.3	125.6	177.0	206.2	217.0	258.1	258.9	241.8
Iron, steel	38.8	42.9	18.3	12.1	5.2	-	356.0	392.8	541.1	581.6	584.5	590.5
Non ferr. metal basic ind.	72.5	90.3	97.3	100.5	103.8	104.6	115.8	109.9	88.8	119.8	125.6	149.9
Cutlery & other non ferr. met.	55.2	51.9	46.2	47.9	55.2	63.2	83.3	99.9	124.0	102.4	116.4	116.4
Electrical equip.	51.0	31.5	47.1	13.5	25.5	40.0	46.3	52.6	29.8	42.9	53.5	67.8
Transport	-	-	-	-	-	-	11.0	-	-	-	-	-
All manufacturing	54.2	56.8	62.1	63.0	63.5	71.3	76.9	87.3	101.2	109.9	115.0	101.0

Note: *Provisional.

Source: Statistical Service Ghana, *Quarterly Digest of Statistics*, March 1998.

largely African owned, have low levels of technical and managerial skills, and generally produce low quality goods for the domestic market. The informal sector is entirely African, uses even simpler technologies and serves local demand for low-cost low-quality products.

Evidence from five SSA countries (Cameroon, Ghana, Kenya, Zambia and Zimbabwe) in the mid-1990s provides an indication of the relative standing of Ghanaian enterprises (Bigsten et al., 1998). Ghanaian firms are smaller, have less than a third of capital per employee compared to the other countries, and use a less educated workforce.

Textiles, garments, electrical equipment, chemicals and tobacco are the sectors that suffered the most in the 1980s (Table 6.3). In common with most other African countries, but in sharp contrast to East Asia, the labour-intensive industries that fuelled manufacturing and export growth (garments, textiles, toys) showed no growth in Ghana.

After the easily usable capacity had been brought into production after import liberalization, the growth of manufacturing called for more investment in refurbishing and modernizing facilities, adding new productive capacity, and increasing the efficiency of operations. However, the investment rate has been low, as in most of SSA (Bigsten et al., 1999), capacity utilization has risen only marginally, and technical efficiency has remained low. There were minimal efforts to raise technological capabilities after liberalization, with predictable consequences on growth, as import competition started to erode domestic market shares (Lall et al., 1994).

Ghana's manufacturing sector does not compare well with other countries in SSA in terms of labour productivity. According to Bigsten et al. (1998),

Table 6.3 Estimated rate of capacity utilization in manufacturing, Ghana, 1984–93 (large and medium-scale factories, %)

	1984	1987	1989	1991	1993
Textiles	17.3	24.0	45.0	45.0	41.3
Garments	20.2	25.0	22.0	30.0	53.3
Food processing	22.9	42.0	51.0	51.0	52.3
Metals	20.1	42.0	45.0	58.0	80.0
Leather	11.9	15.0	25.0	7.0	10.0
Chemicals	22.3	30.0	30.0	30.2	40.0
Wood processing	28.1	43.0	70.0	65.0	65.0
All manufacturing	18.0	35.0	40.6	40.5	45.7

Source: Ghana Statistical Service, Quarterly Digest of Statistics, March 1998.

Ghana's value added per employee is almost identical to Zambia's, but median labour productivity in Cameroon is 3.7 times higher and in Kenya and Zimbabwe 3.5 times higher.[2] A survey conducted by the World Bank confirms these results. Growth in manufacturing during 1991–95 occurred with no increases in productivity, but mainly due to increases in labour and capital inputs (Teal, 1999; Table 6.3).

The manufactured export record is equally disappointing, as a study comparing Ghana's manufactured export performance with Mauritius and other African countries reveals (Teal, 1999). Although per capita manufactured exports have grown since the mid-1980s, reversing negative or very low growth rates in the previous decade, the absolute values remain tiny, reaching $6 in 1980–90 and $9 in 1990–95. This compares with $56 for Zimbabwe in both periods, and $341 and $823 for Mauritius respectively (Table 6.4).[3] What explains this weak record? Of the many possible factors responsible, one is Ghana's S&T system, which affects the capability of enterprises to import technology from abroad, use it efficiently and adapt it to local needs.

Policy Framework for Industry

The Ghanaian government has attempted to encourage industrial investment since 1959, when it enacted the Pioneer Industries and Companies Act. It followed this with several other measures, including the Capital Investment

Table 6.4 Manufactured exports: Ghana and other SSA countries, 1980–95

	Manufactured exports as % of total exports		Manufactured exports (US$ million)		Manufactured exports per capita (US$)	
	1980–90	1990–95	1980–90	1990–95	1980–90	1990–95
Cameroon	9	13	169	224	15	18
Ghana	9	13	83	147	6	9
Kenya	14	17	174	232	8	9
Mauritius	48	67	352	899	341	823
Zambia	6	16	70	132	9	16
Zimbabwe*	33	34	492	573	56	56

Note: *Zimbabwe is 1980–94.

Source: Teal, 1999, from World Bank data.

Act of 1963, the 1973 Investment Decree and the Investment Policy Decree of 1975, the 1981 Investment Code, and the 1985 Investment Code that established the Ghana Investment Centre (Baah-Nuakoh et al., 1996). All these measures included tax holidays, accelerated depreciation allowances, exemption from import duties on machinery and equipment, investment allowances and arrangements for profit repatriation. Capital expenditure on R&D approved by the Minister of Trade and Industry was fully tax deductible. However, the measures failed to evoke a significant response from the business community.

The Ghana Investment Centre played more a regulatory than a promotional role: as approvals had to be obtained from numerous individual ministries and institutions, it did not act as a true one-stop shop. The code was revised with the Ghana Investment Centre Act in August 1994 to convert the Centre into a promotional institution, the Ghana Investment Promotion Centre (GIPC).

The GIPC presently performs the following functions: [4]

- The initiation of, support for and participation in investment promotion activities;
- The collection, collation and dissemination of investment information;
- The identification and promotion of specific projects;
- The linking up of investors with government agencies and institutional lenders, and the provision of investor support services;
- The registration of all enterprises and technology transfer agreements to which the GIPC Act is applicable.

GIPC employs 20 professionals, with salaries accounting for nearly 50 per cent of the annual Cedis 880 million budget (about $250 000 at the 1999 exchange rate). A prospective investor still needs to spend substantial time and effort getting through bureaucratic requirements. While prior approval is not now required to establish in the country and 100 per cent ownership is permitted (on certain conditions), there remain many official obstacles, for instance in access to land, utility installation and services, and import procedures.[5] Access to land is especially problematic, and a Lands Commission notes that a three to six-month delay is typical, though delays can often reach one or two years. Industrially zoned land is especially scarce, no industrial estates with standard factory buildings are available for lease, and utility services are costly and difficult to obtain. Moreover, there is little coordination with other government bodies. The response of the business community to investment promotion has been weak, as falling FDI inflows in the late 1990s reveal (see Table 2.16).

The institution in charge of export promotion is the Ghana Export Promotion Council (GEPC), which is mainly involved in trade fairs and trade promotion. In 1999 its revenues were about Cedis 2000 million ($570 000), slightly higher than GIPC.[6] Together with MOTI, GEPC helps set up incentive schemes for exporters, including export retention (100 per cent of foreign exchange export proceeds may be retained), corporate tax rebates (between 40 and 75 per cent of tax liabilities), customs duty drawbacks and bonded warehouses.[7]

The Ghana Free Zones Board (GFZB) is an integrated programme to promote processing and manufacturing of goods through the establishment of EPZs and the strengthening of seaport and airport services. Investment may occur - and be promoted - anywhere in Ghana. The programme is managed by the private sector, with a Malaysian consulting firm coordinating most components. The following incentives are granted, following the Free Zone Act (Act 504, August 1995), conditional upon at least 70 per cent of annual production being exported:

- Total exemption from direct and indirect import duties, and from income tax on profits for 10 years, and from withholding taxes from dividends from free zone investments;
- Maximum tax rates after 10 years shall not exceed 8 per cent;
- No import licensing requirements, and simplified customs formalities, with customs' officers inspecting inside the factory;
- No restriction on 100 per cent foreign ownership (as for all investments in Ghana), and on repatriation of dividends or profits, or of proceeds from sale of any Free Zone activity;
- No limits on foreign exchange accounts (for all activities in Ghana).

The scheme appears to suit an increasing number of foreign investors, as the cases in Box 6.1 illustrate. Several business associations exist in the country, such as the Association of Ghana Industries (AGI), the Association of Small-Scale Industries (ASSI), and the Private Enterprise Foundation (PEF). They all play an advocacy role for the private sector, but their focus is mainly on such issues as access to credit, trade policies and management training. Technology issues are conspicuous by their absence.

BOX 6.1 GHANA FREE ZONES BOARD: TWO TNCs' EXPERIENCES AFTER LIBERALIZATION

The Ghana Free Zones Board (GFZB) was created in 1995 to attract export oriented foreign investors in the context of Ghana Investment Promotion Centre Act (1994). It aimed to present

Ghana as a 'Gateway to Africa', explicitly targeting the West African market. The following two cases, based on the experience of two TNCs in the free zone, show responses to the policy shift. Both companies value the GFZB highly.

Pioneer Food Cannery was operating in Ghana for many years under different ownership arrangements. It started as a joint venture between Star-Kist Heinz, the large US based food corporation, and a Ghanaian partner, in 1976. It ceased operations from 1987 to 1993, when it was purchased by the European branch of the US shareholder. The initial investment amounted to almost $7 million, and $2 to 3 million have been added yearly since then.

The new FDI policy induced the firm to reopen and expand the factory. Its main product, canned tuna fish, is almost totally exported. Exports rose from $25 million in 1994 to about $80 million in 1999, employing almost 1300 floor-level workers and 50 supervisors and managers.

Under the Ghanaian Managing Director, four expatriate managers control the financial and technical functions of the company. The company is exploring the possibility of establishing some collaboration with the University of Science and Technology in Kumasi and the University of Ghana on issues like waste management or uses of fish bones and skins in agriculture. They need to work in close collaboration with GSB, which has the mandate to certify fish exports to the European Union. Substantial linkages have been developed with local producers, and the company estimates that its indirect employment is 1494 people in fishing companies, can makers, contractors, distributors, printers and transporters.

Carson Products West Africa is a subsidiary of Carson South Africa, itself a subsidiary of the parent company based in Chicago. It started in Ghana in 1997, and now employs about 100 people making hair care and cosmetic goods. It specialises in high quality products and pays higher wages than its competitors in the country.

All its technology comes from the parent company. Second-hand machinery and equipment come from the parent company, and the technology in use is much more labour-intensive than in the US. Samples of the products are sent via express-mail to South Africa every day for testing to ensure compliance with company standards. Local sourcing of inputs has increased – especially in plastic containers and labels – but all chemical inputs are imported from the parent companies. The company targets the regional market, in particular Nigeria and Ivory Coast. The Director of Operations is a dynamic South African mechanical engineer, supported by the Factory Director, a Ghanaian chemist, and two Ghanaian chemical engineers, responsible for the Quality Control Department. Some testing and adaptive research is carried out in this Department, but all results are tested in the parent company's laboratories in the US.

Source: Interviews by Carlo Pietrobelli during field visit, Accra, January 2000.

SCIENCE AND TECHNOLOGY POLICIES

Antecedents[8]

Ghana has long acknowledged the importance of science and technology to development. However, during the colonial period and even after independence, no coherent attempt was made to develop a national science and technology policy with explicit goals, objectives and strategies. S&T policy was implicit in the work of government departments like medical services, agriculture, mines, geological surveys, industry and education. Before independence, the organization of research was handled by inter-territorial research institutions set up by the colonial administrators to cater to the needs of the whole West African region. The setting up of the National Research Council (NRC) in 1958 marked the first attempt at institutionalizing a national structure to act as a focal point for science and technology policy (Government of Ghana, 1958).

Though a national S&T policy document was not prepared at this stage, S&T was the cornerstone of the Seven-Year Development Plan of 1963-64 to 1969-70 (Government of Ghana, 1964), which aimed at using S&T to restructure agriculture and industry, with the emphasis on applied research. However, the strategy was dogged by continued political instability, which persisted with the transformation of the National Research Council into the Ghana Academy of Sciences. The Academy's principal policy contribution was the drafting of a 'Seven-Year National Programme for the Promotion of Science'. The Ghana Academy of Sciences was succeeded in 1968 by the Council for Scientific and Industrial Research (CSIR) (Government of Ghana, 1968).

The Five-Year Development Plan for 1975-76 to 1979-80 tried to integrate S&T into the national development plan (Government of Ghana, 1977). CSIR provided substantial inputs into the plan, identifying the inefficient management of S&T as a major constraint on national development (CSIR, 1973). This document focused on crucial elements such as the lack of priority setting, insufficient funding, lack of inter-agency coordination, ineffective transfer of research results, inadequate infrastructure and human resource deficiencies. During the implementation of this plan, the government was also helped by a UNIDO mission with preparing a national technology plan. However, the results were meagre. The Five-Year Development Plan of 1980–81 to 1985–86 also failed to formulate and implement a S&T plan. The creation of a new Ministry of Industry, Science and Technology (MIST) did not improve the situation.

Efforts during the last decade appear to have been more purposeful. An elaborate effort by the CSIR resulted in the preparation of a document on S&T options for the country, reflecting an innovative approach (CSIR, 1990). In addition to the usual constraints on S&T, such as poor funding, inadequate facilities, and the lack of an S&T culture, this plan brought to the light the concept of the *transfer and adaptation of technology*.

Subsequently, an S&T policy statement prepared by the MIST in 1992 set out government policy for S&T in explicit terms (MIST, 1992b). In addition to the well-known weakness of poor funding and inadequate facilities, this paper addressed issues that revealed a broader concept of S&T, with an awareness of the need to acquire international competitiveness. Thus, among the issues addressed are raw material development, improvement of product quality, transfer and adaptation of technology, and entrepreneurial development. However, implementation fell short of these objectives, essentially due to the lack of political will.

In recognition of these difficulties, the Science and Technology Policy Research Institute (STEPRI), the body officially in charge of designing and proposing S&T policies, made another effort. STEPRI conducted a comprehensive study to deal with the S&T challenges facing the country (Gogo et al., 1998). The study identified six main challenges:

- Funding of R&D and innovation management;
- Linkage of R&D to industry;
- Strategic use of information and communication technology;
- Human resource development and utilization;
- S&T acculturation and awareness creation;
- Stable and high-level political commitment, which was deemed most important for substantial and rapid progress.

A new S&T policy has been formulated under the Ministry of Environment Science and Technology (MEST, 1998). The principal focus of Ghana's S&T policy is now:

> To support socio-economic development goals with a view to lifting Ghana to a middle income status by the year 2020 through the perpetuation of a science and technology culture at all levels of society, which is driven by the promotion of innovation and mastery of known and proven technologies, and their application in industry and other sectors of the economy. (MEST, 1998)

The directive principles for government action are to:

- Create the enabling environment and advocacy for the promotion of S&T as a key factor in Ghana's development process;
- Promote the development and utilization of S&T capabilities including entrepreneurial skills development;
- Promote science and technology capacity building;
- Encourage the improvement of the quality of research and development (R&D) activities, especially within private sector institutions;
- Strengthen national engineering design capacity activities;
- Arrange for the protection of intellectual and innovative property rights;
- Ensure environmental sustainability;
- Promote participation of women in S&T;
- Safeguard the generation, use and application of S&T;
- Promote international and local cooperation and linkages;
- Promote a science and technology culture;
- Establish mechanisms for the finance, management and performance of S&T.

In addition to these measures, MEST proposed the appointment of a 'Presidential Adviser on Science and Technology' to help raise the political profile of S&T and ensure cross-sectoral coordination. This proposal is clearly in the right direction, in line with best practice in the developing and developed worlds. The successful implementation of any S&T policy in Ghana will require that the S&T needs of industry are well understood and given high priority by the government. In early 2000, this new policy document was being deliberated upon by Cabinet, after which parliamentary approval was to be sought. If implemented, the policy could help raise national industrial capabilities and enhance industrial competitiveness. Moreover, the policy could enhance the financing of R&D at the enterprise level, and enable micro, small and medium-sized enterprises to access technology from national and international sources.

These intentions show a positive attitude towards S&T policies. However, since similar intentions have been stated in the past, it remains to be seen how well they will be implemented in the future.

Policy Making Structure

The policy-making structure in Ghana's S&T system, and the interactions among the various actors is illustrated in Figure 6.1. This figure has been abridged for clarity, and a larger number of actors operate in this sector (see Frempong, 1998).

Ministry of Environment Science and Technology (MEST)

The apex of the system is the Ministry of Environment Science and Technology (MEST), the main government ministry supervising S&T institutions and coordinating their activities in the country. It was originally a division of the Ministry of Industry, Technology and Trade (MITT), but in 1994 it was made independent following the new key role that S&T

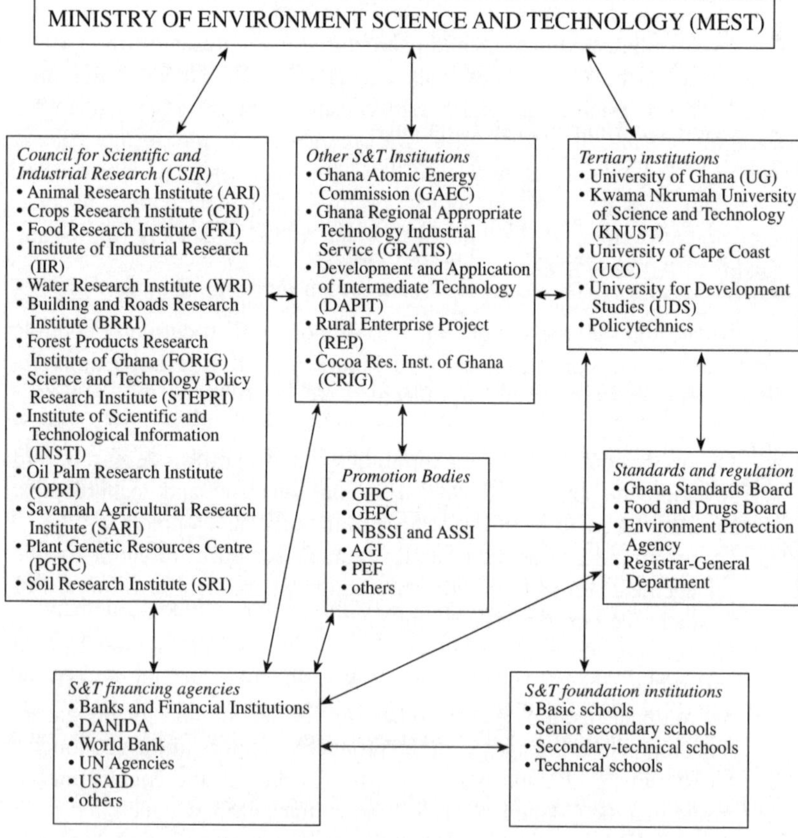

Figure 6.1 The science and technology system in Ghana

development should play in Ghana's economy, as reflected in the *Ghana 2020* exercise. It enjoys Cabinet status, but it is a small ministry with only 77 employees (20 professionals).

MEST has developed an integrated policy framework in six areas: human settlement planning and management; sanitation and waste management; environmental standards; education implementation; S&T promotion, education and acculturation; commercialization of S&T research; and institutional arrangements for collaboration on the management of environment and S&T policies.[9]

Council for Scientific and Industrial Research (CSIR)

The most prominent and largest S&T institution under the direct supervision of MEST is the Council for Scientific and Industrial Research (CSIR). CSIR is an umbrella organization supervising 13 specialized research institutions, with a central secretariat in charge of administration.

CISR was established in 1968 and restructured in its present form in 1996. The genesis of the CSIR dates back to the erstwhile National Research Council (NRC), established in 1958 to organize and coordinate scientific research in Ghana. In 1963, NRC was merged with the former Ghana Academy of Sciences, a statutory learned society. Following a review in 1966, the Academy was reconstituted into its original component bodies, national research organizations, a redesigned CSIR and a learned society (the Ghana Academy of Arts and Sciences).

CSIR employs around 4 800 people, of whom approximately 390 are research staff and 400 are senior technical support staff. It currently controls 13 institutes, centres and projects (see Figure 6.1). It is a large umbrella organization with a broad range of objectives (CSIR, 1999):

- To implement government policies on scientific research and development, and to advise MEST on scientific and technological advances likely to be of importance to national development;
- To encourage coordinated employment of scientific research for the management, utilization and conservation of the natural resources of Ghana in the interest of development;
- To encourage the national interest in scientific and industrial research of importance for the development of agriculture, health, medicine, environment, technology and other service sectors and to this end to encourage close linkages with the productive sectors of the economy;
- To coordinate all aspects of scientific research in the country and to ensure that the Council, the research institutes of the Council and other organizations engaged in research in Ghana, coordinate and cooperate in their research efforts;

- To review, monitor and periodically evaluate the work of the institutes administered by the Council in order to ensure that research being carried out by the institute directly benefits identified sectors of the economy and is within the national priorities;
- To institute a system of contract research to ensure that research being carried out in the Council is relevant and cost effective, and to encourage and promote the commercialization of research results;
- To coordinate human resource development in institutes of the Council and to encourage the training of scientific personnel and research workers through the provision of grants and fellowships;
- To cooperate and liaise with international and local bodies and organizations on matters of research.

The 1996 Act has two distinctive features: it emphasizes private sector concerns, and it introduces market principles into the Council's operations for the first time. The Council is now expected to generate 30 per cent of its income through the sale of products and services and to institute a system of contract research. Some fears have been expressed that this would discriminate against basic research and in favour of development and routine service work. This is a real danger, and may crowd out the development of a private sector testing and laboratory service industry. However, there is still a very long way to go before this effect is felt: at this time, efforts to make research activities more demand-driven and useful to industrial users are welcome. At the time of writing, only one CSIR institute has managed to reach the 30 per cent target (see below), and there is practically no private sector provision of R&D and laboratory services. However, in the longer term, it would be advisable to reorient CSIR to more basic research work.

The World Bank-supported Private Sector Development Project (PSDP) has substantially supported the commercialization programme. Three CSIR institutes have been targeted in the industrial sector, namely the IIR, BRRI, and FRI, to enable them to provide technical support to industry and meet the needs of the private sector. Other non-CSIR institutions are also participating in the PSDP, like the Ghana Standards Board (GSB), the Ghana Trade Fair Authority, and the Attorney General's Department. A related project designed to help the matching of demand and supply of S&T, and to ensure its effective marketing, has been sponsored by the UNDP.

In the following section we focus on the research institutes most relevant to industry, such as the IIR and the FRI.

Coordinating the S&T System in Ghana

The S&T system in Ghana is not well coordinated. It is highly fragmented, with different constituents pursuing their own objectives with little regard to national S&T goals and with almost no linkage between their activities. Other key actors in the S&T system, such as promotional, business and financial institutions, do not take into account the effects of their actions on national science and technology. The educational and training institutions do not meet S&T human capital requirements in terms of numbers or skills. The coordinating role assigned to MEST cannot be performed by it (or by any other ministry alone). Several proposals have been put forward to overcome this problem, and will be discussed below.

Financing Science and Technology in Ghana

The main sources of finance for S&T are government budgetary allocations,[10] donor grants and funds generated from the sale of technology. These do not provide adequate funding. MEST is solely financed by central government consolidated funds (Table 6.5 shows the annual budgetary allocations to MEST from 1996 to 1999). The total amounts involved are very small and barely reach 0.2 per cent of GDP in any year. Development expenditures, directed to research activities rather than salaries and wages, are minimal, between 0.066 and 0.095 per cent of GDP in 1996–99. This is a continuation of earlier patterns (Enos, 1995).

About 90 per cent of R&D in Ghana is undertaken by government funded institutions such as the CSIR (Gogo, 2000, p. 22).[11] This contrasts with the experience of more dynamic developing countries, where private enterprises are engaged in both financing and executing large shares of national R&D (Lall, 1999b, table 7). Thus, in the four East Asian NICs taken together, the productive sector carried out 50 per cent and financed 51 per cent of R&D

Table 6.5 Annual government budget allocations to MEST (million Cedis and %)

Year	Recurrent exp.	Development exp.	% of GDP	Total	% of GDP
1996	13 727.6	8 500.0	0.075	22 227.6	0.196
1997	19 277.4	9 978.0	0.071	29 255.4	0.207
1998*	25 132.0	11 711.6	0.066	36 843.6	0.209
1999*	32 690.3	20 051.7	0.095	52 742.0	0.249

Note: *Computed on the basis of an estimate of GDP.

Source: own elaboration from GOG, Ministry of Finance Annual Budget Estimates.

activity. In Latin America, these percentages amount respectively to 18 and 9 per cent. The figures for Ghana are in line with the low SSA average.

The financial pattern at CSIR is not significantly different from other S&T institutions in the country. An examination of the CSIR budget for 1996–98 suggests that government funding has not only been very inadequate (Table 6.6), it has also declined over time (1998 represents a slight improvement in absolute terms over 1997). In 1998, personnel payments made up 90.2 per cent of the total budget. The government released only about half of the requested budget. Releases of development funds, the most important for R&D, only reached 13–18 per cent of requested values, while those for current operations reached 18-30 per cent. In these years, development expenditure from multilateral donor sources provided the bulk of funds for R&D (Table 6.7), with the agricultural sector receiving the bulk of the funds.

The new policy of making CSIR laboratories earn 30 per cent of their expenditures has, as noted, yielded poor results to date (Table 6.8). The average for CSIR, although rising, is only 4.4 per cent after three years. Some

Table 6.6 Total government funding of CSIR, 1996–98 (million Cedis and %)

Total funds requested/released				
Year	Amount requested	Amount released	% released	% of GDP
1966	32 552	17 812	54.7	0.157
1997	46 955	20 849	44.4	0.147
1998	48 504	24 134	49.8	0.137*
Development funds requested/released				
Year	Requested	Released	% released	% of GDP
1996	17 074	3 224	18.8	0.028
1997	24 418	3 302	13.5	0.023
1998	24 085	3 175	13.1	0.018*
Operational funds requested/released				
Year	Requested	Released	% released	% of GDP
1996	7 038	2 090	30.0	0.018
1997	9 485	1 897	20.0	0.013
1998	9 790	1 760	18.0	0.010*

Note: Computed on the basis of an estimate of GDP.

Source: CSIR Secretariat, 1999.

Table 6.7 R&D funding released: multilateral donor and Ghana Government, 1996-98 (million Cedis)

Source	1996	1997	1998	Total
NARP	6481	12363	10822	29665
PSDP	350	46	1525	1921
UNDP	240	930	245	1415
GOG	3224	3402	3870	10496

Note: NARP: National Agricultural Research Project; PSDP: Public Sector Development Project; UNDP: United Nations Development Programme.

Source: CSIR Secretariat, 1999.

clients have withdrawn because of the increase in service fees (Gogo, 2000). The Oil Palm Research Institute (OPRI) is by far the biggest earner within the CSIR, and is expected to meet the 30 per cent target.

Intellectual Property Regime

The Patent Law of 1992 deals with industrial property such as patents, trademarks and designs, while the Copyright Law of 1985 deals with the works of authors both as individuals and corporate bodies. The latter law also deals with permissible use of protected works, transfer of their copyright, reproduction and translation, and penalties for infringement. In principle, these two laws, together with the Food and Drugs Law, offer considerable protection to inventors. In practice, however, their implementation is deficient and offers inadequate IPR protection. The legal system is cumbersome and lacks the expertise needed to handle modern IPR issues.

Table 6.8 'Commercialization' of CSIR activities, 1996-98 (million Cedis and %)

Item	1996	1997	1998
Approved GOG grant	13941	20957	24626
CSIR revenue earnings	272	674	1091
Percentage earned	1.9	3.2	4.4

Source: CSIR Secretariat, 1999.

The Registrar-General's Department is responsible for registering companies as well as patents, trademarks and industrial designs. The Patent Law authorizes the Registrar-General to register patents locally, as well as those granted under international protocols to which Ghana is a signatory. Patents filed in Ghana are verified with other patenting authorities and are granted if found patentable. The Food and Drugs Board, created in 1997, supervises standards for food and pharmaceutical products in the country, whether locally manufactured, imported, exported, distributed, sold or used. The law also allows the accreditation of analysts or laboratories to carry out testing at the district level. The Food and Drugs Law is not, however, effectively enforced. In January 2000, the board only had a technical staff of five and one testing laboratory, with inadequate office and laboratory space.

The Patent Law does not grant the right to patent (among other things) plant or animal varieties, or the biological processes for the production of plants or animals (Gogo et al., 1998). In light of the current developments in other parts of the world where living things (for example, genetically engineered crops) are being patented, this may need to be changed in the near future.

TECHNOLOGY TRANSFER AND TECHNOLOGICAL ACTIVITY

Foreign technology can be transferred from abroad through several formal and informal channels.[12] As with other countries in this study, Ghana imports relatively little technology in the form of capital goods or licensing (Table 6.9); certainly technology imports are minuscule compared to East Asian countries (see Chapter 2).

The earlier cumbersome policy framework that discouraged FDI and private sector activity more generally in the pre-reform period was changed in 1994. There is now a liberal and competitive investment code embodying 'best country' practice (Botchwey, 1998). Investment licensing has been abolished, while constraints on foreign ownership and technology transfer have been eased. Tax incentives have been vastly improved, and dependence on income-

Table 6.9 Ghana: payments for royalties and licence fee (US$ million)

	1991	1992	1993	1994	1995	1996
Royalties and licence fees	0.5	0.9	0.9	0.7	0.9	1.0
% of total exports	0.05	0.09	0.08	0.06	0.06	0.06

Source: IMF, Balance of Payments Statistics.

based taxes, which characterized much of the 1980s, has been greatly reduced. Although the corporate tax rate remains high compared to the average in Asia, they have been reduced significantly (World Economic Forum, 1998). In spite of the more liberal regime, FDI inflows have suffered a recent decline. In any case, much of the inflow goes into the primary sector or services (Table 6.10). During the period 1995–98, manufacturing accounted for only 25 per cent of inflows. This does not bode well for industrial capabilities or upgrading.

HUMAN CAPITAL

Ghana has a relatively good system of education by SSA standards, with higher secondary enrolments than three of the case study countries. However, its record in creating high level technical skills (as measured by the engineering enrolment index) is poor relative to the other sample countries. More importantly, its performance is very weak by international standards, showing an enormous and probably widening skill gap with other developing countries that are going to be major competitors in industry.

Verner (1999), using sample data on 215 manufacturing enterprises, presents recent evidence on firm-level skills and training in Ghana. The majority of workers in the formal manufacturing sector have middle or secondary education, with middle school as the most common level of completed education. Higher education is positively correlated with increased productivity; the productivity gap is significantly larger than the wage gap, suggesting that productivity-enhancing factors like education are not fully reflected in wages.[13] The incidence of training in the Ghanaian manufacturing sector appears respectable compared with industrial and semi-industrial economies. Around 64 per cent of employees receive formal training, and 28 per cent of the total receive in-house training (Table 6.11 and Verner, 1999). However, the effects of in-house training on productivity are not significantly different from zero. This may reflect the intensity and quality of the training provided, though it may also be due to the fact that the impact on productivity (and wages) takes time to show itself. However, this finding contradicts other findings (Lall and Wignaraja, 1996), which suggest that the level of training in Ghana is well below that of other developing countries like Sri Lanka.

Main Training and Educational Institutions in Ghana

The main institutions include the four main universities: the University of Ghana in Legon, Accra, the Kwame Nkrumah University of Science and Technology in Kumasi, the University of Cape Coast and the University for

Table 6.10 Registered direct investments, Ghana, 1995-98*

	1995		1996		1997		1998		Cumul. 1995–98			
	No.	$	No.	$	No.	$	No.	$	No.	%	$	%
Total	150	183.8	187	257.9	237	636.7	187	177.4	761	100	1.107	100
Manufacturing	41	75.3	57	4.3	68	100.8	39	29.1	205	26.9	275	24.8
Services	49	66.7	43	145.9	58	435.5	47	44.4	197	25.9	741	66.9
Foreign (%)		81.8		74.8		75.3		92.9			78.7	

Note: *Includes foreign equity and foreign loans in investment project.

Source: Ghana Investment Promotion Centre.

Table 6.11 Training in Ghanaian manufacturing enterprises (%)

		Gender		Residence	
Training	Full sample	Female	Male	Accra	Other
In-house	28.0	33.0	27.0	25.1	34.2
Outside	36.2	24.7	38.7	38.0	35.4
None	35.8	42.3	34.3	36.9	30.4
Total	100	100	100	100	100

Note: The values show the percentage of each category of workers with each level of education. For example, 28.0 per cent of the manufacturing workers in the sample received in-house training.

Source: Verner, 1999. Round Three of the 1994 RPED for Ghana, The World Bank.

Development Studies. All have faculties of science, medicine and agriculture. KNUST is the principal professional training institution in S&T, and it also has faculties of engineering, pharmacy and architecture, as well as a programme in industrial management. Business management training is run by the University of Ghana. However, the numbers of graduates required by the local industrial and service sector exceeds by far those produced by these institutions

Other important training institutions include the Ghana Institute of Management and Public Administration, established in 1961, which provides management training in commerce, industry and public administration. With a staff of 25 lecturers, it is actively engaged in improving its information technology and setting up a distance learning centre sponsored by the World Bank. The Management Development and Productivity Institute provides short-term training aimed at improving management practices, efficiency and productivity in industry, commerce and related fields.[14] It also runs an Entrepreneurship Development Programme for the private sector.

Middle-level S&T manpower is produced mainly by polytechnics, set up in most regions of the country. They provide hands-on training of technicians up to the Higher National Diploma level in most fields of science, engineering, commerce and management. However, detailed analysis of their efficiency goes beyond the scope of this study.

SCIENCE AND TECHNOLOGY INFRASTRUCTURE

Ghana's S&T infrastructure is primarily composed of public institutions, in charge of policy design and scientific information provision, of the setting and promotion of industrial standards, and of R&D. Some private or mixed institutions also resulted from foreign funded projects.

Technology transfer to Ghana's industrial sector was given impetus in 1981 when the Technology Transfer Centre (TTC) was established within the CSIR. By 1987, the government realized that the TTC, as established, could not bring about the desired technological transformation. In 1988, a UNDP funded project was launched to strengthen TTC, which was transformed and in 1996 gave birth to the Science and Technology Policy Research Institute (STEPRI). STEPRI is the policy research institute of the CSIR, with a mandate to provide research support for national S&T policy development, monitoring and evaluation. It is in charge of policy design, and addresses identified policy research issues in technology transfer and technology policy formulation.

STEPRI has a staff strength of 38 (12 of which are senior members) and provides advice to industrialists on technology transfer agreements, technology choices and technology management. Its clients include ministries and other government institutions. In principle, STEPRI could play an important role in the development and modernization of the S&T system in Ghana. However, to do this effectively, it has to have considerable political status to influence and coordinate the relevant agents and institutions. This is not the case today.

The Institute for Scientific and Technological Information is another CSIR institute, set up to collect and disseminate scientific information. Its customers are mainly researchers and students rather than private industrial firms.

Standards and Quality

The Ghana Standards Board (GSB), the institution in charge of standards, metrology, testing and quality assurance, was established in 1967. A study in 1993 by one of the present authors had the following to say on standards in Ghana and on the role of the GSB:

> The engineering sector in Ghana lacks a comprehensive range of product standards, and tends to use a variety of foreign standards which may not match each other, and some of which may not represent a good choice of technology. Along with the absence of quality control systems, there is a widespread *lack of appreciation of standards in Ghanaian industry*. This reflects the previous protected regime under which it operated, as well as the lack of qualified personnel able to understand and implement the technical aspects of standardisation. The GSB lacks the resources (financial and human) to prepare engineering standards, to encourage industry to use them, and to enforce standards in a meaningful way. Its attitude to promoting standards has been very passive. GSB operates a mandatory system of product certification under which all manufacturers are required by law to have their products certified as being of acceptable quality. This requirement is largely

> theoretical, since the severe shortage of resources means that there is no way the GSB can check satisfactorily the quality of a range of manufactures ... *GSB certification has correspondingly little value in countries that adhere to international standards.* (Lall et al., 1994, pp. 44-5)

The situation has not improved greatly since this was written. GSB still suffers from several weaknesses. Funding is a major constraint, especially the budget devoted to raising quality and standards awareness in local industry. Salaries account for an increasing and disproportionate share of the budget (up from 60 per cent in 1994-95 to 77 per cent in 1998-99), while only 2 per cent is spent in staff training. No funding is available for any kind of R&D (Table 6.12). Total revenues amounted to about $2.2 million, twice that of the standards institution in Uganda, but much less than in other SSA countries. Although the share of self-financing is increasing, the government still contributes 82 per cent of total revenues. The equipment in use is old and outdated. The GSB staff interviewed noted that no other institution in the country possesses comparable equipment, but this may simply be suggestive of the low technological level overall of Ghana's industry.

Table 6.12 Summary financial indicators of the Ghana Standards Board

	1994-95	1998-99
Revenues (Ghana Cedis and US$ million)		
Ghana Cedis (bn.)	1.4	6.3
US$ mill.*	1.46	2.25
Sources of Revenues (%)		
From Government scheduled	90	82
From services sold	10	18
Expenditures (%)		
Salaries	60	77
Materials & buildings	4.5	6.6
Training	1	2
Equipment	10	5
R&D	–	–
Others	24.5	9.4
Total	100.0	100.0

Note: *Approximate figures obtained due to variable exchange rate.

Source: Interviews with GSB Staff during UNCTAD field mission.

GSB has five technical divisions. These are Standards and Specifications, Chemical Laboratories, Physical Laboratories, Quality Assurance, and Metrology. These divisions carry out the following core activities:

- Standards development;
- Testing services: chemical and microbiological analysis of food and drugs, industrial raw materials and toxicological samples, and physical testing of plastics, leather and rubber, building materials, electrical cables, engineering fabrications, packaging materials, and textiles, garments and paper products;
- Calibration services;
- Certification;
- Training;
- Consumer complaints on product defects and expiry dates, and public educational campaigns to sensitize the public on relevant issues such as labelling rules and good trade practices.

Employment at the time of the visit was 403, with surprisingly high numbers employed in financial and administrative functions (250). The chemical and physical laboratories follow, with respectively 46 and 27 employees, most responsible for scientific tasks (37 and 23 respectively). Overall, the administrative staff appears disproportionately large relative to the scientific and technical staff, imposing a further burden on the institution without providing to the technical excellence required. The level of the technical and scientific expertise available in-house is deemed adequate by the business community, and 49 hold Masters' degrees. However, the level of pay, according to the government scale, is not sufficient to attract the best graduates, and does not motivate them to stay.

Among the positive achievements of the Board are the acceptance by the European Union of its testing and health certificates for exports of fish and fishery products to the EU. In March 1999 the Japanese Government accredited the GSB Chemical Laboratory for chemical analysis and certification of food and food related products exported to Japan. This is bound to facilitate Ghana's food exports to Japan, though the Japanese market accounts for only 3–5 per cent of total exports in recent years (ISSER, 1999). GSB enjoys a strong reputation in the African region, and the United Nations Drugs Control Programme (UNDCP) has selected it as a centre for the training of analysis of controlled drugs for the anglophone sub-region of Africa.[15] The Board has also undertaken training in ISO 9000, and at the time of the field visit it was near to being certified.

In sum, the GSB has good technical personnel and some strengths. It is gaining international acceptance in such areas such as food, fish and fish products. However, it suffers from important drawbacks in terms of industrial technology promotion, the main ones being:

- Insufficient funding;
- Excessive administrative compared to scientific staff, with poor pay levels;
- Low involvement of clients in setting the standards, and insufficient outreach to SMEs;
- Weak awareness of quality and standardization in the country.

It is important for GSB to be more active in promoting standards and quality improvement among industrial enterprises. The mandatory system of product certification has little value if it is not accompanied by a clear perception of the need for industrial standardization, and its usefulness for international competitiveness.

R&D Institutions

The main R&D institutions directly concerned with industry are the Institute of Industrial Research (IIR) and the Food Research Institute (FRI).

Institute of Industrial Research (IIR)

In 1996 the two original CSIR institutes, the Industrial Research Institute (founded in 1967) and the Scientific Instrumentation Centre (1978) were merged to form the Institute of Industrial Research, in an attempt to avoid duplication of effort. The mandate of the IIR is to undertake research into process and product design and development and promote technology adaptation, scientific instrumentation and calibration and repair of precision equipment. In fact, its activities today are largely confined to repair, maintenance and calibration of equipment and machinery, and the emphasis has been increasingly on servicing manufacturing enterprises. IIR's work consists increasingly of 'development' rather than basic research, mainly in the areas of process technology, agro-industrial machinery development, materials studies, repair, maintenance, installation and calibration of sophisticated industrial equipment, and science and technology equipment development.

While this emphasis on applied work is positive in the Ghanaian context, its scope and impact are fairly limited. The institute, by admission of the senior staff interviewed, is underfunded, lacking in infrastructure and equipment, and provides insufficient training to its research and technical staff. It serves a relatively small number of clients (rising from 30 in 1997 to 114 in 1999), 50 per cent of which are in the food industry, 10 per cent in the mining industry and another 10 per cent in hospitals, medical laboratories, schools and universities. Clearly much more needs to be done to reach the private industrial - and especially the SME - sector.

According to official reports (CSIR, 1999) the IIR has developed several new processes and products. These include groundnut dehullers, production of soap from cocoa hulks and palm "brunch", refining of crude soy oil, glazes and alumino-silicate refractors, LPG cook stoves and extraction of essential oils from local plants such as citronella and orange peels. Moreover, the IIR offers consulting services in equipment specification, installation of precision and industrial equipment, instrument surveys, bio-gas technology, industrial and technological information, chemical and biochemical analyses, room acoustics design, noise and vibration measurement and noise pollution control, environmental impact assessment and environmental management plans. Some of these technologies have been transferred to industry and the general public. Prominent among these are food industrial technologies related to cassava processing, production of liquid soap from the ash of agricultural waste, and crude soy oil refining.

However, the institute lacks a systematic strategy to reach and respond to industrial customers. There is little sustained interaction with manufacturing firms, and the institute's activities appear essentially supply-driven. Linkages with industry consist mainly of private sector representatives sitting on its Board, rather than through collaboration at the shop-floor level.

IIR has 135 staff, comprising 38 research grade staff, 44 non-research grade technical and administrative staff, and 53 junior staff. In 1989, before the two institutes merged, IRI and SIC together employed 147 people with a similar proportion of technical and research staff (Lall et al., 1994). Thus, the institute has not grown in the last years. The director and his deputy hold PhDs, and the heads of the five technical divisions hold Masters' degrees. The five technical divisions are industrial chemistry, materials S&T, mechanical engineering, industrial and applied physics, and glass technology. The staff is paid according to government scales, which compare unfavourably with other scales. This makes it difficult to recruit and retain good staff.

The 1996 merger further reduced government financing, already very low in 1989 (Lall et al., 1994, p. 43; Enos, 1995). In 1999 the institute received Cedis 1300 million from the government, equivalent to about $370 000 at the prevailing rate of exchange. Only Cedis 78 million ($22 000) was for research and development.

Food Research Institute (FRI)

The second main R&D institute of the CSIR is the FRI, established in 1963 and incorporated into the CSIR in 1965. Its mandate is 'to undertake applied research through laboratory and pilot scale investigations into the processing, preservation and storage, transportation and distribution of staple and non-staple plant and animal foods in the country with a view to producing new foods and improving upon traditional ones' (CSIR, 1999).[16]

FRI has a larger and better-qualified staff than IIR. It has 172 employees, of whom 36 are research grade staff, 37 are senior technical and administrative staff and 99 are junior members of staff. The research staff includes engineers, food scientists and technologists, biochemists, microbiologists, economists, nutritionists and myco-toxicologists. Five hold PhDs. FRI actively supports training by helping junior staff to get scholarships and complete doctoral studies, sometimes paying fees and keeping them in paid employment during their years of education. Sometimes it hosts trainees from university to work on projects and use the material for their theses. As a result, FRI has a good reputation in the country for its research staff. However, low pay levels and service conditions are a disincentive, and lead to high staff turnover and loss of experienced scientists.

FRI has three scientific divisions in addition to the administration and business development divisions. These are food microbiology, food chemistry, and food processing and engineering.

Over the years, FRI has been substantially funded by international aid, with sponsors ranging from the World Bank, IFAD, UNDP, DANIDA, DFID, the Dutch Government, and USAID. This reflects the priority attached by foreign donors to the development of the agricultural sector, and mainly to staple food production and storage. This suggests that FRI has relatively little impact on non-traditional agro-industrial activities, and therefore on manufactured exports by Ghana.

Official reports state that FRI has been actively transferring its technologies to industry and the general public (CSIR, 1999). These include improved fish smoking equipment (locally known as the *chorkor* smoker), instant foods (*fufu* flours from plantain, *cocoyam*, yam and cow-pea), fermented cassava meal, and improved *kokonte* powder. The FRI has also developed technology for refining and deodorizing vegetable oils. The institute offers technical services in food analysis, product quality improvement, identification and selection of equipment and training of quality control and food processing technicians. These services offer the best prospects for earning fees, which in 1999 reached 7 per cent of the budget. In this year, more than 100 clients benefited from these services.

In the past, one of the main weaknesses of FRI was the absence of a unit responsible for providing services to the public. This was remedied with the creation of the Business Development Division, but its capability to disseminate scientific information with commercial potential and to generate commissioned research projects is still limited. FRI scientists tend to regard their main objective as pure research; the dissemination of research findings, undertaking of pilot projects and provision of consulting services are often viewed as secondary or undesirable. This can only be remedied by a wholesale *change in corporate values.*

In sum, FRI is better financed and equipped than IIR. Foreign aid is contributing significantly to its activities. Its research and technical staff, although paid non-competitive salaries, is well qualified and enjoys a good reputation. Exchanges and cooperation with universities are frequent. However, its activities are essentially related to food staples for local consumption. Some less traditional products are being researched and improved, but they have little relevance to new manufactured exports. The ability to disseminate and market research results, and to link basic and applied research with production, lags behind national needs.

Other R&D institutions

The Ghana Regional Appropriate Technology Industrial Service (GRATIS) is one of the leading institutions to promote the transfer and utilization of industrial technology. In 1987, with the assistance of two donor agencies - the Canadian Agency for International Development and the European Commission - the government created GRATIS under the Ministry of Industries, Science and Technology 'to promote grass-root industrialisation in Ghana'. This was to be achieved by providing consulting services and training to micro and small-scale industrialists. The reason for the establishment of GRATIS was the success of the Technology Consultancy Centre in transferring intermediate technology to the craftsmen in the largest informal sector in Ghana, 'Suame Magazine', a well-known cluster of workshops and small factories in Kumasi (McCormick, 1999). The mandate of GRATIS is to transfer intermediate technology to the ten regions of the country. This would also help reduce migration to towns and cities, and encourage educated and experienced people to return to rural areas and set up enterprises.

Apart from its head office, GRATIS has under it nine Intermediate Technology Transfer Units (ITTU). In addition to providing technical information and training, the units' main functions include the manufacture of equipment for rural industries and provision of advice on small-scale engineering and manufacturing industries. Demonstration workshops are set up in each ITTU to show potential clients new industrial processes suitable for their workshops. In addition, GRATIS assists clients to obtain machinery under a hire-purchase scheme, and provides subsidized loans for a maximum of seven years at about 20 per cent interest rate.

It claims to have some 16000 beneficiaries (micro and small entrepreneurs, apprentices and trainees).[17] It has provided these with a variety of services, such as technical training in textiles, design of industrial parts and equipment, manufacturing of industrial spare parts, repair of industrial machinery, and apprenticeship training in automobile repairs. Most clients are SMEs to whom the intermediate technologies transferred by GRATIS are well suited. The GRATIS network employs a total of 287 people. As with other technology institutions, it has to pay low salaries that result in high personnel turnover. In January 2000, it was in transition from a project under the MEST to a non-profit limited liability foundation, with the active agreement and participation of the government and donors such as CIDA, the EU, JICA and others.

GRATIS has provided useful technology services to micro enterprises in Ghana. Among its strengths are:

- Close contact with enterprises, with monthly clients' associations meetings;
- National coverage with ITTUs in all 10 regions - although it is a weakness that the ITTUs are not connected through the Internet;
- Practical and problem-solving orientation;
- ISO 9000 awareness training.

However, its contribution to industrial technology and competitiveness more generally is limited by its focus on micro and small enterprises and on *intermediate* technology. Moreover, its dependence on government subsidies and donor support constrains its effectiveness. Its loan recovery ratio is estimated to be only around 52 per cent. In 1997 the percentage of total costs covered by the sales of goods and services was only 46 per cent, reaching 53 per cent in 1998.

GRATIS is exporting some services to other African countries. For example, it has sold shea-butter machinery to Burkina Faso on three occasions (in 1990, 1992 and 1999), cotton-spinning wheels to Uganda to make thread oil extraction, and helped develop fish smokers in Mauritania.

A few other technological organizations exist in Ghana, engaged mainly in technology transfer activities. However, none is large enough to have an impact on industrial technology transfer and development in the country.

Outside the public technology institutions mentioned above, there is a privately established organization, Technoserve, set up in 1971 as an international NGO. Its main aim is to increase rural productivity, rural incomes and rural access to jobs through a process of agricultural business development and farmers' training. It charges for services, and having rural development as its focus, the bulk of its clients are micro and small-scale rural enterprises.

EMPRETEC was created in 1990 as a joint project of the UNDP, Barclays Bank Ghana and the National Board for Small Scale Industries. Its mandate is to offer entrepreneurship and management training, consultancy and extension support services, and credit packages with the help of financial institutions. As far as technology is concerned, the 35 professionals (of a total of 65 employees in five offices) often provide technical advice to their clients and help them to buy technology in Denmark through a DANIDA project. The foundation appears very successful, with good access to international funding (World Bank, EU and DFID). However, its main focus is on business services rather than technology, and its links with the national technology system are virtually nonexistent.

The Technology Consultancy Centre (TCC) was established in 1972 as a production unit of the University of Science and Technology (UST) in Kumasi, and now serves as a conduit through which the results of research in each faculty are made available to industry. A large majority of TCC clients are SMEs in the informal sector, to which technology has been transferred in the form of capital goods for food processing, fabrication of small-scale machinery and parts, and ceramics manufacture and foundry works. TCC enjoys substantial financial assistance from international organizations.[18] It has played a useful role in promoting technology transfer and adaptation for local SMEs in simple industrial activities in Ghana, but its relevance for industrial efficiency more broadly, and for upgrading competitiveness, is relatively limited.

Development and Application of Intermediate Technology (DAPIT) is a project set up with the assistance of USAID to focus on technology transfer to rural industries. The technologies transferred to rural entrepreneurs include solar dryers, rice planters, improved maize cribs, wooden grain storage silos, and equipment for snail production. Other technologies being considered for transfer are the manufacture of liquid soap from agricultural waste; the extraction of oil from plant material, including simple vegetable oil extraction machines; and a cassava slicer machine for producing cassava chips for export. Since DAPIT does not develop new technologies, it has close collaboration with some CSIR institutes, especially IIR and FRI, as well as the TTC. The Rural Enterprise Project is focused on the rural economy, seeking to replace inefficient traditional technologies with more appropriate ones in agro-based small-scale industries.

CONCLUSIONS AND POLICY RECOMMENDATIONS

Ghana's efforts to develop technological capability go back at least three decades, but very little has been achieved in terms of effective technology transfer and competitive industrial development (Lall et al., 1994; Pietrobelli, 1994a). For many years Ghana pursued strongly inward-looking, protectionist policies with a heavy reliance on public enterprises. As in many other countries, this strategy did not furnish enterprises with the incentives needed to stimulate technological activity and capabilities. Structural adjustment reintroduced competition forcefully and relatively quickly. However, weak capabilities and the lack of support for improving them has evoked a weak supply and export response. MVA per capita is stagnating at the same value as in 1980. Several industries have suffered significant closure in these years, and there is little sign of emergence of new competitive and dynamic industrial activities (Lall et al., 1994; Teal, 1999a). To achieve sustained industrial growth in this new environment will require a comprehensive strategy for upgrading capabilities and institutions. It will have to include the development of local skills and technological capabilities, securing larger inflows of FDI, restructuring, and the improved functioning of the institutional structure to provide the public goods of technology development.

At present, S&T policy remains largely on paper. Policy-makers attach low priority to technological issues and the implementation of the policies that exist is weak and uncoordinated. There is little understanding of the importance of S&T and of the need for technological effort at the enterprise level in dynamic competitiveness. The role that government institutions can play in stimulating and supporting enterprise technology development is also neglected. The meagre R&D carried out in CSIR institutions is isolated from production. There seem to be serious skill deficiencies at practically all levels of industry, from the shop-floor to the highest of technological and managerial levels. Few specialized training institutes exist, and most firms are forced to use only the limited capabilities available in-house.

There are several policy implications of this analysis.

Improving technology strategy formulation

The document *Ghana Vision 2020: The First Medium-Term Development Plan (1997-2000)* emphasises the importance of S&T. To quote,

> The enormity of the advantages and benefits from science and technology development in our socio-economic venture seems to have been lightly appreciated, even at the highest level of decision making. Recognition by decision-makers at the highest level of the importance of S&T as a tool for the rapid development of the country, and by the public in general is crucial to any effort to adopt a science and technology culture.

However, as of January 2000 the official policy paper submitted by STEPRI on National S&T Policy was still at a draft stage and was being discussed in Cabinet. This document contains a clear set of short, medium and long-term measures, but it is not clear how well it will be implemented.

STEPRI is in charge of making and implementing S&T policy. However, to perform this role effectively, it has to be highly placed in the political hierarchy so that it can influence and coordinate the relevant agents and institutions. This is not the case at present. It is clear that a major restructuring of government structure is needed if S&T strategy is to be effective.

Co-ordinating and planning the S&T system

The S&T system in Ghana is highly fragmented, with different agencies pursuing different objectives with no reference to national goals and needs. The private sector is hardly involved in the design and implementation of strategy. The coordinating role assigned to MEST cannot be effectively performed by it (or by any ministry alone) under these circumstances; it is imperative to raise the political status and reach of the agency. Several proposals have been put forward to address this issue, including one to set up an *Office of Science Adviser to the President* or a *National Science and Technology Commission*. In addition, the government has to improve skill levels in the S&T system. It has to start using such tools as skill and technology audits and the benchmarking of technical performance against international levels, in line with practice in more advanced countries.

Improving human capital and skills

Ghana's education system has deteriorated over time, and its skill gaps vis-à-vis dynamic developing countries are enormous and growing. Enterprise training does not fill these gaps. The government has to strengthen skill creation at both the educational and enterprise levels. The new strategy should involve all stakeholders in design and implementation, from S&T institutions, education and training establishments and universities to private enterprises. The skill needs of the economy should be monitored continuously, and the education and training system made responsive to these needs.

It is particularly important to raise and improve enterprise training. This would involve measures on both the demand and the supply side. On the demand side, it may, for instance, mean giving fiscal incentives for training and persuading firms to undertake more training. On the supply side, it may include setting up, improving and coordinating industrial training institutions. The enterprise sector has to be induced to strike closer linkages with training and educational institutions, and the latter to be fully responsive to their needs.

Accessing foreign technology and attracting FDI

Ghana is importing insufficient amounts of foreign technology in any form: capital goods, licensing and FDI. Although the policy regime for FDI has improved, bureaucratic obstacles remain in areas like access to land, utilities and import procedures and should be removed. The main focus of technology transfer policy has to be information provision to enterprises, particularly SMEs, on sources and costs of foreign technologies. This information needs to be backed by technical extension services to help them absorb new technologies. The Ghanaian government should consider launching benchmarking exercises to help firms evaluate their technological weaknesses and needs.[19]

Create an R&D culture in industry

About 90 per cent of the R&D in Ghana is carried out by government-funded institutions, in strong contrast to more dynamic developing countries where private enterprises finance and execute large shares of their national R&D (Lall, 1999a). There is little awareness in industry of the importance of in-firm technological effort. Most enterprises operate at small scales, use simple machinery, have low levels of technical and managerial skills, and generally produce lower quality goods. Their exports are concentrated in a few, relatively stagnant, non-traditional manufactured products.

Most firms importing technology tend to use it passively, often at below international best practice levels, with no effort to absorb, adapt and improve upon it (Lall et al., 1994; Teal, 1999a). The need for such effort is not understood, and there is no attempt by the government to improve awareness. It is vital for the government to undertake such effort, by information and persuasion campaigns, selection of leading technology performers as 'technology models' for the rest of industry, and effective advocacy work in collaboration with private business associations.

Strengthening the technology infrastructure and institutions

Ghana's technology infrastructure needs substantial reform and improvement. The system suffers from an absence of economic analysis of technology policy. The whole public S&T system employs only two economists. There is no effort to calculate the cost and benefit of technology investments or to financially evaluate S&T activities. An explicit effort should be made to rectify this deficiency.

The 1996 Act sought to introduce greater market orientation into CSIR by setting a target of 30 per cent self-financing over five years. This target appears overly ambitious and is unlikely to be achieved. The government needs to make additional effort to explain the policy shift to CSIR institutions and support them in restructuring and improving their activities.

As it stands, the Institute for Industrial Research is of little use to industry. It clearly needs to improve its capabilities and strengthen linkages with the productive sector. The Food Research Institute is better financed and endowed with laboratories and scientific equipment (and better supported by foreign aid). However, it faces difficulties in disseminating and marketing its research and in linking research with production. A change of corporate values is needed: scientists and technical personnel have to be convinced – through persuasion and incentives like research grants and promotions - of the importance of linking basic research, applied research and industrial activity.

The Ghana Standards Board has good technical personnel, and has international accreditation in selected food, fish and fish products. However, it suffers from insufficient funding and poor links with business enterprises, especially with SMEs. Its range of competence has to be widened and it needs to engage more actively in promoting standards among enterprises. It should promote the development of a private testing industry. Its metrological capabilities should be improved to reduce the cost to enterprises of meeting stringent standards in export activities.

NOTES

1. There is a huge literature on the ERP in Ghana, its features and results. See for example Caputo and Rabellotti (1990), Chand and van Til (1988), Kapur et al. (1991), Lall et al. (1994) and Leechor (1994).
2. Evidence from a stratified sample of 230 enterprises, with average value added per employee of $4868, and median value equal to $2203 in purchasing power parity terms (Bigsten et al., 1998).
3. Ghana exports less manufactures than it should on the basis of its comparative advantage, calculated on the basis of the proportions of skilled labour to natural resources by Wood and Mayer (1998). The share of manufactures in total exports was 3 per cent compared to an expected 30 per cent, with exports dominated by traditional goods such as gold and cocoa (37.5 and 36 per cent of the total, respectively) in 1998.
4. GIPC leaflets. One of the authors could visit most of the institutions analysed in this chapter during an UNCTAD field visit in January 2000.
5. See the extensive compilation of material in the Africa Region of the World Bank, and Lall (2000a).
6. Other export-specific programmes have been established over the years with the help of foreign donors, like for example the Trade and Investment Promotion Programme (TIP) sponsored by USAID - 5-year $80 million programme started in 1993 - and the Private Enterprise and Export Development (PEED), a $51 million credit facility sponsored by the World Bank (Baah-Nuakoh et al., 1996, p. 20).
7. The Export Development and Investment Fund Bill was approved and published in the *Gazette* on 10 December 1999 to address the problems associated with the supply-side constraints of exports by creating a financial facility. At the time of writing, it is too early to assess its effects.
8. This section is based on Gogo (2000).
9. MEST also has ministerial control over the following agencies: Town and Country Planning Department (TCPD), Environmental Protection Agency (EPA), Council for Scientific and Industrial Research (CSIR), Development and Application of Intermediate Technology (DAPIT), and Ghana Regional Appropriate Technology Industrial Service (GRATIS).
10. The financing of public research institutions is categorized in four main items. Item 1 covers personnel expenditures; item 2 recurrent expenditures (electricity, petrol, phone, running expenditures of vehicles, etc.); item 3 includes development expenditures for project execution; and item 4 groups investment and capacity building expenses. In fact, only item 3 is actually directed to finance research activities, and it is the one that is most easily cut, promising essentially long-term results. In most CSIR institutes item 3 has not been financed for years.
11. Every year each Institute proposes a budget to CSIR justifying its request with the activities

it plans to execute. A technical assessment is carried out by CSIR, an overall budget is prepared and passed to MEST for approval. Then the budget is sent to the Ministry of Finance that has still the right to repeal it. The approved budget is the official document required to finance all the operations of the CSIR institutes.

12. See Chapter 2, and Pietrobelli (2000) for a discussion on the various channels of technology transfer and their policy implications.
13. Similar evidence is provided by Bigsten et al., 1998. Their five-country study reveals that the rates of return for education in the sample are highly non-linear, rising from 3 per cent for primary to 14 per cent for secondary completers and 43 per cent for university completers. The average return for education would hide the extreme non-linearity. To quote 'insofar as advanced skills are those used intensively in a successful manufacturing sector, the relative scarcity of such skills is consistent with the failure of Africa to develop a successful manufacturing sector' (Bigsten et al., 1998, p. 9).
14. Now MDPI is fully owned by the government, after being a project of UNDP, ILO and the government of Ghana until 1977.
15. Analysts trained by the GSB over the years have come from Eritrea, Ethiopia, Mauritius, Zanzibar, and other countries.
16. FRI research covers cereal processing and preservation, grain legume processing and preservation, fish and meat handling, processing and preservation, root and tuber crop processing and preservation, fruit and vegetable processing and preservation, fats and oils studies, food packing studies, storage of staple food crops, extension of food preservation and processing, solar energy application and mushroom cultivation.
17. This amounts to the remarkable figure of an average of 53 beneficiaries per employee in 1998.
18. Intermediate Technology Development Group of Rugby, UK, British Voluntary Services Overseas, CIDA, GTZ and the EU, among many.
19. In the UK, large firms use PROBE software with data on thousands of leading European firms, this is provided by the Confederation of British Industry. SMEs, on the other hand, are provided benchmarking help by the Department of Trade and Industry, which has developed a simple questionnaire to this aim. Around 10 000 SMEs per annum are benchmarked, comparing company performance with national, regional or sectoral standards.

7. Zimbabwe

Zimbabwe is the most industrialized economy in SSA after South Africa. It launched industrial development earlier than most other African countries, and during UDI (Unilateral Declaration of Independence, when a white government was subjected to sanctions that cut the country off from trade with Europe and the USA) it pushed industry into making products that could no longer be imported. As a result, by independence (1980), Zimbabwe had a relatively deep and diverse industrial sector, with considerable capabilities in engineering and intermediate products. In this, it displayed significantly higher levels of technological capability than all the other countries in the sample. After some time, it undertook a series of structural adjustment programmes that started to expose industry to global competitive forces. The impact of adjustment was not, on the whole, beneficial, though it is difficult to distinguish this impact from the effects of other economic and policy variables (note, however, that this chapter uses information collected in 1997, well before the current political crisis caused by the takeover of farms).

Over the 1980s, Zimbabwean GDP grew at 3.2 per cent and manufacturing at 3.4 per cent per annum. The policy regime was still highly inward-oriented, continuing largely intact the controls of the UDI period. Manufactured exports grew by only 2.8 per cent per annum during 1981–90, while 'pure' manufactured exports (defined in Zimbabwe to exclude sugar, cotton lint, ferrochrome and iron and steel) grew at 5.1 per cent. There were two sub-periods: 1981–86 and 1986–90. Export performance was much poorer in the former than in the latter. Total manufactured exports declined by 1.7 per cent and 'pure' manufactured exports by 1.4 per cent per annum over 1981–86. Over 1986–90, they rose by 8.6 per cent and 13.7 per cent per annum respectively, reflecting new incentives for exporting (to obtain imported inputs for domestic market-oriented production). Subsequent export growth in the 1990s was somewhat lower.

At the start of the 1990s, Zimbabwe launched a major economic reform programme. The Economic Structural Adjustment Programme (ESAP) of 1991–95 led to a dramatic change in the trade regime, from a strongly inward-oriented to a far more outward-looking and market-oriented stance.

On the external front, the exchange rate was devalued, import trade liberalized (with quantitative restrictions on imports removed and tariffs reformed and lowered) direct export incentives abolished, and investment policies liberalized. On the internal front, prices and trade were deregulated, competition policies improved, industrial relations reformed and a start made in the restructuring and privatization of public enterprises.

The launch of ESAP coincided with two severe droughts and with declining prices for important commodity exports. While these had ended or been reversed by 1996, several macroeconomic problems persisted. The fiscal deficit was large (10.2 per cent of GDP in 1995–96). The real exchange rate appreciated significantly, and the interest rate was at uncomfortably high nominal and real levels. As a consequence of stagnating domestic demand and import liberalization, industrial production declined over the ESAP period (by a total of 21 per cent over 1991–95), with manufacturing declining at 6 per cent each year, faring worse than mining. The share of MVA in GDP was reduced from 22 per cent in 1980 to 18 per cent in 1997. Real per capita income fell from around Z$1 950 in 1991 to Z$1 600 in 1995 (in 1990 prices).

Though manufactured exports grew at a respectable rate (about 10 per cent per annum) during 1990–95, this was not in response to structural adjustment. It was a continuation of trends during 1985–90 (when manufactured exports grew at 9 per cent), based more on using existing capacity and better access to imported inputs than on adding to capacity or raising technology or competitive capabilities. There was, in other words, little structural response to the new trade and domestic industrial regime. This can be illustrated by looking at the skill and technological base of Zimbabwean industry.

SKILLS

Education System

To quote a 1995 World Bank report on Zimbabwean human resources:

> Zimbabwe recognises that human resource development is fundamental to longer-term sustainable growth, particularly given the globalisation of production and the increasing importance of human capital. Furthermore, human resources development is probably the most equitable form of social investment. Investment in health and education has been one of Zimbabwe's top priorities... Despite its significant investments in this area so far, Zimbabwe still faces the question of whether the country is investing enough in education and health for long-run sustainable poverty reduction, and if resources are allocated efficiently across activities, regions and ethnic groups...
>
> Zimbabwe's achievements in education are among the country's most impressive gains since independence, putting Zimbabwe near the top of the list in Africa in

> terms of absolute achievements and the pace at which these results have been attained. (World Bank, 1995, paragraphs 3.9, 3.10 and 3.20)

As the World Bank notes, Zimbabwe's educational base is relatively advanced by regional standards, and its expansion over the 1980s has been impressive. Chapter 2 showed enrolment rates at all levels and in technical subjects at university relative to selected countries. At the primary and secondary levels, Zimbabwean enrolments (117 per cent and 44 per cent of the relevant age groups) are ahead of all African countries with the exception of South Africa in 1995. The comparable rates for sub-Saharan Africa as a whole are 78 per cent and 23 per cent. At the tertiary level, Zimbabwe's 6 per cent again compares well with the 2.9 per cent for SSA, though it comes well behind South Africa's 16 per cent. Zimbabwe's enrolments also compare favourably with China and South Asia, though they lag in relation to East and South East Asia. In general, Zimbabwe can be described as having a broadly literate and trainable work force, one of the best in the region.

The general enrolment figures are less interesting for industrial competitiveness than are the figures on *tertiary enrolments in technical subjects*, the main source of high-level technical skills for industry, research and services. Here comparisons with other regions are less favourable. Zimbabwe barely approaches the level of South Asia, and the lag with respect to the mature Tigers is very large indeed. In terms of the number of students enrolled in technical subjects as a percentage of the population, for instance, Korea enrols over 25 times more than Zimbabwe.

This is not to suggest that Zimbabwe should match East Asian enrolment levels at this stage of its development. It is clear, however, that if it is to gain something of the technological dynamism and industrial competitiveness that East Asia has displayed, it has to boost its technical human capital significantly. Even latecomers like Malaysia, Indonesia and Thailand have twice the percentage of their populations enrolled in tertiary level technical subjects. These countries are, it must be remembered, still at relatively low levels of technological sophistication in their manufacturing activity and are highly dependent on foreign investors to provide high-level skills and training. Singapore, with an MNC dependent strategy, has been able to move into much more sophisticated technologies by investing heavily in education and training, with the highest proportion of higher education financed by the government in Asia.

Enrolment figures can be misleading as indicators of human capital: the *quality* of education is equally important. It is generally accepted that the quality of schooling in Zimbabwe has suffered as a consequence of the rapid expansion in the 1980s (Knight, 1996). According to the World Bank (1995), government expenditures on education as a per centage of GDP have declined steadily since 1991. The cutbacks have hit primary education the hardest; teachers' real wages have dropped and this is 'threatening the morale and quality of teacher input' (paragraph 3.14). About 20 per cent of primary school teachers, and over 30 per cent of secondary school teachers, are unqualified. Moreover, while all able children enter school in Zimbabwe, about 25 per cent drop out before reaching 7th grade and another 25 per cent after finishing primary school. The pass rates of O-levels are *only 12-15 per cent of those sitting*, so that in the end under 5 per cent of those entering primary school pass their O-levels. In general, girls perform more poorly than boys, and rural areas worse than urban ones. About 25 per cent of students leave secondary schooling after 2 years. The situation is likely to have deteriorated since 1995.

Vocational education is held in low esteem in Zimbabwe, leading to low quality of applicants and under-utilization of capacity, poor staffing and equipment (Knight, 1996). In 1993, the most popular subjects - agriculture, commerce, accounting and fashion - were not in areas directly relevant to industrial needs. By 1994, there were 8 technical colleges in Zimbabwe, with a total enrolment of over 13000 (Knight, 1996). There were also 14 youth training centres, over 100 private colleges and five correspondence schools, in addition to the many training courses offered by foreign donors and NGOs. Many technical colleges, however, suffered from inadequate equipment and staffing; their overall staff vacancy rate in 1992 was 40 per cent.

While higher education receives more government support than other levels do, the emphasis is on academic subjects rather than on vocational or technical training. The public sector is short of teachers for technical and vocational training institutions. The situation is exacerbated by the fact that training centres fall under four different ministries. Even the relatively small number of graduates at the tertiary level do not find it easy to get employment in their subjects, suggesting that Zimbabwean enterprises are not aware of their skill needs or find the training of graduates deficient. The general figures suggest, nevertheless, that Zimbabwe would face severe technical skill constraints if its enterprises were to upgrade technologies, attract export-oriented FDI in larger volumes, and compete directly with East Asian counterparts.

In 1990, before the launch of ESAP, it was estimated that the Zimbabwean manufacturing sector faced a shortage of up to 60000 skilled artisans. The gap in engineering skills was set at 37 per cent of needs (Biggs et al., 1995, p. 118). These estimates may be outdated, but they confirm that there is a skill gap in industry. There is no sign that the gap has been closing in recent years.

Employee Training

Formal education is only a part, often a small part, of the system for creating human capital for industry. Employee training, within firms and externally, is just as important (Tan and Batra, 1995). Since independence, the employee training system in Zimbabwe has not expanded at the same pace as the education system. To correct the racial bias of the earlier apprenticeship system (confined to whites) the government centralized the recruitment of apprentices under the Ministry of Labour, and those selected were offered to employers (Knight, 1996). The number of apprentices declined over time, partly because employers were hostile to the role played by the ministry, and most apprentices had to be employed in public sector firms. Private enterprises preferred to hire workers with little previous training or job experience and provide on-the-job training. This trend continues. Private firms regard formal training as of poor quality and irrelevant or harmful for their needs (it leads to inflexibility and unrealistically high expectations among trainees). As the head of one major packaging firm put it, 'We have well-educated, not well-trained, people in Zimbabwe.'

While Zimbabwean firms provide a fair amount of on-the-job training to recruits (more than in Ghana, Kenya or Tanzania, see Lall et al., 1996), this does not mean that such training is adequate to the needs of competitiveness. The training is essentially to impart basic operational skills, with little effort to raise the skill level or retrain workers in new methods. This limits the ability of firms to introduce new technologies or organizational techniques. While there is considerable use of external training facilities, relatively little of this pertains to technical personnel except in food processing (Biggs et al., 1995). It is the large firms, especially foreign affiliates, that are the most aware of training needs and invest most in internal and external training. Smaller enterprises are less aware and invest much less, and also tend to lack an appreciation of the value of formally trained engineers and technicians. There is a dearth of training institutions suited to their needs and resources.

Traditional attitudes toward formally educated employees mean that relatively few high-level technical personnel are employed in Zimbabwean enterprises. A large survey of manufacturing firms found that, of total employment of 56400, the proportion of scientists was 0.19 per cent, engineers 0.17 per cent and technicians 1.43 per cent, yielding a total of 1.79 per cent (Biggs et al., 1995, p. 142). Over 98 per cent of scientists were employed in food processing firms because of the specific nature of quality control and testing needs. Engineers were more widely spread over woodworking, metalworking and food, as were technicians. Large firms accounted for most of these employees.

In general, these numbers are far below comparable figures in Asian industrializing countries: the proportion of engineers in total employment ranges from a low of 3 per cent in Sri Lanka to a high of 12 per cent in Korea (Lall et al., 1996). Perhaps more surprisingly, they are also below those found in similar surveys, in the same industries, in Kenya and Ghana, both with distinctly less complex industrial structures. Thus, of a total of 26600 employees surveyed in Kenya, 0.15 per cent were scientists, 0.74 per cent engineers and 2.42 per cent technicians, a total of 3.31 per cent. In Ghana, the figures (based on a smaller sample of 32 firms with 3800 employees) were 0.3 per cent scientists (all in food processing, dominated by a large MNC), 0.6 per cent engineers and 5.6 per cent technicians, a total of 6.5 per cent (Biggs et al., 1995). Figure 7.1 shows these distributions.

Some deterrents to firm-level training often found in other developing countries - like rapid turnover of workers, indiscipline or union problems - are not often mentioned in Zimbabwe.[2] Most workers appear to be stable, loyal and disciplined. The deterrents to training lie elsewhere, as noted, in the lack of awareness of the benefits of training, the lack of suitable training facilities for smaller enterprise or for specific industrial needs (for example, textiles and garments), and the inefficiencies in the operation of the levy scheme (see below). Clearly much remains to be done to raise general awareness and change attitudes.

Unfortunately, there is no systematic survey of industrial training provision or needs in Zimbabwe. This is a major gap - without such basic information, it is difficult to formulate or evaluate the training system or to devise

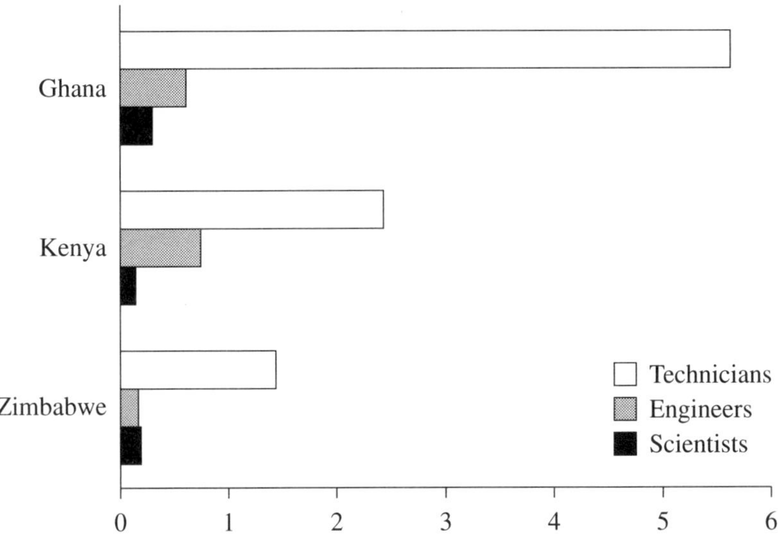

Source: Biggs et al., 1995.

Figure 7.1 Percentages of technically qualified personnel in total employment in manufacturing enterprises, 1993–94

strategy. Most successful industrializing countries undertake regular and detailed surveys of this sort, and build manpower strategies on their findings. Most also benchmark training levels and practices in more advanced economies.

At the time of the field visit (1997), the most important government initiative in the field of training was the *Zimbabwe Manpower Development Fund*, based on a 1 per cent levy on the payroll of formal sector firms. The levy was used to compensate employers who provide approved training to their employees, the proportion of the refund depending on the numbers of people trained. The majority of the budget was directed to training provided by government colleges. The levy raised Z$247 million in 1995 (about US$28 million), of which Z$185 million 1995 (about US$21 million) was spent and the rest invested to earn interest.

The way in which the fund was operated meant that most funds went to larger firms, which were able to send more employees on training courses. It was unrelated to the cost of specific training, and complex and costly training received the same grant as others, which tended to discriminate against more advanced training. SMEs need to be given additional support in providing training, and refunds should be related to the cost of specific courses. Informal sector firms, by definition, get no support for skill development. The fund did not base its strategy on a detailed and up-to-date analysis of training provision or needs in Zimbabwean industry, another anomaly that needed correction. Many industrial enterprises complained about the efficacy of the fund in promoting effective training. Despite having businessmen, as well as trade unions, employee representatives, academics and accountants on its Board, the fund was yet to establish its credibility with manufacturing industry.

One of the best training systems in the developing world is, by common acknowledgement, that of Singapore, which has mounted numerous policies to encourage pre- and post-employment training. Singapore has the highest percentage of government support of higher education among Asian industrializing economies, and it is the proactive stance of the government (generally in close consultation with business, in particular MNC affiliates) that accounts for its efficacy (Green et al., 1999; Manzocchi and Pietrobelli, 2001; Soon, 1993). Another interesting case is the Penang Skills Development Corporation in Malaysia, which has involved private firms (led by multinationals) in training, with little direct government support.

There is growing awareness in Zimbabwean industry and government of skill shortages, but the response has been tepid. In industry, only a small number of large, especially export-oriented, firms feel the need for better skills.[3] Several have good in-house training programmes, and consider the institutional structure for training inadequate. SMEs do not appreciate the need to employ qualified manpower or to invest in upgrading employee skills. The government has been forced to reduce education spending, with very undesirable effects on educational quality. It does little to monitor training by enterprises or to develop effective measures to promote it.

Textile and Clothing Industry

A digression into the textile and clothing industry is useful at this point, since this is a potential area for Zimbabwean industrial competitiveness. Its competitive position is illustrative of the broader range of competitive challenges in Zimbabwe, particularly in terms of human capital.

Real wages declined in Zimbabwe in the 1990s, as in many other African countries. However, data on hourly labour costs in the apparel industry show that Zimbabwean wages are still not low relative to several Asian competitors (Chapter 2). Zimbabwe clearly cannot establish a competitive edge based on cheap 'raw' labour; its edge must lie in intermediate levels of skill, quality, and design. Yet lower wage countries in Asia are investing massively in design, technology and other capabilities in this industry. Table 7.1 provides additional data on labour costs and salaries for higher-level staff. Zimbabwe is relatively expensive at the supervisory and management levels, with a higher dispersion of remuneration than other countries. This may reflect the racially biased pay structures before independence, which the government has tried to change down but without complete success (Knight, 1996). It may, however, also reflect the relative scarcity of the skills at higher levels.

A 1996 study on skills in textiles and garments in Zimbabwe notes a wide range of skill deficiencies in this industry, and makes several policy recommendations (KSA, 1996). Among the main deficiencies are weak middle management, craft-oriented management approaches in smaller firms, poor cost management, and weak product promotion and design skills. The study recommends, among other things, the formation of an association to promote skill formation, and the setting up of a fashion institute to monitor trends internationally, diffusing information to Zimbabwean firms and providing design assistance. Hong Kong has such a centre, regarded as vital to the quality upgrading of its clothing industry. India has a very successful institute, described in Box 7.1.

It is also important for Zimbabwe to have larger training facilities for textile and clothing operatives, designers and production managers. A Danish-run Clothing Design and Technical Institute (CDTI), set up in 1993, provides such training on a small scale, including a 3-year course on mechanical work and short-term courses in production management and different aspects of clothing manufacture. Despite the demand for its services, CDTI has been experiencing serious problems with the bureaucracy and Danish support may be withdrawn.

Table 7.1 Comparisons of various wages

Country	Minimum wage for unskilled labour (US$/day)	Average wage for unskilled labour (US$/day)	Average wage for skilled labour (US$/day)	Average wage for technicians/supervisors (US$/month)	Average wage for middle manager/ engineer (US$/month)
Bangladesh	1.58	1.66	2.33	63(min)	N/A
Vietnam	0.70	1.15–1.22	1.75–1.90	55–150	152
Sri Lanka	1.15	1.25	2.20	90–279	210–400
India	0.82–1.17	2.40–3.33	4.2–6.2	128–200	285–430
Indonesia	0.60–2.62	2.00–2.87	5.98	215	359
Philippines	4.00	4.00	7.00	237	625
Mauritius	2.66[c]	5.5–6.8[d]	6.8–10.3	210–400	560–1100
Thailand	5.22	9.05	15.72	274–630	730–964
Malaysia	No minimum wage	5.20–8.08	12.86	321	780–1150
Zimbabwe	No minimum wage	2.71	3.7–4.7[a]	190–300[a]	700–1300[a]
Taiwan	22.50	32.50	42.50	1300	1500–2500
South Africa	Set by agreements	7.33-12.0	11.7-14.8[b]	N/A	N/A
China	N/A	2.05-5.18	4.03-9.65	N/A	N/A
Pakistan	1.44	N/A	N/A	N/A	N/A

Notes:
Wage rates are prevailing averages for workers in light manufacturing; for China, wages are for Special Economic Zones. Countries ranked by columns 5 and 6.
(a) Mid 1994, data collected for World Bank RPED survey and reported by Velenchik (1995); (b) Salary and benefits of qualified machinist in clothing from CloFed (1997); (c) Statutory minimum daily wage in 1995 for export enterprise workers; (d) Mauritian data on average wage rates in different occupations from Central Statistical Office, *Digest of Labour Statistics 1995*.

Sources: Interviews, various official and private publications, the Services Group, CloFed (1997).

It is important for the government to resolve these problems and to expand CDTI operations and encourage similar industry-run centres.

BOX 7.1 NATIONAL INSTITUTE OF FASHION TECHNOLOGY, INDIA

The National Institute of Fashion Technology (NIFT) was started in 1986 by the Indian Government, under the Ministry of Textiles in New Delhi to train fashion technologists, provide industry with up-to-date information and help craftsmen and manufacturers, with the main focus on the textile and garment industries. It received collaboration from the Fashion Institute of Technology, New York, Nottingham Trent University (UK) and IFM, Paris. Within a few years its services were in such demand that various regional centres have been set up, including Bombay, Ahmedabad and Bangalore.

NIFT offers diploma and certificate courses to full and part-time students as well as training to industry personnel. The main campus has 40 faculty staff, around 70 specialized guest teachers and 486 students. The main programme is a 3-year diploma on fashion design, whose trainees find instant employment in industry as designers, pattern makers, stylists, coordinators and fashion illustrators. There is also a 3 year diploma in accessory design. It is not just the garment industry which seeks these skills but also makers of costume jewellery, leather goods, precious jewellery and other accessories. NIFT also offers a number of 2-year courses: apparel marketing and merchandizing; garment manufacturing technology; leather garment design; knitwear design and technology; textile design and development. Admission is purely on merit, and a number of the top designers in India today are graduates of the NIFT.

NIFT has a well-stocked library on Indian and foreign designs and materials. Its resource centre conducts fashion forecast seminars in major garment manufacturing centres in the country, and has compiled a directory of resources used by the garment industry. It gets constant feedback from industry on its designs and training programmes, and is constantly redesigning its courses to meet industrial needs.

NIFT is implementing a World Bank project to improve its CAD training facilities for industry and to provide design consultancy services for smaller garment firms. There has been growing demand for such consultancy as SMEs have sought to upgrade their export activities, and NIFT plans to develop a network of linked computer design facilities with manufacturers (initially in the region near to Delhi). This would greatly speed up the process of disseminating new design concepts to firms, helping their flexibility and response times.

Source: Information collected by Sanjaya Lall.

To conclude, human capital formation is critical to competitiveness in Zimbabwe. Its lead over neighbouring countries is an asset that needs to be cherished and enhanced, but it is not one that can sustain its competitiveness in open markets. The government needs to form a careful strategy of using resources effectively to create the skills that will upgrade activities and allow new competitive activities to emerge. Apart from generally improving the education and training system, there is an important policy consideration: there has to be *targeting* of industrial skill creation. Production, supervision, process and product technology, industrial engineering, design and development skills are not generic but activity specific: a textile engineer is not much use in developing electronics.

TECHNOLOGY IMPORTS AND TECHNOLOGICAL ACTIVITY

Comparative Technological Performance and Capabilities

How does Zimbabwe compare with other countries in access to foreign technology and technological effort? Purchases of foreign equipment are the predominant form of technology imports by Zimbabwe. There is relatively little use of disembodied technology transfer, that is, licensing, turnkey contracts or the use of foreign consultants - these exist, but impressionistic evidence suggests that they are low. The data presented in Chapter 2 show that all five SSA countries studied import relatively few capital goods, less than most dynamic developing countries. Zimbabwe appears to be relatively better off than other SSA countries, with the usual exclusion of South Africa, but still lags behind most of the developing world.

Zimbabwe does not provide data on R&D to UNESCO. According to figures reported in Biggs et al. (1995), some 50 out of 200 sampled enterprises, mainly large firms, claimed to do R&D: as a percentage of sales, they spent 0.11 per cent in food processing, 0.16 per cent in textiles, 0.42 per cent in woodworking and 1.85 per cent in metalworking. However, most of this apparently involved minor process or product adaptation rather than what is normally understood as R&D. Another survey found that R&D in the conventional sense was absent in Zimbabwean firms (Latsch and Robinson, 1999). Certainly the impression that most enterprises were highly dependent on foreign sources of technology and did little R&D was confirmed during the field visit.

While R&D performance is weak in Zimbabwe, its industries have relatively good mastery of the technologies they use, at least in comparison to neighbouring countries. Thus, a study of technological capabilities in Kenya, Tanzania and Zimbabwe, devised a 'technology index' of the main technological functions in samples of garment and metalworking firms. It found that Zimbabwean firms have higher scores than counterparts in the other two countries (see Chapter 2). This confirms that Zimbabwean industry is technologically in advance of neighbouring countries. It is also in line with the results of total factor productivity analysis in the World Bank's RPED study (Biggs et al., 1995) which shows that average technical efficiency was higher in Zimbabwe than in Kenya or Ghana. However,

> the detailed 'snapshot' of endowments of firm technological capabilities reveals levels that are *significantly lower than international standards* ... In comparison to countries outside Sub-Saharan Africa, however, all three countries show low firm endowments of production capabilities. (Biggs et al., 1995, pp. 3–4, emphasis added)

The impact of liberalization has been mixed. Some firms, mainly large ones with export experience, have used the easier access to imported capital goods, and to a lesser extent licensing, to improve their technological base. However, the recession caused by the drought and the subsequent high interest rates and uncertainty has probably deterred a larger commitment to new technology and facilities. Many others have adopted a passive 'wait and see' strategy, with some firms withdrawing from export markets that they had entered under the previous incentive scheme. There have been inter-industry differences: the clothing sector has reacted largely defensively while the engineering goods sector was more offensive, investing in new equipment and training. This may be traced to the speed and intensity of the competitive threat - the garment industry was threatened by a sudden influx of second-hand products and firms at the lower end of the quality scale found it difficult to react; by contrast, engineering firms had more 'natural protection', faced a more gradual increase in import penetration, and had much better links with customers. Thus, the latter had more time to react.

In general, however, the impact of ESAP on technological activity in Zimbabwe has been fairly muted. Weak inward FDI has meant that one major avenue of technology inflow has not been exploited. Licensing has not risen significantly, and domestic technological activity has not shifted to a higher plane. The shocks administered by the drought and recession, together with general policy uncertainty and the high interest rates, have also contributed. Note that some UDI-bred capabilities may not be competitive in an open regime. Given the extent of isolation that much of Zimbabwean industries operated under, this is a real danger.

Of course, since technological capabilities are best developed in a dynamic setting, where old skills and technologies die out and new ones emerge, the dying out of the 'dinosaurs' of UDI may not, as such, be undesirable. However, it should be noted that some UDI capabilities are valuable and may be preserved if they can be upgraded to competitive levels with relatively modest investment in equipment, skills, technological effort and restructuring. The existing base should be seen as an asset that most other Sub-Saharan African countries lack - and may not be able to build in the new trade environment. Thus, technology policy should provide a supportive setting in which viable capabilities do survive and improve, and only the really uncompetitive ones die out.

This will probably not be enough to dynamize Zimbabwean competitiveness in manufacturing: fresh entrants will be needed to enter new activities and take up new technologies. The government will need to give strong signals and encouragement, particularly to the SME sector. This may be difficult in the present macroeconomic and political environment, which deters investment or favours only short-term investment. Liberalization itself tends to favour, as in other countries, entry into quicker paying service activities rather than manufacturing. However, the current political instability and uncertain future tend to deter *all* investments. But even if the macro situation were more favourable and manufacturing itself more attractive to entrants, technological advance would need strong support, an efficient and responsive technology infrastructure, a financial system capable of supporting risky and technology-based ventures and an education and training system capable of providing the skills. How the remaining requirements are being fulfilled is taken up in the rest of this chapter, with special emphasis on the S&T infrastructure.

SCIENCE AND TECHNOLOGY INFRASTRUCTURE AND POLICIES

Setting Technological Priorities

There is no institutional mechanism in Zimbabwe for evaluating and setting technological priorities. There is no science and technology plan, nor is there a separate department in charge of S&T activity. While most science and technology plans in developing countries have been grandiose affairs with little practical relevance for industrial development or competitiveness, such plans have also served very useful roles in some instances. Asian economies with strongly export-oriented industrial sectors, good skill bases and a responsive institutional environment have used S&T plans to good effect. Each of the mature Asian Tigers apart from Hong Kong has formulated elaborate technology plans identifying strategic technologies for future development (one of the most active being free trade Singapore). These priorities have been readjusted every few years, and they have guided the allocation of technology resources. Malaysia has a similar technology plan, as does Indonesia, though these countries are not technologically anywhere as active as the mature Tigers (Lall, 1996, 2002).

It is not only the NIEs that undertake technology targeting. In some form or another, targeting is an integral part of technology resource allocation in many advanced countries. In many OECD countries, much of the process is implicit rather than embodied in formal plans, largely driven by defence and mission-oriented objectives. More interventionist governments like Japan and France have laid down explicit technology targets to promote national technological capabilities and selected industries or champions. More recently, however, national technological priorities are being set in practically all mature industrial countries, including the USA, UK, Germany, Japan, France and elsewhere, by the use of 'Technology Foresight' Programmes. Foresight programmes are lengthy exercises by which all parties concerned with science and technology - industrial leaders and researchers, academia, services, financial institutions and the government - interact to decide on technological trends and needs for their country. A number of developing countries, including India and Korea, are considering launching similar exercises.

As noted in previous chapters, S&T plans in the other countries described here have often remained wish lists. By avoiding such plans, the Zimbabwe government has probably saved itself some waste. However, it is necessary at this stage to mount a more explicit analysis of technological needs and priorities, along with a strategy to meet the needs. This could be helped by a Technology Foresight Programme, enabling all stakeholders to take stock of national technological resources and to assess how to allocate resources in the future. As in developed countries, the process could be more useful than the results, bringing Zimbabwe closer to building a technology 'culture'.

Promoting an R&D Culture in Industry

Despite the significant base of operational capabilities built during the UDI period, Zimbabwe lacks a technology 'culture', a tradition of enterprise-driven dynamic technological activity improving upon imported technologies and developing indigenous products and processes. The UDI period was an aberration in that it forced industry into a great deal of technological effort to overcome shortages, but it did not lead to a basic change in attitudes to technological activity. These attitudes remained geared essentially to relying on imported technologies and developing local capabilities only to the extent necessary to produce for the home market. The drive to compete with moving world best practice frontiers was largely absent. Also absent was the urge to develop new products and processes for export markets. Formal R&D remained minimal.

These attitudes must be changed if manufactured export growth is to be dynamized. Zimbabwe seeks to raise national R&D to 1 per cent of GNP,[4] the proportion reached by countries like South Africa, India and Singapore. Since the present level is not known, it cannot be judged how distant the target is; however, impressionistic evidence suggests that it is fairly far away. Given the low propensity of enterprises to undertake R&D, moreover, much of the increased research spending will have to come from the government rather than the private sector: not necessarily a desirable outcome. Setting up a large and expensive public R&D infrastructure which does not feed directly into industrial operations is relative easy, but very wasteful. Public R&D is certainly needed, but mainly as a complement to private effort. The policy priority should be to stimulate R&D in private enterprises. There does not, however, appear to be any consideration being given to *how* this may be done in Zimbabwe. On the other side, enterprises or industry associations are also uninterested: R&D is at this time very low on their list of priorities. This is not the basis for strategic policy-making.

There are no special incentives in Zimbabwe for undertaking industrial R&D activity. Apart from its allowance as a legitimate business expense, there are no other schemes to persuade enterprises to launch or expand technological effort. This contrasts with Asia (Lall, 1996).

A related issue is *technology finance*, an essential ingredient of R&D promotion. Large companies generally have sufficient internal reserves and standing with financial institutions to be able to finance technological investments. By contrast small and medium-sized companies, and start-ups without a track record, need special financial facilities to undertake technological investment. Normal financial institutions are not competent to assess, finance, monitor and assist technology investments, and a technology-based venture capital industry exists in relatively few countries. Moreover, even where large firms are concerned, financial support is generally needed to catalyse collaborative research between industry and technology institutions, or to guide R&D into new areas of technology considered to be in the national interest. Zimbabwe has very little of all this.

SCIENCE AND TECHNOLOGY INFRASTRUCTURE

The technology infrastructure in Zimbabwe is, by most standards, not very developed.[5] The research support system was just being launched in 1997. There were no productivity centres, SME support was weak and linkages of institutions and universities with industry were feeble. Though most technological activity relevant to competitiveness takes place within enterprises, there remain many activities with strong 'public goods' characteristics, such as basic research, standards, information on sources of technology or support for SMEs, that need government support. Other activities include capital-intensive testing or other services, requiring specialized skills and coordination between different agents. These can only be conducted efficiently by specialized institutions.

Very few firms collaborate with technical departments in the University of Zimbabwe, other colleges, or the polytechnic. At the time of the field visit, only two companies (both engineering firms) were working closely with the university and the polytechnic to devise training programmes and internships for students, but these are not technological linkages. These two firms, and one other engineering firm, also had technical connections with the university, but for metallurgical and chemical testing rather than for technological upgrading or research. Three firms occasionally sent people on training courses at these institutions (again, only fairly large engineering firms). Generally, the university is regarded as too far removed from the needs and requirements of industry. The clothing firms tend to have no links with any institutions, except the occasional training link with a technical college, usually for supervisory or technical and maintenance training.

Technology institutions are generally passive. Firms regard their abilities poorly and expect little from them. There is no contracting of industrial research to government technology institutions. The few companies that have any links at all use mostly testing facilities, and are either foreign-owned, or well-established, or have entrepreneurs with engineering degrees. This seems to reflect both the lack of initiative within the institutions, and possibly their lack of suitable equipment and skill, as well as the weaknesses in the technological capability of the firms themselves. Experience elsewhere suggests that some research capability within firms is generally required before they can make good use of technology institutions, and this is certainly lacking in Zimbabwe. The poor link between firms and technology institutions is an especially weak area in most of SSA, as shown in previous chapters and in Box 5.2.

STANDARDS AND QUALITY

The institution charged with promoting standardization and quality improvement in Zimbabwe is the Standards Association of Zimbabwe (SAZ). This was set up in 1957 (originally as an outpost of the British Standards Institution) as a non-government and non-profit making body. It is governed by a General Council, which comprises representatives of government, local authorities, industry, commerce and professional institutions.

SAZ is, according to its brochure, 'subsidised by monies from the Standards Development Levy Fund and also derives income from the Mark Certification Scheme, Registration under Quality Management Standards, Laboratory Testing fees and sales of publications'. The Levy Fund is operated by the Ministry of Industry and is charged on the wage bill of larger companies (an earlier system of voluntary membership did not produce sufficient revenue). This provided some 70 per cent of SAZ's income in 1996, another 21 per cent coming from its earning for inspection, laboratory fees and publications. The levy is a cause of general complaint among companies, which do not feel that they get sufficient value for money, but this could not be investigated in detail. The one-fifth proportion of own earnings is low by standards of similar bodies in East Asia.

The functions of SAZ are to encourage the use of standards and publish Zimbabwe standards, provide testing facilities, operate certification schemes, register international standards such as ISO 9000 and 14000 and provide information on international standards and other standards. These functions are intended, among other things, to improve the quality of local goods, raise awareness of quality among producers and consumers and enhance the competitiveness of Zimbabwean exports. SAZ had a staff of just under 100, of which about half are scientists and technicians. By 1997, it had prepared a total of approximately 500 standards, mainly for the construction industry: it adopts international standards wherever possible, writing its own standards only when these are not applicable. Practically all standards are voluntary (the only mandatory ones are for seat belts and motorcycle helmets). It had no capability to accredit private testing laboratories though this is an objective in the longer term. There did exist a number of private testing laboratories which operated under foreign accreditation.

Apart from the inability to accredit laboratories locally, SAZ is handicapped by not having a metrology facility. Most calibration is done in South Africa and some (for mining equipment) in Zambia. A new metrology facility is to be set up in Zimbabwe, but under the SIRDC (see below). The rationale for putting standards and metrology under two different institutions is not clear, since their work is often closely related and most countries have them under one administration.

SAZ can play a crucial role in promoting export competitiveness, particularly by encouraging the adoption of internationally recognized quality management standards such as ISO 9000 and 14000. While not compulsory except in some health-related exports, the series is becoming de rigueur for selling to Europe, and increasingly elsewhere. A widespread adoption of the standards can also lead to a more rapid diffusion of techniques and skills. SAZ has developed some capability in this area, and by 1997 had certified around 20 companies with ISO 9000 (Zimbabwe ranks third in SSA, after South Africa and Kenya, see Table 2.14). While there has been promotional work in Zimbabwe, it has not been very forceful. No financial assistance has been offered to firms, even SMEs, to bear the cost of getting consultancy services, training and equipment for ISO certification.[6]

One of the difficulties facing SAZ in launching a more aggressive campaign is the shortage of trained staff. The private sector is able to attract good technicians away from SAZ. This is not necessarily undesirable from the economic perspective, since it improves quality management in industry. However, it is important for the country's standards body to have strong capabilities.

Industry is fairly complimentary about the quality of testing services offered by SAZ. However, most services are used by large companies; SAZ lacks the ability to reach out to and help SMEs. A more proactive approach to SMEs can be a powerful means of disseminating modern technology and raising their potential as subcontractors to large enterprises. Again, manpower shortages constrain SAZ from being more aggressive in this area.

It is difficult to comment on the more technical aspects of SAZ capabilities and equipment, but the physical facilities appear to be better than in most neighbouring countries. Subject to more expert assessment, a strengthening of its staff and a reorientation of purpose towards aggressively helping the technological upgrading of SMEs would be valuable.

R&D INSTITUTIONS

In Zimbabwe there have been practically no public R&D institutions for manufacturing technology. The only bodies that could do research for industry were the technical departments of the university but, as noted, industry had few links with them. In 1997 the government launched on an ambitious programme of building several R&D institutes under the Scientific and Industrial Research and Development Centre (SIRDC), located in the President's office. The first phase of this programme involves the setting up of seven research institutes. Their status in 1997 was as follows:

- *Biotechnology Research Institute* This institute, with five divisions, will work on such projects as the development of drought-resistant maize species, micro propagation of disease-resistant potatoes, and food irradiation. The building programme is behind schedule, but the director and six research scientists (all MScs) have been selected.

- *Building Research Institute* The initial projects of this institute will be to use local materials and waste materials for lower-cost construction, get lower-cost technologies from other countries and develop cheap concrete panels for walls and roofing. The director and two research scientists have been appointed.
- *Environment and Remote Sensing Institute* This institute is fully functional, with a German-funded remote sensing and information system and an environment management unit. The director is supported by nine scientists, of whom two have doctorates.
- *Production Engineering Institute* Originally called the 'mechanical engineering institute', this institute is supposed to provide a range of common services and technological assistance to manufacturing industry. It will have a foundry, machine shop, fabrication workshop, CNC machine section, workshop with tribology, corrosion and other testing facilities, and materials science. It will provide pilot plant facilities and provide consultancy services to industry. This institute is not intended to do research and development; thus, it will be more of a productivity centre than a normal technology institute. This is likely to be extremely useful if it lives up to expectations: it will help industry to improve quality and develop new products and processes, diffuse technology and provide trouble-shooting services. However, the building is not complete yet and the staff complement is not full (only four have been appointed so far). The intention is to work a great deal with SMEs and informal sector enterprises, providing training for free and also management, finance, business and other forms of assistance that such enterprises need. It plans to have a team to work with managers, giving advice on entire production systems and devising systems for improving them. It is starting to work with a Norwegian (aid funded) team to develop the capabilities of this team.

While it is obviously premature to judge the design of the institute, it does seem to have many attractions, especially its very practical orientation and emphasis on helping SMEs. Much will depend upon how proactive it is in reaching out to SMEs (rather than waiting for them to come to it) and how well it can combine technical services with other forms of assistance. It is universally found that technical assistance by itself is far less successful because SMEs find it difficult to define their technological needs, cannot spare the time or personnel to go and look for help and find bureaucratic procedures very irksome.

In addition, many cannot make use of technical help unless it is supported by a package of financial, management and marketing assistance. While the institute is intending to provide this, it does not have any financial resources of its own and will have to draw on other sources. This may be a major disadvantage. Another handicap that this institute may face is that it has no means of subsidizing the sale of technical services to SMEs. Most countries offer this sort of subsidy because of the inability or reluctance of SMEs to pay full costs for such services, at least in the medium term until they realize their value. Malaysia, for instance, has a fund which pays up to 50 per cent of all costs for quality, process and product improvement by SMEs. In some countries, the subsidy element is higher to start with, and is gradually reduced over time. The fact that the institute is only designed to provide productivity services also means that Zimbabwe still lacks a research centre for industry. While this may not seem important in the near future, the gap may become more important in the future as industry seeks to build up advanced capabilities. Contract R&D is assuming increasing significance in newly-industrializing countries, and can be a vital competitive asset.

- *Electronics Technology Institute* This institute is intended to provide systems engineering services rather than electronics manufacturing or design technology. It will allow Zimbabwe to 'open up' and adapt software packages that are presently imported in their entirety. It may give it a head start in software production and may be a source of comparative advantage in the region. It is, however, difficult to see Zimbabwe emerging as a competitor in the larger arena when lower-wage countries like India have already established a strong base of software exports. This institute is still to be built but a director and three engineers have been appointed.
- *Energy Technology Institute* This will work on energy conservation, non-conventional sources of energy and efficient generation from conventional sources. The director and four scientists have been appointed.
- *National Metrology Institute* This was already mentioned in the section on standards, and is still at the planning stage.

This is the complete list of institutions to be set up. Unfortunately, we lack recent information on the progress of the programme, and on whether subsequent economic and political difficulties have affected its implementation. The potential benefits and problems of the institute that will serve manufacturing have already been noted above, but it is difficult to say more at this stage.

SME SUPPORT SYSTEMS

There are several institutions in the public and private sectors offering technical and other services to SMEs in Zimbabwe.[7] Some important ones are reviewed briefly here.

Business Extension and Advisory Services (BESA) BESA was set up in 1991 to provide training, counselling and business support services to SMEs; it has a network of five regional offices. By 1997 it had dealt with around 4000 clients, of which 80 per cent were new start-ups. BESA receives support from the international donor and local business communities, and has a budget of around Z$3 million per year. It charges for some services but offers initial business advice for free. Its earnings provide about 10 per cent of its budget, but it seeking to raise the proportion to one-half.

BESA has useful contacts with local financial institutions, and occasionally accompanies its clients to negotiate loans. However, it has no system to monitor performance by clients, and there is a high failure rate (around 70 per cent). Many of its clients are staff retrenched by enterprises in the wake of adjustment. The focus of its work is more on business facilitation than on technology.

EMPRETEC Zimbabwe EMPRETEC is an UNCTAD programme to develop entrepreneurship in several countries. It provides management training and consultancy/advisory services to facilitate overseas contacts, with offices in Harare and Bulawayo giving intensive two-week courses on Entrepreneurship Development. Its Management Assistance Programme also uses consultants from the local industrial sector to provide help in marketing, technology and financing,

Zimbabwe Enterprise Development Programme This is a programme started in 1996 by the Confederation of Zimbabwe Industry (CZI) to provide ‘match-making’ services to large and small companies. Funded mainly by USAID, it has three offices in the country with a database on (around 200) potential SME suppliers and subcontractors. It provides training support to SMEs and helps place foreign business executives with local firms. It does not deal much with technology issues.

Small Enterprises Development Corporation (SEDCO) SEDCO is a parastatal organization formed in 1983, with World Bank assistance, to help SMEs access finance. It provides loans to enterprises with fewer than 50 employees at commercial rates, aiming mainly at manufacturing, construction and agro-based companies. It is also seeking to serve the micro enterprise sector. However, its remit does not cover technological assistance.

Small Business Support Unit (SBSU) This is part of the Zimbabwe National Chamber of Commerce, with a staff of 12 and a focus on management development and information provision.

Venture Capital Company of Zimbabwe (VCCZ) VCCZ offers equity finance to SMEs. Formed in 1991, it is supported by the private sector, the Reserve Bank of Zimbabwe, IFC and the Commonwealth Development Corporation. It takes stakes of 26–49 per cent in clients, with a minimum of Z$250 000 and a maximum of Z$3 million. By 1997 it had supported over 50 firms, with a failure rate (reasonable by international standards) of 15 per cent. The assistance and guidance provided to clients are mainly on business planning and management rather than on technological issues.

This list illustrates that Zimbabwe has a broad range of support institutions for SMEs, with a greater spread and coverage than the other countries in this study. The support available for financing is particularly noteworthy, as is the participation of the private sector in helping SMEs. However, as noted, the technological needs of SMEs are not well served, and many institutions are not sufficiently proactive in reaching out to their clients. Some are rather bureaucratic and are weak in marketing their services. Most SMEs are unaware of the services on offer and have little understanding of the terms of service provision. Large areas of the country are not served, particularly in small towns and rural areas. The institutions do not network with each other, leading to overlaps and duplication.

In general, therefore, the SME support system in Zimbabwe, while advanced by regional standards, is not able to meet properly the technological needs of local enterprises.

POLICY RECOMMENDATIONS

Skill Formation

Zimbabwe has a good human capital base by regional (except South African) and South Asian standards, but suffers from underinvestment in high-level technical manpower. The quality of education has declined at all levels with its rapid expansion. Dropout and failure rates are high. Vocational training is held in low regard by employers, and fails to meet emerging industrial needs. Though there are ample technical colleges, their equipment tends to be poor and staff weak. Apprentice training offered by the Ministry of Labour also suffers from lack of credibility with industry, and numbers have declined over time. Industry generally employs low levels of formally trained people. In-house training by industrial enterprises is used to compensate for the deficiencies of the formal system, and is fairly good by regional standards. However, such training is concentrated in large (particularly foreign) enterprises, and is aimed essentially at providing basic operational skills rather than upgrading them. Yet it is the latter that is necessary to tackle the more advanced technologies that will be needed to enhance competitiveness. Coupled with the 'anti-education bias', this can be a severe constraint to future upgrading.

There is therefore a pressing need to upgrade the education and training system and make it more responsive to industrial needs. Only this can reverse the 'anti-education bias' in employment practices in large firms and provide the basic input into long-term technological upgrading of Zimbabwean industry. However, by itself this is unlikely to suffice to meet the human capital needs of competitiveness. The training system must *anticipate* new skill needs and even temporarily over-supply specialized manpower in order to encourage industry to enter into new technologies and activities. The private sector, in particular smaller enterprises, must be persuaded to invest more in training; for this it must be better informed of the benefits of and returns to employee training.

The recommendations on skill upgrading are as follows:

- Conduct a comprehensive *survey of skill needs*, not just at present but in the future, and continue such surveys on a regular basis. This can serve as the basis for prioritizing training needs at all levels; the government should *target new skills* that are likely to be critical for future competitiveness. There is also a need to evaluate the skill needs of supporting service activities, for example, information technology, finance and marketing.
- The government must ensure effective *interaction between employers and training institutions*, possibly by setting up a unit to sponsor and implement such interaction on a continuous basis.
- The operations of the present financial provisions, namely the *Manpower Development Fund* need to be examined, to help overcome its continuing lack of credibility with industry.
- There may be a need to launch new types of training institutions more *directly linked with, and in some cases managed by, industry*. Industry associations in Zimbabwe have been rather inactive in promoting training services for their members, and the government should provide incentives or seed money for them to launch centres on their own.

- *Firm-level training* must be encouraged by information and persuasion and, where desirable, by incentives and the setting up of institutions and programmes. The training levy is not seen by much of industry as productive, though such a levy is in use in many other countries.
- *SMEs* have to be targeted by special information and incentive programmes to recruit better-trained labour and to invest in formal training. Their method of skill transmission tends to be confined to apprenticeship systems, where craftsmen teach young workers, largely with little formal education, traditional methods that have been used over time without much change.

Technology Support

The technology infrastructure in Zimbabwe is of long standing, but is not geared to building dynamic competitiveness. It has been a relatively passive provider of basic testing and quality services. There is no tradition of research support for manufacturing. The relevant institutions are being set up now, but their programme seems very ambitious; in any case, subsequent developments may well have knocked the programme off track. There are no productivity centres to help firms to benchmark and improve their technology. Other forms of SME technology support are also weak. Linkages between industry and technology institutions and universities are practically non-existent - industry knows little about the technology institutions and has low regard for their capabilities.

Firms themselves do very little formal R&D, also explaining partly why they do not seek help from universities or institutions. All this does not matter greatly at low levels of technology serving protected domestic markets where operational capabilities are easy to master and no further effort is needed to compete. It does matter when efforts have to be made to reach world levels of efficiency and new, complex products and processes have to be introduced.

While more Zimbabwean firms have been certified with ISO 9000 than in most other African countries, there is a large (and widening) lag with respect to Asian competitors. The Standards Authority is promoting the ISO standards but lacks the resources to do this forcefully; it cannot, for instance, offer financial support to SMEs to meet the consultancy costs involved. It also lacks the qualified staff to undertake more ambitious campaigns.

There is no institutional mechanism for deciding and implementing technological priorities in Zimbabwe. Grand science and technology plans, common in many developing countries, are not generally a good way to direct national technological activity. However, an indicative plan with a clear set of priorities can help focus effort and allocate resources, and should be considered in Zimbabwe. Nor is there any consistent set of policies in place to stimulate R&D by private industry. What is needed is a campaign of information, persuasion, support and incentives, along with measures to strengthen linkages between industry and technology institutions. A 'technology culture' is not easy to create, but there are strong demonstration and positive spillover effects once a few enterprises start to conduct R&D. Thus, an immediate aim could be to encourage in-house R&D by a few leading enterprises, and to publicize this to other firms.

The policy implications that follow are:

- *Technology infrastructure institutions* should be strengthened in manpower and resources to be more proactive in improving quality standards and obtaining ISO 9000 certification. Financial support should be provided for this purpose to smaller enterprises.
- A *Zimbabwe Productivity Centre* should be established to help SMEs benchmark and upgrade their technologies and meet international levels of product and process technology. Existing SME support agencies should be more proactive and market their services more effectively. The government should consider consolidating the large variety of available institutions to provide one-stop services at various locations in the country. This is the strategy adopted in the UK in its 'Business Links' programme. An attempt should also be made to strengthen SME clusters, to allow them to reap the benefits of closer networking and economies of scale.
- The *research infrastructure* being set up seems well conceived and practically-oriented. It is important to ensure that its practical objectives are really met. There is a risk that overambitious plans will spread human resources too thinly and lead to a 'supply push' programme where there is little demand for institutional support from the industrial sector.
- The Zimbabwe government could consider setting up regional *Technology Transfer Centres* (along the lines of Northern Ireland and the Asian Tigers) to help local enterprises define their technological needs and problems; this would supplement the work of the central Zimbabwe Productivity Centre. The regional centres could be involved in conducting 'technology audits', providing information on appropriate sources of technology, and helping with training, testing, computer aided design and manufacture, equipment repair and maintenance and generally raising awareness of technological activity.
- *Enterprise-level R&D* should be strongly promoted by a programme devised in consultation with industry, including fiscal incentives, and a government campaign to persuade and help enterprises in this endeavour. Industry associations may play an important role in catalysing such activity.

- *Collaboration between technology institutions* in Zimbabwe and abroad, in particular South Africa, should be encouraged. Research staff could be exchanged, joint projects launched and funding sought for research of interest abroad.

NOTES

1. This chapter draws upon Lall et al. (1998).
2. Evidence gathered during Commonwealth Secretariat field visit (1997).
3. See Wangwe (1995) for some case studies of training by export-oriented firms in Zimbabwe.
4. Interview with SIRDC.
5. Evidence collected during a Commonwealth Secretariat field mission (1997), Lall et al. (1998), and others.
6. The UK government, in the heyday of the Thatcher laissez-faire approach to manufacturing, promoted the ISO 9000 series by offering subsidies of 50 per cent of consultancy services; the aggressive promotion campaign has led the UK to have the highest number of ISO certificates in the world (Lall et al., 1998).
7. This draws upon contributions by Mike Sellek from the Department of Trade and Industry of the UK government.

Annex: Attracting manufacturing FDI to Africa

In common with other developing regions, Africa is actively seeking FDI - in particular export-oriented manufacturing FDI - to build industrial competitiveness and enhance economic growth. Most African countries have improved their FDI regimes in recent years. They have removed most restrictions on foreign entry and participation. Many are privatizing state-owned enterprises and utilities, and welcoming foreign investors to participate. Several have launched programmes to attract export-oriented MNCs into EPZs or similar facilities, offering generous tax and other incentives. They have liberalized their trade regimes and are negotiating or implementing a range of regional trade arrangements that promise larger markets to investors.

These developments reflect not just the growing liberalization of investment and trade regimes in the developing world but also the changing international technological and competitive climate. Continuing and rapid technical change has made access to new technologies and skills more crucial for growth than ever before. Competition for scarce investment, technologies, skills and market access that MNCs embody has intensified. At the same time, liberalization has placed enormous stresses on existing industrial activities in much of Africa. Many enterprises facing direct import competition have found adjustment difficult; many have not survived (Lall, 1999c). Their ability to gear up to world competition is relatively limited, and the pace of change in global markets threatens to leave them further behind. Thus, FDI has become a vital source not just of capital but of most tangible and intangible assets that enterprises need to survive and grow. This annex analyses the FDI promotion and incentive strategies pursued by African countries in the light of these changes in the international environment for investment flows.

FDI LOCATION IN A GLOBALIZING WORLD

The location of FDI is determined by the interaction of firm and industry specific variables with host country factors. The former affects the initial propensity of firms to undertake overseas investment, while host country factors influence the *location* of the investment. Table A.1 shows the nature of the decision-making process on site location in multinational enterprises.

International experience suggests that most foreign investors go through a

Table A.1 Investment location decisions by MNCs

Location decision-making steps	Factors affecting location decision-making process
Step 1: Initial decision to invest in an offshore location	Better access to end-user markets Global or regional production and supply strategy Staying ahead of the competition Lowering per unit production costs Technological changes affecting competitiveness Securing access to raw materials Gaining access to technology or skills
Step 2: Selection of national location	Political and economic stability Favourable and predictable foreign investment climate Efficient and honest FDI policy administration: low red tape, streamlined procedures, transparency and honesty Preferential access to target end-user markets Adequate physical infrastructure and transport services Supply of trainable labour and skills Good supplier network and support services Competitive set of investment incentives
Step 3: Selection of individual site	Physical suitability of the site for industrial process Distance from labour pools and transportation hubs Availability, cost and quality of area labour supply Condition of transportation network and frequency and cost of ground, air and sea freight services Cost and quality of utilities Access to raw material and other inputs Land lease rates and conditions Facilities, services and amenities Capabilities and reputation of management group Good local supplier network and support services

Source: The Services Group

three-step process to select a particular industrial location. The first step is the large number of the firm-specific variables that 'push' or 'pull' the firm to make the initial decision to invest overseas (through relocation, expansion or consolidation). The second is the selection of an individual country or region. Here a number of factors come into play, including such fundamentals as political stability, investment policies and, in economic terms, the competitiveness and attractiveness of the country. Once a particular country has been chosen the investor has to decide on a particular site. Depending on the needs of its production and sales business, the MNC will evaluate, among many other factors, site suitability, distance from transport, labour and input sources, availability of local inputs and distribution network, reliability of services and cost of utilities, lease rates and facilities and so on. Many location determinants are changing in the new competitive environment, as discussed below.

Host *government policies* affect FDI location directly, by acting on the immediate profitability (or feasibility) of direct foreign investment, and indirectly, by changing underlying location costs. For instance, the profitability of FDI can be changed temporarily by offering fixed term tax holidays or over a longer period by setting relatively low tax rates. The feasibility of using FDI as a means of exploiting location advantages can be affected by government rules on foreign ownership. Location costs can be lowered by raising the quality or lowering the cost of local inputs, or by offering foreign investors privileged access to local inputs (or privatized assets).

Not all policies to attract FDI are equally desirable: much depends on *how* governments act to make the FDI option attractive. Traditionally, the most important policy to attract FDI has been offering high and varied levels of import protection, making the production of selected products cheaper than importing. While a powerful means of fostering industrial investment (both local and foreign), import substitution has often created large inefficiencies, fostering infant industries that never matured. Many governments also sought to promote the development of nationally-owned firms by restricting foreign shares. This also tended to create inefficiencies, by promoting domestic enterprises protected both from import competition and MNC affiliates: unless the enterprises faced international competitive pressures they tended to stagnate with high costs and lengthening technological lags.

Many such selective policy interventions, particularly those related to trade and ownership, are now being abandoned, partly because of the general disillusionment with import substituting strategies and partly as a result of changing international pressures and 'rules of the game'. This is as true of Africa as elsewhere, though in practice the speed and spread of economic liberalization varies by country and period (World Bank, 1994).

One of the most important consequences of the emerging environment is that

FDI location will *increasingly depend on economic factors* (reflecting competitiveness in terms of cost, quality, reliability and logistics) rather than on policy interventions and short-term incentives. However, this does not mean that policy is unimportant. On the contrary, policies that affect national competitiveness are now even more important than before. These include a broad range of measures, for instance to facilitate private investment (national and foreign), enforce competition policy, provide stable and transparent rules for private business and, over time, improve the quality of local productive factors. Before coming to the analysis of these factors in Africa, it is worth looking at the changing context for FDI location at a little more length. Table A.2 illustrates the main determinants of FDI location in developing countries.

The traditional determinants of FDI attraction - welcoming policies, political and economic stability, large markets, import protection, cheap labour, natural resources and the like - are well known and need not be discussed here. These remain important, but the significance of 'new' factors is growing (Table A.3). What are these new determinants?

Technological progress, globalization of production and policy liberalization means that the relative importance and nature of the traditional determinants of FDI location are changing. To take them briefly in turn.

- *Technological change* implies that host economies have to provide the (more skill and technology intensive) inputs, institutions and infrastructure needed for efficient production in almost all branches of activity. Falling transport costs mean that they face more immediate competition from across the globe, and also have the prospect of serving more markets. Falling communication costs (with the ability to exchange massive amounts of data and information instantaneously) allow for different kinds of activities to be undertaken. They also allow parent companies to exercise much tighter control over affiliates and to integrate them more closely into their activity. The provision of higher quality inputs is not a once-for-all matter. Skills, information, institutions and capabilities have to be upgraded constantly. The growing role of proprietary technology in competitiveness also means that investors in technology-intensive activities demand tighter intellectual property protection and better enforcement of the relevant laws and rules.
- The *globalization* of production and the emergence of *integrated structures* across countries also affect location determinants. Leading MNCs face increasing competition from potential host countries for their tangible and intangible assets. Thus, they can demand better terms and services in selecting sites, particularly for activities not based on local natural resources; this makes effective promotion (or, as Wells and

Table A.2 Host country determinants of inward FDI

Major determinants	Principal elements
1. Policy framework: general and FDI related	Political and social stability Transparency, predictability and (lack of) corruption Entry, exit, ownership, staff and ownership rules Efficient legal and dispute settlement system Operational costs, licensing Treatment standards for foreign affiliates Competition policy M&A and privatization policies Tax rates and agreements Other FDI-related treaties, guarantees, insurance Foreign exchange controls and ease of repatriation Regional agreements and access to major markets
2. Economic determinants of FDI by type of investment	Local market seeking Efficiency seeking Natural resource seeking Intangible asset seeking
3. FDI promotion and facilitation	Image building Investment generation, including ability to create necessary skills/institutions for targeted FDI Investor facilitation (one-stop) Investment incentives Administration of FDI rules, incentives and facilitation Post-investment services, responsiveness to MNC needs

Wint, 1990, call it 'marketing a country') very important in FDI attraction. The increased 'choosiness' of MNCs also reflects the fact they face more intense international competition, forcing them to rationalize and restructure their global operations. Their strategies tend to change: they now exercize tighter control over their affiliates, with majority or complete equity shares and closer managerial links. In many cases, this leads MNCs to adopt what UNCTAD (1998a) calls 'complex integration strategies'. In contrast to traditional strategies, where stand-alone affiliates reproduce all major functions of parents, MNCs use affiliates to provide specialized functions for the whole corporate

Table A.3 Main economic determinants of FDI

Local market seeking FDI
Size of market
Per capita income
Growth prospects
Access to regional or OECD markets
Non-tradability of product or service
Need to customize product for local tastes
Import barriers
Market structure, interaction with other MNCs
Privatization strategies
Efficiency seeking (export-oriented) FDI
Low-cost, trainable labour for simple activities
Specialized skills for complex activities
Ease of access to foreign personnel
Efficient local supplier networks
Efficient local technology, training institutions
Competitive infrastructure and efficient EPZs or industrial estates
Access to world price inputs, efficient import and export procedures
Conducive, open trade regime
Special incentives for transferring regional or global MNC functions
Resource seeking FDI
Availability of valuable resources
Secure property rights
Import and export costs
Infrastructure
Intangible asset seeking FDI
Ample skilled, especially technical, workers
Strong R&D in local firms
Presence of other high-tech MNCs
Advanced clusters of SMEs in relevant activities
Developed university and research infrastructure
Incentives for local R&D, training and linkages
Strong intellectual property protection
World class communication links

network. Host economies with the smallest endowments receive the simplest assembly functions, or just serve as markets for products made more efficiently elsewhere. There is a risk of growing discrepancies between 'insiders' and 'outsiders' in emerging multinational production networks, that is, between countries that are able to cope with the demands of new technologies and organizational methods and those that are not. While some FDI will go to most countries, it is the insiders that are best placed to attract sustained new investment and to benefit from it in development terms.

- *Policy liberalization* permits greater play to the technological and economic factors noted above. It reduces the role of trade policy in attracting FDI or raising local content. It also minimizes the role of host government technology policy in making investors externalize their intangible technological or marketing assets (selling or licensing them to local firms). Liberalization enables MNCs to choose freely the optimal mix of ownership, local content, technology and skills to use in each location.[1] At the same time, the spread of large firms in developing countries means that host governments have to design and implement effective *competition policies* to counteract the potential abuse of market power (by large domestic firms as well as MNCs). A clear and efficient framework for such policies not only provides a good environment for investment decisions, it also allows host countries to maximize their benefits from MNC entry.

Three aspects of liberalization are particularly important for FDI today.

- The opening of domestic capital markets to *mergers and acquisitions* (M&As) of domestic by foreign companies. M&As are now the driving force in FDI between developed countries, and also in flows to developing regions such as Latin America and parts of Asia.
- Foreign participation in *privatization*. As Pigato (1999) notes, privatization to foreigners, particularly of utilities, provided about 44 per cent of total revenue generated by privatization in developing countries during 1990–97. In SSA the foreign exchange contribution to privatization revenue was higher, at 59 per cent, and about 80-90 per cent came from FDI (rather than portfolio inflows).
- FDI in new *infrastructure projects* under a variety of contractual and ownership arrangements, which were largely closed to FDI earlier (in developed as well as developing countries). The emergence of the new contractual forms (build-own-operate, build-operate-transfer and so on) has allowed operators and contractors from industrialized countries (and some NIEs) to go multinational in a big way. Many large new foreign investments in SSA are from infrastructure operators from Southeast Asia (for example, Malaysia in telecommunications).

FDI location in the emerging global environment will be increasingly driven by the ability of host countries to provide *two kinds of competitive assets*: a competitive FDI regime and competitive factors of production. A competitive FDI regime entails, among other things, a stable, efficient, and service-oriented setting for investors, which welcomes them into most economic activities without discrimination (on conditions comparable to other host economies). It includes a strong and modern legal and intellectual property system and effective competition policies. Note that a welcoming regime does *not* mean large tax incentives: if other factors are unfavourable, offering large incentives will not result in a sustained increase in desirable FDI. As CBI (1999) notes, low taxes are better than selective tax incentives. Competitive factors will be the ultimate determinants of efficient, sustained FDI, calling for more than cheap raw labour and basic infrastructure, and involving a constantly improving base of skills, capabilities, suppliers and institutions. The possession of valuable natural resources remains an important draw for FDI, but using it as a springboard for further industrial development will need the skills and capabilities called for in all other activities.

Given this evolving FDI scene, how does Africa rank in the developing world as a destination for FDI?

THE ECONOMIC AND POLICY DETERMINANTS OF FDI IN AFRICA

This section compares Sub-Saharan Africa with other developing regions in terms of the locational factors for FDI. The recent pattern of FDI in much of Africa reflects relatively static advantages, with a very low skill and technology specialization. Pigato (1999, p. 16) concludes, 'much FDI [in Africa] is either in the primary sector, particularly petroleum, or in infrastructure. And, with the exception of South Africa, other SSA countries have seen very little inflows into the manufacturing sector in recent years.' What does go into manufacturing is mainly in simple processing for local markets, with minimal exports (especially to demanding OECD markets).

There are thus two broad strategic challenges facing the region:

- Increase FDI inflows into *existing areas of comparative advantage* – resource-based activities and privatization or private-sector development of infrastructure;
- Improve the 'quality' of FDI by *creating new sources of advantage* – adding more value to resources, enlarging simple export-oriented activities, and building the potential for more complex industrial and service activities.

Relevant policy implications, however, can be drawn only if we understand the current base of policies and endowments in the region. Let us start with the economic factors.

Economic Factors

The economic location factors, and their weaknesses in relation to 'the competition' (other developing regions), have already been discussed in Chapter 2. To reiterate the main points:

- *Labour and skills* While SSA is often thought to have a competitive edge in cheap labour, on a par with many Asian countries, it has not been able to exploit this edge in attracting FDI. There are widespread skill deficiencies, particularly in specialized technical, managerial and marketing areas. The quality of education in the region has been declining. Scattered evidence on enterprise training (Lall et al., 1994; and Lall, 1999c) suggests that African enterprises do very little; far less than comparable firms in Asia.
- *Technological activity* While it is difficult to compare technological effort, the few measures that exist point to very little such effort in SSA. R&D data and case studies of enterprises suggest that technological capabilities are extremely low even by developing world standards. One result is that the region attracts FDI only in very simple activities; its ability to draw in FDI in more complex - and more dynamic - activities is necessarily very limited. MNCs that do invest transfer the lowest end of technologies and functions to the region relative to other host countries. The ability of MNCs to increase local content is constrained: domestic firms simply do not have the ability to make the technological leap needed to meet international standards of quality, technology, cost and delivery.
- *Infrastructure* Measures of infrastructure cost, quality and availability place SSA near the bottom of the pecking order in the developing world. Modern infrastructure like telecommunications and logistics, particularly important for attracting export-oriented FDI, are uncompetitive by world standards. Shipping costs tend to be high and connections from Africa infrequent. The quality of infrastructure has deteriorated in recent years in many countries, a result of economic hardship and crises. Landlocked countries lack adequate access to shipping through other countries. In addition, as Collier and Gunning (1999b, pp. 12–13) note, 'most Africans live much further from the coast or navigable rivers than in other regions and so face intrinsically higher transport costs for exports … Much of the population lives in

countries which are landlocked, so that the problems of distance are compounded by political barriers.'

One aspect of infrastructure is particularly important for export-oriented FDI: *export processing zones* (EPZs). These have worked extremely well in Southeast Asia and Mexico in attracting new export activities to areas insulated from the domestic policy regime and endowed with a concentration of good infrastructure. Many African countries have also set up EPZs, South Africa being a notable exception (EPZs have not been permitted because of trade union objections). However, apart from Mauritius, hardly any African EPZs can be regarded as successful in terms of attracting FDI or stimulating exports and employment. Most have been set up by government, along rather rigid traditional lines; most appear to fall well short of best-practice standards. Some, like Kenya, allow private operators to set up EPZs, but the amount of FDI flowing into them is minuscule and the value of exports tiny (Chapter 3). Box A.1 describes the evolution of EPZs in recent years, and suggests some reasons why African countries are lagging in this critical area.

BOX A.1 FREE TRADE AND EXPORT PROCESSING ZONES IN EVOLUTION

Free trade zones have been used internationally to promote exports, attract foreign direct investment, and spur economic growth. Modern free zones, including as one variant EPZs, are recent variants of the traditional freeport or free zone concept, which has been existence for several centuries. Free zones were established to encourage entrepôt trade, mostly within harbours along international trade routes. Since the first modern zone in the United States in 1945, the number of zones worldwide has multiplied rapidly. The first modern industrial free zone *in a developing country* was established in Shannon, Ireland in 1959, followed by the Kaoshiung EPZ in Taiwan in 1962. Today, over 850 free zones are operating in some 100 countries, directly employing almost 30 million workers, and accounting for over US$250 billion in global trade. There are over 240 Foreign-Trade Zones in the United States; in 1998, they employed over 370000 people and generated some US$16 billion of exports.

The generic free zone concept has evolved internationally over time, and many developing countries have failed to keep up with the evolution of the concept. Free zones were traditionally developed as isolated enclaves, both in terms of the underlying policy framework, and in terms of geographic location. Access to a generous set of incentives and privileges were tightly controlled. Qualifying firms typically had to be 80–100 per cent export-oriented (for EPZs), engaged in recognized manufacturing activities, and at times only foreign-owned. Zones were physically located in relatively remote areas or near transport hubs, viewed primarily as 'growth poles' for regional development.

This rather rigid concept has changed significantly over the past decade. Countries now wish to integrate free zones with the domestic economy and use them as catalysts for the liberalization and modernization of the host economy. They now encompass a broader range of activities, directed at both export and local markets. Commercial and manufacturing zones have evolved into large-scale special economic zones and freeports. EPZs have changed from the traditional 'pure EPZ' concept of industrial estates solely for export-oriented manufacturers to various 'hybrid' EPZs (see table). The other major development is the establishment of *specialized zones* catering to specific sectors or industries. Most Latin American countries, for instance, have commercial free zones for trans-shipment and other trade services. Malaysia has a separate law governing these zones. Science and technology parks have been established in Taiwan, Singapore, China and elsewhere. Zones catering to specific industries like petrochemicals, forestry products and gems/jewellery, are found in Thailand and Malaysia. Financial service zones have been established in Israel and Malaysia.

Changing concepts of EPZs in different regions

Zone	Northeast Asia	Southeast Asia	South Asia	Middle East/ NorthAfrica
Pure EPZ	Taiwan S. Korea Philippines	Indonesia Vietnam Pakistan	Bangladesh India Sri Lanka	Cyprus Morocco Gaza
Hybrid EPZ	China	Indonesia Philippines Thailand Vietnam		

Pure FTZ		Malaysia		Egypt Iran Jordan Turkey UAE
Commercial free zone	China Japan	Malaysia		Iran Israel Jordan Kuwait Lebanon Syria
Special economic zone	China	Philippines		
Freeport		Indonesia Malaysia Philippines		
Science/ technology park	China Japan Taiwan	Malaysia Singapore	India	

Note: A country listed in more than one category means that several free zone concepts are available in that location. Pure EPZs are those that permit entry of EPZ-registered firms only, and exclude those registered under other schemes. Hybrid EPZs are divided into a fenced in, EPZ area open only to EPZ-registered firms, and a general industrial estate open to all firms. Pure FTZs are for industrial or commercial users, without an export requirement.

In much of Africa, on the other hand, EPZs continue to follow the traditional enclave, assembly-for-export-only pattern. Government domination of zone development and operation has restricted the number and vitality of zones. Zones have not specialized to cater to the needs of specific groups of industries. The net effect of these factors has been greatly to restrict zone activity, and circumscribe their economic impact. A number of zones have failed to materialize, those on the drawing board are taking a long time to come into operation. The lack of critical scale is a major competitive weakness of the region's free zone programmes. In many cases, zone physical development has not been properly phased; facilities have been heavily subsidized or poorly designed, sometimes poorly maintained or not promoted to prospective investors.

Where private zones are permitted, most face unfair competition from government-run free zones operating on a subsidized basis. In contrast, the most notable trend over the past 15 years has been the growing number of privately owned and operated zones and industrial estates worldwide. While Latin America still accounts for the largest number of private zones, an increasing number are found in East Asia, especially the Philippines, with 80 operating special economic zones, and another 30 under development. The increasing role of the private sector in zone development is changing the way in which the public and private sectors interact in zone development. In traditional projects, the government provides on- and off-site infrastructure, facilities, and basic services. To facilitate private zone development, innovative public-private partnership approaches have been established, which appear to be lacking in Africa.

A major reason behind the poor performance of some EPZs in Africa may also be restrictive policy frameworks. While investment incentives provided are often generous, restrictive provisions and bureaucratic procedures erode their effectiveness. The regulatory framework governing free zone activity, and the efficiency with which it is implemented and administered, has proved to be one of the key determinants of free zone success or failure worldwide. The cornerstone of a successful free zone programme is the transparency and comprehensiveness of the incentives offered and their automatic application, without the need for elaborate qualifying criteria. Other weaknesses may be elaborate procedures and heavy documentation.

A competitive weakness of these programmes is their continued reliance on tax holidays. This may lead to significant distortions for several reasons. A tax exemption is of little benefit if the company is not making profits, which is usually the case in the initial years of operation. Firms that are profitable from the outset might not have needed incentives in the first place. Tax holidays can facilitate income shifting from non-tax-exempt enterprises to tax-exempt companies through transfer pricing of inter-company transactions. They reduce the appeal of debt financing of capital investment by removing the benefits of interest deductibility. This funding bias is accentuated if dividends of tax-exempt firms are also exempt from personal income tax. Tax exemptions tend to benefit investments with a short-term time horizon. Longer-term projects that generate profits beyond the tax holiday period do not benefit, unless firms are permitted to accrue and defer asset depreciation deductions beyond the tax holiday period. Finally, tax exemptions do not benefit investors from many OECD countries that tax income on a global basis, unless a 'tax sparing' agreement is in place.

The weak performance of some programmes may also be due to weak government bodies established to develop and operate zones, and to regulate free zone activity. This is likely to be especially true where regulatory authorities lack the basic power, autonomy and funding to function effectively. Some lack control over their budgets and have restrictive civil service limitations on remuneration and employment conditions. With the entry of the private sector into zone development, most countries have either set up specialized public sector free zone development and management agencies, or increasingly have divested the physical project development function to the private sector, and transformed their free zone authorities into purely regulatory and promotional bodies. Many free zone authorities are becoming more user-responsive by reorganizing themselves as corporate entities (to get out of civil service limitations) and have substantial private sector participation at the Board of Directors level. An example in Asia is Thailand's Industrial Estate Authority, but this approach is more commonly found among the industrial free zone programmes in Latin America (notably, Costa Rica and the Dominican Republic).

International experience has shown that countries embarking on private free zone development find it difficult to reconcile the divergent functions of zone management, regulation and investment promotion. In many free zone sponsoring countries, conflicts of interest have arisen when regulatory bodies are also engaged in zone development activity, especially when existing public zones would directly compete against new private zones. Opportunities for perceived and actual conflict of interest are multiplied when the entity charged with guiding and monitoring free zone performance is simultaneously one of the free zone operators being monitored.

Source: Rao (1999).

FDI POLICIES AND PROMOTION IN AFRICA

FDI Policies

Background and 'image'

The policy framework for FDI has clearly improved in much of Africa. Many countries now have 'liberal' or 'relatively liberal' regimes towards foreign investors. Most have concluded bilateral treaties to protect and promote FDI. Some are starting to conclude double taxation treaties: for instance, Uganda signed four in 1997 alone. The majority have signed multilateral agreements such as the convention establishing MIGA and ICSID. In general, therefore, FDI regimes in most of Africa are in line with those of other developing countries.

At the same time, 'most countries are failing to attract sufficient savings and investment. The main reason is the absence of one or more of the essential conditions for attracting investment: political stability, good governance, macroeconomic reform and stability, free trade and open foreign exchange systems, investment deregulation, and (for large investors) sufficient market size … In addition, there is the problem of perception' (CBI, 1999, p. 3). Many of these elements fall under the heading of policy (that is, under the control of governments), though some do not. This section deals with policy factors, particularly FDI policy in the narrow sense.

To start with, the CBI report is correct in noting the 'perception problem': SSA has a poor image in the international investment community. As noted in Chapter 2, the region is seen as an undifferentiated area of instability, poverty and stagnation. This may be understandable as far as investors with low exposure to Africa (say, from East Asia) are concerned. However, even investors from countries with long historic links with Africa - from Europe - tend to invest less in researching investment opportunities there than in Asia or Latin America. Risk ratings of many African countries tend to be high, the highest in the world apart from such obvious exceptions like Iran or Iraq. The World Bank's Country Policy and Institutional Assessment for Africa, a weighted sum of 20 elements as rated by the Bank's country economists, shows some recent improvement for Africa but also rates it lowest in the developing world. The *International Country Risk Guide Index*, which measures political risk and is based on views expressed by banks, MNCs and institutional investors, has a more mixed picture. The overall index for the region improves after 1991. While its index on 'rule of law' ranks SSA about the same as South Asia and Latin America (below East Asia), its index of 'corruption' ranks the region poorly.

Image problems apart, economic management is also important. It is, in fact, heartening to note that the African countries that have improved economic management have attracted more FDI. While this is difficult to establish rigorously, Pigato (1999) provides an interesting finding. She identifies the *16 best African FDI performers* in the late 1980s and mid 1990s[2] and notes some common characteristics:

- All the 'best performers' have reformed their economies in the past 10 years. They have liberalized trade, production and marketing significantly, and introduced market-based exchange rates (though the process has been varied and sometimes reversed).
- All have enjoyed higher real per capita GDP growth than before.
- The ratio of gross private domestic investment has increased significantly in all these countries (though it remains negative in Namibia and Zambia). So has gross private investment in GDP. This indicates that growth is supported by a build-up of productive capacity rather than just better capacity utilization.
- The 'best performers' received twice as much aid relative to GDP as the region as a whole, though there is no particular pattern in the amount of aid received or the share of ODA.
- Privatization has played a major role in attracting FDI, particularly in South Africa, Côte d'Ivoire, Ghana, Lesotho, Tanzania, Uganda and Zambia.
- Most of these countries have abundant natural resources and attract large FDI inflows into exploiting these resources.

This suggests that general policy reform is making countries more attractive to FDI, both directly and indirectly. Apart from the obvious draw of better macroeconomic management, liberalization is helping in two ways: privatization and improved conditions for resource-based investments. The most important indirect benefits for FDI have been improved growth performance and aid inflows.

FDI policies

Coming to FDI policies narrowly defined, we can draw some conclusions from the available information on leading African countries.[3] While this does not permit a detailed evaluation of the *effectiveness* of policies and their *implementation*, it provides a useful starting point for comparison within the region and externally.

There is considerable variation in FDI *entry procedures and requirements* across African countries. While some countries, like Ghana or Tanzania, have removed most bureaucratic impediments to rapid entry without onerous conditions, in many countries, entry procedures remain sub-optimal by international standards. CBI countries 'have agreed to simplify and codify all regulatory provisions into a single published document that would be widely available, and to establish one-stop centres that will process all applications within 45-60 days and grant automatic approval in the absence of objections at the end of that period' (CBI, 1999, p. 6). Despite this, implementation is lagging in several countries (Table A.4 gives some comparative data). There are instances of unnecessary duplication of approval processes or of the application of (vague and obsolete) economic criteria. Special sectors like tourism, petroleum and minerals are often placed under special approval regimes. Some governments still put (implicit) pressures on investors to have joint ventures with local enterprises. Take some examples.

In *Botswana*, a prospective manufacturing investor has to obtain both an investment licence and approvals from the land board and district councils. The investment has to satisfy criteria on adequacy of capital, technical skills, and the interests of the economy. Incentives can be granted only to registered companies, which are only allowed one application per 12-month period. MNCs are not allowed in activities kept for SMEs, while in *Cameroon* investment in SMEs must have 35 per cent local equity. In the *Republic of Congo*, investors from outside the Central African Customs and Economic Union (UDEAC) region have to deposit 1 per cent of invested capital.

In *Gambia*, investors have to go through several government departments to get their applications approved. Tourism investors for instance have to go through the State Department for Tourism and Culture, the State Department

Table A.4 Average processing time for FDI approvals in selected countries

Africa	
Ghana	No approval for non-mining/petroleum FDI
Tanzania	Under 1 week
Zimbabwe	2–8 weeks
Mozambique	Up to 90 days
Mauritius	9–30 weeks
Asia	
Singapore	1 day to 3 weeks
Sri Lanka	4 weeks
Thailand	4–5 weeks
Indonesia	5–6 weeks
Taiwan	4–8 weeks
Malaysia	8–12 weeks

Source: Lall, et al. (1998).

for Trade, Industry and Employment, the State Department for Finance and Economic Affairs, the immigration department, the Central Revenue Department and the Attorney General's Chambers to get the necessary approvals.

In *Kenya*, a large number of specific licences are needed before the investor can set up. Some of these, like land title transfer and registration, can take from 6 months to 8 years (TSG, 1998). Special authority is needed for oil and mineral prospecting. The Kenyan government also places pressure on investors to increase Kenyan ownership shares. While *Ghana* does not require investment approval, land titles can take up to two years to obtain. Investors regard the policy climate as unconducive to investment, partly due to cumbersome and corrupt customs procedures.

Mozambique reserves several activities for the public sector and encourages local equity participation, even in EPZs. *Nigeria* requires approval from both the Ministry of Internal Affairs and the Ministry of Finance for new investment; applications have to provide biographical information to the Industrial Development Coordination Committee. Here too utilities are not open to FDI, and procedures are cumbersome and bureaucratic. In *Uganda*, potential investors have to establish that the project generates economic benefits like foreign exchange, employment, use of local raw materials, skills or technology transfer. *Zambia* requires a variety of different approvals by different agencies. In *Zimbabwe*, the approval process is cumbersome and slow.

In general, company registration procedures in many countries are inefficient because of ill-equipped offices and underinvestment in staff and technology (CBI, 1999, pp. 20–21). This is confirmed by the evidence on our sample countries in previous chapters. National registries are not linked to each other, making it impossible for a foreign investor registering in one country to automatically open offices in another. Standardized registration systems and procedures 'would also facilitate trade as buyers and sellers will be able to access publicly disclosed information on potential corporate suppliers and customers across borders'.

The *granting of investment incentives* is similarly variable, with some countries still operating on a discretionary, case-by-case basis that gives rise to delays and non-transparent procedures. *Kenya* is a good case in point, and may be associated with the generally negative image the regime has acquired in terms of corruption and rent-seeking. In *Angola*, the situation with respect to rent-seeking behaviour is even worse. However, in many other countries, the process has become much more transparent and automatic; there is also considerable effort under way to make procedures more so with new investment codes.

The *nature of investment incentives* is also variable, and sometimes lagging behind best practice. Most countries conform to international norms of granting tax holidays for 5–10 years; only a few, like *Ghana*, have moved to the system of abolishing tax holidays in favour of low general tax rates. Most countries grant depreciation allowances on a straight-line basis, with differing rates for different items of capital. Relatively few, like *South Africa*, allow accelerated depreciation, though this appears to be the preferred tool in most modern tax regimes. The South African government grants several industry-specific incentives (for example, for textiles and automobiles) and activities (innovation, SMEs); this opens the door for confusion and discretion unless handled very efficiently. *Kenya* also has industry specific incentives. The Kenyan tax regime does not recognize R&D expenditures as legitimate tax deductible expenses.

Tax systems are still far from ideal. While many countries are bringing tax rates in line with international norms, the desirable degree of rationalization and harmonization still has not been achieved (CBI, 1999, p. 8). Double taxation treaties have to be finalized by many countries. The treatment of such important items as R&D, training and new equipment purchase is out of line with current international standards. Assessment and collection procedures are lagging. Customs procedures still constitute major transaction costs. Government officials in the relevant ministries have yet to learn to be responsive, efficient, honest and 'user friendly'.

Loss carry-forward provisions vary, with some countries allowing 3–5 years and others (like Mauritius) giving indefinite periods. *Withholding taxes* on royalties, fees, interest payments and dividends are similarly variable by country. Some, like *South Africa* and *Zimbabwe* (in EPZs, do not impose such taxes, while in others they are high (*Kenya* imposes 20 per cent on royalties) and can vary by origin of investor (for example, *Uganda* and *Zambia*). *Royalty and technical fee limits* have been removed in most countries, but some, like *Nigeria*, still impose limits on such fees.

Work permit regulations are highly variable, with many countries still making it difficult and cumbersome to obtain expatriate permits quickly and efficiently (on Kenya and Tanzania see TSG, 1998, 1999). The situation contrasts sharply with countries like Singapore, where the government recognizes local skill gaps and seeks to compensate by allowing MNCs relatively easy access to international markets for skilled workers.

Legal and judicial systems are inadequate in many African countries. 'Changes are needed not only because of outdated laws and the rationale for harmonisation but also because courts are not functioning properly ... Too often, the excessive time needed to process recovery action through the courts and the unpredictable outcome of what should be a straightforward legal process to recover debt have led to a lack of confidence in the judicial system' (CBI, 1999, p. 8). The CBI report goes on to note that reform is needed in the following: *corporate law, contract law, bankruptcy, labour law and property rights*. Moreover, 'there is widespread recognition that redrafting of legislation will not of itself introduce the requisite changes. Judicial reforms are essential to ensure that the laws are applied properly. Only then will investors begin to acquire greater confidence that there is legal support for claims to payments and for property rights' (ibid.). Thus, it becomes vital for African countries to update and harmonize the relevant laws and improve the judicial systems.

In general, while FDI regimes are improving in Africa, and generally appear - on paper - to be in line with regimes elsewhere, *serious deficiencies remain*. These are partly in the regimes themselves, and partly in the general investment climate, the implementation of policies and the regional image. Small and fragmented markets in Africa combined with the slow pace of regional integration add to the problems - the whole of SSA, excluding South Africa, is in economic terms about as large as Thailand. The above summary does not go into the various transaction costs faced by investors in each country, but the Tanzania Investor Roadmap described in Chapter 4 above illustrates these in a country that has a fairly liberal regime by regional standards.

There remain policy obstacles in the two main areas of FDI inflow relevant for the region – *privatization* and *natural resource exploration and extraction*. Few privatization programmes in Africa can be considered successful. Many have been undertaken reluctantly and many have been badly managed. As CBI (1999, pp. 13–14) notes,

> In particular, there are concerns about insufficient public information and transparency. The recent trend for major utilities to enter the privatization process has only highlighted these issues, with reports from several countries of behind the scenes manoeuvring (involving bribes to give preferential treatment to particular investors) in an attempt to bypass official procedures which were designed to ensure a level playing field. Recently in Uganda, a well publicised example of this led Parliament to suspend the privatization program there.

Needless to say, it is imperative for African governments to conduct privatization programmes in a transparent, professional and business-like manner if this vital source of FDI is to be fully and economically exploited.

A related issue is the promotion of *private sector participation in infrastructure* projects in Africa. The region lags behind most NIEs in such participation because of official reluctance and lags in fixing appropriate tariffs and setting up necessary regulatory rules and institutions. In their absence, investors are unwilling to undertake the massive investments entailed. While pure political risks have been met by joining MIGA and other schemes, the economic risks remain large.

As far as *resource-based FDI* is concerned, the available information does not allow us to assess how well existing legal, administrative and economic provisions in the region match up to international best practice. It is vital to carry out such an assessment to establish how more FDI could be attracted on terms and conditions beneficial to host economies. As with other reforms, however, such large and long-term investments require *credibility*. The government has to assure potential investors of its stability and ability to deliver on its promises of the life of the project.

Investment Promotion in Africa

Introduction: Investment Promotion Agencies (IPAs)

It is increasingly recognized that effective FDI promotion greatly enhances the flow and quality of investment into a country. International investors have a great deal of information on investment possibilities, but they do not have perfect information; in addition, their interpretation of the information they have can be changed by a better presentation of information. Most importantly, a potential host economy can significantly alter its attractiveness by improving its facilitation and coordinating its critical 'endowments' with the needs of investors. This sub-section provides a survey of promotion practices and agencies (IPAs) in the developing world.[4]

There are a wide range of institutional structures for investment promotion in different countries, reflecting differences in governmental systems, investment priorities, resource availability, and private sector role and capabilities. In general, IPAs can be grouped into the following categories:

- *Government organizations* This is the most common but not the most effective organizational form for investment promotion activities. They are usually staffed by civil servants seconded from line ministries, and operate as a direct organ of government. Institutionally, these organizations may be contained as a department within a line ministry (usually the industry ministry); may be an authority reporting directly to a line ministry; or may be organized directly under the office of the president or Prime Minister. As government organizations, these agencies are often primarily responsible for screening and approving investments, and the promotion function may be conducted as a secondary responsibility. Overseas marketing is typically conducted through the country's embassies or consulates.

- *Quasi-governmental organizations* Quasi-governmental or 'mixed' agencies are typically autonomous in operation, and operate outside civil service guidelines and salary structures. As a result, salary levels are usually higher than civil service scales, enabling the competitive requirement of staff members from the private sector. As autonomous organizations, overseas marketing is usually conducted through independent offices. These agencies typically have their own board of directors, often with private sector membership. There are direct linkages with government, usually in the form of a reporting relationship with a government ministry and through direct government funding.
- *Private organizations* While still uncommon, investment promotion and investment approval activities have been carried out by corporations formed under the private sector companies law. Sometimes, these are projects of business or exporters' chambers of commerce, or independent foundations. Private organizations generally do not receive any government funding, although many have senior government representatives on their board of directors.

There are *advantages and disadvantages* to each of these organizational types. Purely government organizations are usually those initially set up to screen and approve investments, and have a regulatory rather than promotional focus. In practice, however, these are entirely different functions, requiring different skills and the flexibility to respond quickly to investors' needs. These capabilities are found more commonly in the private sector than in government organizations, and civil service salaries are typically inadequate to attract personnel with such abilities. The resulting lack of appropriate personnel and autonomy lessens the effectiveness of this approach.

Quasi-government organizations offset many of these weaknesses by offering competitive salaries and greater autonomy. These attributes, and the presence of senior level private sector representatives on the board of directors, give these institutions the skills and flexibility for effective promotion. The establishment of overseas marketing offices are generally more effective than operating through embassies, because they are staffed with business-oriented personnel with specialized marketing skills.

Wholly private investment promotion organizations have all these advantages, usually with the added benefits of being more able to offer competitive salaries, hire the most qualified people, and operate in a flexible bureaucracy-free environment. Substantial funding can be accessed through direct contributions from the private sector - usually private utilities services companies - and international donors. In some cases, however, the effectiveness of these organizations is compromised by the lack of adequate ties and support from government bodies. By contrast, quasi-government agencies can often be very effective in assisting investors with the acquisition of needed permits and licences because of their close ties to government. Moreover, the long-term financing of wholly private agencies is often difficult to secure on a sustainable basis.

In addition to variations in structure, investment promotion agencies vary in function (Wells and Wint, 1990). Primary functions include:

- *Investment approval and regulation* (for example, screening and approving investments; monitoring compliance; compiling statistics on investment impact);
- *Investment facilitation* (for example, trouble shooting problems of investors; assisting in securing of all secondary licences and permits);
- *Research and development* (for example, investment policy impact analyses, policy development and advocacy, publications);
- *Investment promotion* (image building, investor services and investment generation).

The relative emphasis placed on each of these functions varies considerably from agency to agency. A useful typology for analysing the investment approval, screening and regulation function is the following:[5]

- *Non-Coordinated Frameworks* Under this structure the investment approvals process is neither centralized nor coordinated by any one agency. Potential investors must deal with a large number of national and local government bodies to receive an operating licence or register their business. Once approved, these investments are subject to the regulatory requirements of a number of different agencies and departments. As a result, investment approvals can take anywhere from several months to even years. Unfortunately this is the most common investment regulatory structure found in developing countries.
- *Single Ministry Model* Under this approach, the primary investment approvals process is coordinated by one ministry that coordinates other licensing requirements. This has been successfully employed in some countries such as Mexico where there is a single dominant economic ministry. In most other cases, this approach has been unsuccessful mainly because of the delays and bureaucracy resulting from having to deal with multiple government bodies, and the lack of power of any single line ministry.
- *Inter-Ministerial Committees* These committees are usually comprised

of representatives of relevant technical ministries as well as the Central Bank, Customs, and, in many cases, the President's or Prime Minister's office. While often an improvement over the uncoordinated structure, in that approvals may be centralized in the one committee, the large number of participating ministries and agencies tends to slow the decision-making process. Because these committees are generally comprised of high-level officials unable to meet frequently, investments have a tendency to languish under this model. In addition, officials sometimes lack the knowledge base or interest to make effective contributions to the committee. The approval process often becomes one of compromise among agencies with conflicting interests. As a result, approvals are unlikely to be automatic and criteria may vary from one case to another, depending upon which ministries decide to take an active interest.

- *One-Stop Facilitator Frameworks* This is an increasingly common regulatory structure, largely as a result of the failure of attempts to set up true one-stop shops. Under this structure, a potential investor interacts with only one agency that actively facilitates and coordinates obtaining all necessary approvals. The agency does not have the authority to grant all other licences and permits needed to establish an investment and make it operational. In this sense, it basically accepts and allows the flaws in the investment approval process to persist, and processing of potential investments remains cumbersome and lengthy as each relevant agency often conducts its own analysis. From the perspective of the investor, the facilitator agency may merely appear as yet another layer of bureaucracy. Furthermore, its operations may be hindered by other agencies unwilling to give up their approval authority. While this structure is generally more effective than the two previous frameworks discussed, it operates far below the level of service provided by true one-stop shops.
- *One-Stop Shops* True one-stop shops, with the power and autonomy to screen and approve investments unilaterally are relatively rare. When the authority designated to these centres is recognized by all other government agencies, they can be extremely effective in streamlining the investment approval process. The investment process is significantly simplified through a mechanism that triggers automatic granting of all secondary permits, licences, and compliance as soon as the investment is approved by the one-stop centre. But international experience indicates that creation of a true one-stop approval centre is the most difficult to implement successfully, except in countries where investment approval procedures themselves are relatively streamlined.

In addition, investment agencies use different techniques to discharge their core investment promotion function. As summarized in Table A.5, these are generally organized into:

- *Image building,* which uses advertising, media relations and other techniques to create or change the image of the investment location;
- *Investment generation*, which employs a variety of more proactive techniques to generate inward investments;
- *Investor services*, which are comprised of a whole host of activities, designed to rapidly facilitate and realize an investment commitment, and retain and facilitate the expansion of existing investors.

No one model has been uniformly successful (or unsuccessful). Institutional effectiveness is linked to the following factors:

1. Degree of managerial and financial flexibility;
2. Flexibility in hiring, compensating and firing staff without public sector restrictions;
3. An independent board with direct private sector participation;
4. High level of power and autonomy in decision making;
5. Simplified procedures and lack of bureaucracy.

Table A.5 Types of investment promotion activities

Category	Objective	Delivery method
Image building	Create or change an image about a location as an investment site	Public relations General advertising Informational seminars General outbound trade missions Participation in trade shows/conferences
Investment generation	Directly attract new investment	Direct mail campaigns Telemarketing Firm-specific direct selling Targeted advertising Participation in trade shows/conferences
Investor services	Facilitate and realize new investment, and retain existing investors	Arranging investors' site visits Identifying local business partners, sites Assisting in proposal preparation/submission Follow-up and aftercare services

The effectiveness of an investment agency typically has as much to do with its *implementation* as with its structure. One important factor for success is the full commitment and backing from those at the highest level of the government. Without such support, other agencies are likely to push strongly to retain their discretionary powers. One way to assure high-level support has been to place the agency directly under the authority of the office of the head of state, so that its chief executive officer can directly report bureaucratic constraints to the one office that can ensure government-wide cooperation. Another innovation used by the Singapore Economic Development Board is to have a high-powered International Advisory Council to guide FDI strategy. This is largely constituted of the CEOs of leading MNCs, and allows the IPA to have independent business advice to supplement guidance given by the government. This is seen as vital to maintaining the 'business friendly' approach of the IPA.

The traditional government organizational model is found mostly in the older Asian NIEs (the most prominent example is the Industrial Development and Investment Center in Taiwan) and India and Pakistan, both of whom have investment boards with a predominantly regulatory rather than promotional focus. Other countries, such as Thailand, have a hybrid model: the Board of Investment in Thailand is directly under the Prime Minister's Office, but has an independent board of directors with private sector representation. The most common approach is the quasi-governmental structure, with successful models exemplified by the Singapore Economic Development Board, arguably the most successful investment promotion agency in the world; the Malaysian Industrial Development Authority; and the Irish Development Authority. Purely private-sector Investment Promotion Agencies (IPAs) are common in Latin America, with notable examples in Costa Rica and the Dominican Republic. In these countries, faced with the continuing failure of public sector IPAs, governments allowed private foundations to be set up to act as official promotion agencies for the countries. But it is important to note that in most cases where private IPAs have been established, they rarely also undertake the investment regulation and incentives provision function.

In undertaking the investment regulation function, most agencies are facilitators in the sense that, in addition to providing the initial investment approval, they coordinate and facilitate the provision of secondary permits and licences to ensure quick implementation of the approved product. It is important to note that in practice *true one-stop shops are very rare, and are arguably found only in Ireland and Singapore.* In the latter's case, the provision of the initial licence automatically 'triggers' issuance of all secondary permits. In other cases, the one-stop shop is physically located in the IPA, staffed with representatives of various government bodies; the effectiveness of these arrangements has been mixed.

Another significant difference is the extent to which the private sector is formally represented in the IPA. On the one extreme are the wholly private boards in Latin American IPAs; at the other are the purely public sector models in Indonesia, the Philippines, India, and Pakistan, all of which have quite ineffective IPAs. The presence of a mixed Board has had a positive impact on the ethos and performance of the agency, as exemplified by the success of IPAs such as the EDB, Thailand BOI and the Mauritian MEDIA. Private sector support and commitment is extremely important especially since investment promotion does not have a constituency of support per se, unlike export promotion which directly benefits exporters.

But most important of all is the *organization and effectiveness of the investment promotion function*. The most effective promoters are generally the ones that have the most streamlined investment regulation function, and are closest to the private sector. IPAs in Costa Rica and the Dominican Republic receive close to one hundred enquiries a month, mostly generated by proactive promotion efforts. In Sri Lanka over 1990–95, 12.7 per cent of total annual average number of leads generated resulted in projects implemented, in line with international standards.

The African experience

Most African countries now have IPAs. In terms of the above classification, most are *government agencies operating non-coordinated or one-stop facilitator frameworks*. The available evidence suggests that their effectiveness is low: the promotion effort is weak and diffuse, well below 'best practice' levels achieved in East Asia or Latin America. Box A.2 illustrates, with the example of Zimbabwe Investment Centre (ZIC), the problems of many African IPAs.

BOX A.2 FDI PROMOTION BY ZIMBABWE INVESTMENT CENTRE (ZIC)

A recent analysis of export competitiveness in Zimbabwe pointed to two types of deficiencies in FDI promotion by ZIC.

First, *a lack of funds* has constrained the effectiveness of investment promotion efforts. ZIC's total budget increased slightly from US$1.1 million to US$1.2 million between 1994 and 1996. About 35 per cent of this ($420 000) is for investment promotion, a fairly low sum in the context of modern promotion needs. For instance, the Singapore Economic Development Board has an annual budget of $34.2 million and the Malaysian Industrial Development Authority of $11 million. The Mauritius Export

Development and Investment Authority has an annual budget of $3.1 million. The lack of funds hampers Zimbabwe's investment promotion effectiveness in several ways. It limits ZIC's ability to offer competitive salaries to attract the best personnel and curtails overseas advertising and other promotion campaigns. It limits the pre-approval services that can be offered to investors (such as airport-to-airport service). It prevents it from establishing an overseas presence to actively network with potential investors. And it hinders intelligence gathering about overseas investors.

Second, there are *shortcomings in the design of the foreign investment promotion strategy* that have reduced its impact.

- ZIC functions on a short planning cycle with activities closely linked to the annual budgets rather than to a long-term national foreign investment promotion plan. International experience suggests that a one-year planning cycle is inadequate for formulating and implementing a strategic programme, particularly to attract FDI in new industrial and service activities.
- The country's limited financial and manpower resources were spread too thinly for the strategy to have much impact because of an emphasis on too many sectors (in early 1997, the EPZA had 11 target sectors covering much of manufacturing) rather than a few target sectors. There were wasted attempts to try to develop industrial sectors where the country had no obvious short or medium-term comparative advantage (for example, data processing).
- There was insufficient focus on key investor markets. For instance, South Africa could be a major target for promotion. Zimbabwe has cheaper and better-educated labour than South Africa as well as a relatively low crime environment. At the same time, South Africa offers a large dynamic market for low-cost, high-quality goods manufactured in Zimbabwe and transport costs are low between the two economies. Zimbabwe thus seems an obvious production location for South African investors, but ZIC does not target South African investors by special investment promotion activities, incentives and building an EPZ infrastructure oriented to South Africa.
- More generally, Zimbabwe does not have a network of independent investment promotion offices, staffed by marketing professionals, to mount an effective image

building and investment generation campaign. Instead, the country relies on poorly trained commercial attaches to provide information about markets and to act as the point of contact with investors.

- ZIC lacks regular monitoring (along with appropriate performance indicators) of its activities. It did not keep regular track of FDI inflows by industrial branch and country of origin, and used inaccurate FDI approval statistics for publicity purposes.
- There was a passive approach to dealing with potential 'high profile' investors in target sectors and inadequate emphasis on developing long-term relationships with them to induce sustained inward investment. This may stem from an absence of detailed and up-to-date overseas intelligence about potential investors in particular target activities, and weak capabilities to cultivate them on a long-term basis. ZIC lacked a strong and sustained presence in key markets and depended too heavily on the ad hoc efforts of one or two energetic officials in embassies and infrequent outbound missions.

Source: Lall et al. (1998).

The CBI report notes many of the deficiencies of African FDI promotion efforts. It notes that African countries lack a focused campaign to attract investors in areas or from sources of high potential. The promotion effort is not, in other words, based on any analysis of national competitive advantages or 'selling points'. Nor is it geared to any national efforts to improve location determinants, so that new areas of competitive advantage can be developed. The promotion agency tends to be located at a level of government that gives it insufficient authority to mount effective strategy or coordination. It is generally unable to offer true one-stop facilitation. Since IPAs lack the authority to overcome layers of bureaucracy facing investors, transaction costs (including those of corruption) tend to be higher than in many countries in Latin America or Asia.

The promotion effort tends not to have sufficient private sector participation or representation, beyond the presence of private entrepreneurs on the occasional foreign mission. The promotion agencies do not do enough 'homework' on prospective investors to be able to target and attract promising firms. They have not been successful in changing the poor image of the region or of individual countries in the investment community at large. The information they provide to prospective investors does not match that offered by leading IPAs in Southeast Asia. Box A.3 describes the information routinely provided on local conditions by the Thai Board of Investment.

BOX A.3 INFORMATION PROVIDED BY THE THAI BOARD OF INVESTMENT

A major problem facing potential foreign investors is how to obtain reliable data on the costs of doing business in a particular production location. Foreign investors typically solicit such data from national investment promotion agencies (IPAs) in the relevant country but few IPAs appear to maintain up-to-date databases on the costs of doing business. Those that do, tend to have data on a limited range of variables of a rather general nature. The Thai Board of Investment (BOI) is an exception. It surveys enterprises annually to collect information on a large number of detailed factor and transactions costs in Thailand. This data is readily available to potential investors via a web site, by fax or email, at overseas embassies and at investment conferences. The Thai BOI provides data on several aspects of the business costs on a regular basis:

- Indicative company establishment (support staff wages, legal expenses, furnishing costs, car purchase, rental deposit and utilities deposit) and monthly running costs (including wages, rents, telecommunications, transport, official entertainment);
- Labour costs by several categories of skills and locations, and major labour regulations (starting rates for new graduates, daily employee wages, overtime regulations, severance payment entitlements);
- Tax rates (corporate income tax, personal income tax, tax on bank deposits, VAT, excise tax, structure of import tariffs) and double taxation agreements;
- Fuel costs and air, sea, rail and road freight rates;
- Communications costs (telephone, mobile phones, international voice graded leased circuit, fax machines, telex machines);
- Utility costs (water and electricity rates for regional areas);
- Industrial estates and facilities (location from Bangkok, available land, costs of utilities and fees, contact address);

- Indicative expatriate living costs in Bangkok (food, drinks/tobacco, clothing, recreation, medical, education, transport, domestic help, and household utilities).

Source: Thai Board of Investment.

The CBI also notes the lack of such services to investors as airport arrival arrangements, information on hotels and services, quality transportation services and adequate security in high-risk areas. Local businessmen - as sources of information, potential partners, suppliers or buyers - are not adequately equipped to deal with modern business needs. Their financial, managerial, marketing, technological and other capabilities are often not up to the demands of international investors, and the IPAs do little to help them develop these capabilities. IPAs also do not provide sufficient information on local business counterparts.

In addition, national efforts by different African countries are *not coordinated* with each other, though there is a strong case for small economies and agencies to increase such coordination (CBI, 1999). Given the general image problem in the region, countries would benefit by cooperating in FDI promotion. This would involve consolidating investment codes and other regulatory provisions across countries and pooling advertising efforts. If accompanied by effective lowering of trade barriers, this would also exploit the larger market size available, overcoming one of the major handicaps of investing in Africa. A harmonization of tax rates and regulations, along with customs rules and procedures, would significantly lower transaction costs for investors.

POLICY IMPLICATIONS

The setting for attracting international direct investment is changing, in terms both of the economic determinants for competitive production and of the policy and promotion regime within which investment occurs. The best framework for attracting FDI is one that meets both sets of needs. The economic factors for attracting FDI (taking macroeconomic conditions for granted) are the possession of exploitable natural resources, large and dynamic markets, efficient infrastructure and a competitive base of productive factors - skills, technology, suppliers and support institutions.

That the policy regime has to be welcoming to FDI goes without saying. But being 'welcoming' does not mean having lots of fiscal incentives. It means being stable, transparent, honest and fair, with no discrimination by origin of investor and low tax rates set in an open trade regime. This has to be supported by an efficient judicial and arbitration system, low entry and business transaction costs and well functioning labour and financial markets that can match those in competing FDI destinations. Successful FDI attraction now also requires proactive promotion and facilitation. Even mature industrial countries like Britain, with highly developed markets and institutions, find it helpful to undertake such promotion and facilitation where large discrete investments are concerned (Box A.4). While advanced countries tend to offer large up-front grants for such investments, developing countries tend to offer tax or other incentives; however, incentives are not the decisive long-term factor. The critical factors have to do with the competitive base of the site: and with many alternative sites available, an MNC has to be wooed by ensuring that its factor needs are fully met, its search and location costs are minimized and it is made to 'feel welcome'.

BOX A.4 THE UK's APPROACH TO ATTRACTING SIEMENS

An example from the UK's recent experience highlights the value of cultivating foreign investors and the importance of close coordination between government investment promotion agencies. The UK foreign investment promotion system is decentralized - it consists of a central body (the 'Invest in Britain Bureau') that is responsible for overall promotion, and several regional bodies that undertake local investment facilitation.

Effective market research by the Invest in Britain Bureau revealed that Siemens, a giant German electrical and electronics MNC, was considering where to locate its new semiconductor fabrication plant in 1995. Supported by central government, a local partnership led by the Northern Development Company was created to persuade Siemens to invest in the north east of England rather than in other production locations (including Austria and Ireland). A package was rapidly put together with the following elements:

- The Tyne and Wear Development Company identified suitable land;
- English Partnerships developed that land into a low vibration site, with access to essential infrastructure of the type needed for semiconductor manufacture;
- Tyneside TEC and Employment Services provided tailored

recruitment and training support to meet Siemens' requirements for skilled labour;

- Representatives of the region's universities visited Siemens in Germany to demonstrate the strength of the region's infrastructure and its ability to supply high quality graduate technicians and engineers;
- Northern Tyneside Council and the Government's Office for the North-East worked together to offer a rapid response to planning application and Enterprise Zone issues;
- The Department of Trade and Industry, North Tyneside City Challenge and North Tyneside Council put together financial support worth over £30 million.

The package - along with the warm welcome offered to Siemens by the UK Government centrally, good market research, ample supplies of educated, productive manpower, high quality infrastructure and a large local market - was successful. In August 1995, Siemens announced its intention to locate the £1.1 billion facility in North Tyneside, creating up to 1500 new jobs.

Source: UK Cabinet Office (1996).

Some countries have employed proactive targeting very successfully. Singapore is the best example (Ireland is its counterpart in Europe) in the developing world. A more recent case is Costa Rica, which attracted Intel's first semiconductor plant in Latin America in the teeth of competition from larger, more developed neighbours and so transformed its economic structure (Box A.5).

BOX A.5 FDI IN THE CARIBBEAN BASIN: FROM LOW- WAGE ASSEMBLY TO HIGH-TECH CLUSTERS

The main form of international economic activity in the Caribbean Basin historically was the export of natural resources. This started to change in the 1980s, when US MNCs attempted to face foreign (particularly Asian) competition in their home market by spreading their production networks to the Caribbean Basin. As a result, the share of natural resources in exports to North America declined from 84 per cent in 1980 to 37 per cent in 1994, while the share of manufactures rose from 13 to 59 per cent. However, these manufacturing operations consisted mainly of simple assembly of imported components, concentrated in export processing zones isolated from the domestic economy. Much of the FDI in countries like Costa Rica, Jamaica and the Dominican Republic, major recipients of export-oriented FDI, concentrated on garments. MNCs were attracted by low labour costs and fiscal incentives; they used virtually no local physical inputs. This led to an enclave of MNC activity, with few beneficial spillovers in terms of linkages, and technology and skills transfers to local companies of the workforce.

Costa Rica broke this mould in 1997 by attracting a $500 million facility from Intel for manufacturing and testing semiconductors. How did Costa Rica succeed in beating competition from such countries as Brazil, Chile and Mexico for this investment? One reason was a clear definition by the Costa Rican government of microelectronics as a strategic area, followed by an aggressive policy of targeted incentives designed to meet the competitive needs of this company. The government also promised to provide cheap energy to the plant, to improve the necessary physical infrastructure, to give tax incentives and implement training programmes specifically designed for the needs of the company. This represented a radical change from the horizontal incentives previously used; these did not discriminate between sectors and companies, and so treated all FDI as equal in terms of the country's technology and skill needs.

The Intel investment promises much. Exports are projected to reach $3 billion by 2000 and microprocessor exports in 1998 exceeded exports of traditional products such as bananas and coffee. Investment by Intel's suppliers is expected. Some 40 firms are expected to invest an additional $500 million, and start a new high-tech cluster with important spillover effects. Recent policy announcements by the Dominican Republic indicate a similar shift of FDI strategy from horizontal to targeted promotion: its officials have recently unveiled plans to attract investment into computer and telecommunications-based industries. The main instruments to be adopted include training programmes geared to the needs of telecommunication-intensive activities such as call centres and computer-based data handling industries. Judging by Costa Rica's experience with Intel, a more aggressive strategy of targeting key global players in these industries may be a necessary complement to these measures.

Source: UNCTAD (1999a).

In sum, the economic and policy elements of FDI attraction have to mesh together, otherwise the amount and quality of FDI is bound to be lower than its potential. Neither element will work unless the 'fundamentals' are right: political and economic stability, good macroeconomic management, a positive attitude to private enterprise and basic security and rule of law.

The Way Forward in SSA

No progress is, of course, possible on FDI attraction unless countries get their *political and economic 'fundamentals'* right. While some investors may be prepared to invest in highly risky and unstable environments, they will compensate by demanding correspondingly high rates of return, minimizing their long-term commitment and concentrating in exploiting static advantages. This is not the way to attract sustained inflows of FDI, to improve its quality, or maximize its development impact. What then is the way forward for Africa in this sphere? To highlight the points made here:

FDI policy

The *general policy framework* of FDI in Africa has improved greatly and is being further streamlined in many countries. However, it still suffers from deficiencies:

- There remain unnecessary barriers to foreign entry in some countries, with activities restricted to foreign companies or implicit pressures applied on investors to dilute ownership and control. Rules on long-term resource exploration and exploitation may be unclear and inhibiting in some cases. It is imperative to bring entry and other contractual rules in line with best practice, and to remove equity sharing rules or pressures. Registration procedures should be simplified and streamlined. It would be desirable over the medium term to link registration across countries to reduce costs to entrants.
- Apart from the formal entry rules, there are many entry regulations and registration requirements that raise transaction costs to foreign investors. Many of these can be simplified and rationalized without affecting their purpose. More importantly, their implementation can be greatly improved and accelerated, with corruption minimized and a far

more user-friendly approach. A necessary first step for each government is to conduct an 'investor roadmap' exercise to determine exactly where the costs and barriers arise, then to benchmark procedures against international standards. The next step is to develop a more modern system of regulation. This will require improving the quality of human capital involved in regulation and providing appropriate guidelines and incentives for effective delivery of services. Finally, the government must put in place a monitoring system to ensure that the new regulations and procedures are properly implemented, with feedback from the private sector.

- Privatization has not generally been efficiently conducted in SSA, with the result that foreign interest has been lower than it might have been. It is vital for governments to conduct privatization in a transparent, professional and business-like manner, providing a truly level playing field for foreign investors, and to make this fully known to potential investors. At the same time, governments must put in place adequate competition policy and regulatory institutions that can ensure the proper management and operation of privatized enterprises. This also applies to the participation of private investors in new infrastructure projects, where considerable care has to be taken to provide a regulatory framework. These are skill-intensive tasks, and governments need to develop specialized institutes and units with the requisite personnel to tackle these essential tasks as quickly as possible.
- Tax rates and incentives are variable across the region. While some countries, like Ghana, are moving towards modern systems of taxation (with low uniform rates and few or no tax holidays), others retain traditional systems with high rates, obsolete methods and considerable discretionary powers. Many countries do not grant tax exemption to such expenditures as training and R&D; this should be remedied. Tax administration is often inefficient and subject to corruption - this has to be addressed as a matter of priority. In terms of granting tax incentives, the available evidence does not suggest a 'race to the bottom' across the region. Nevertheless, there is a need to harmonize rates and incentives across the region (at least within major trading blocs). This would become imperative if the CBI suggestion of joint promotion is accepted, but it would be desirable even without this initiative to lower transaction costs and improve the region's image. Incentives may be retained if they are moderate and geared to development objectives. Their administration should be transparent and non-discretionary, and access to them rapid and honest.
- Rules governing the use of expatriate personnel need to be simplified and rationalized, and the time taken to grant approvals reduced.

- The legal and judicial system needs reform urgently. As far as FDI goes, the most pressing needs are in the areas of corporate law, contract law, bankruptcy, labour law and property rights. Foreign investors prefer international arbitration provisions, and governments should consider how best to accommodate this preference. Intellectual property legislation and implementation should be strengthened.
- Some of the most cumbersome and costly procedural impediments arise in import and export activity. Customs systems should be greatly improved, with the use of computerized systems and simplified processes that reduce inefficiency and corruption.

FDI promotion and facilitation

The effectiveness of FDI promotion in SSA is generally low. The promotion effort is weak and diffuse by international standards. Promotion agencies are underfunded and have insufficient private sector participation. Their information systems are underdeveloped, and their marketing is not focused on promising investors by area or activity. They do not provide proper one-stop facilities and often lack the authority to help investors cope with the myriad of ministries, departments and agencies involved in their investment activities. More important, they are not able to coordinate investor needs (in terms of productive factors or institutions) with the ability of the rest of the government to improve these factors or institutions. The policy needs are:

- Strengthen the funding and staffing of investment promotion agencies as necessary. Ensure that they are fully oriented to attraction and facilitation rather than regulation or registration.
- Raise their position in the government hierarchy to enable them to deliver effective facilitation and coordination services to investors.
- Encourage them to develop effective strategies for targeting and attracting promising investors by area and activity.
- Involve the private sector more directly in promotion activities. Over time, involve MNCs in such activities – existing investors are the best 'ambassadors' for investment promotion.
- Monitor the effectiveness of investment promotion by the use of standard benchmarks and compare agencies with those in Asia or Latin America.
- Strengthen contacts with and knowledge of local enterprise: their investment needs to be promoted just as much as FDI and they need to establish business relations with MNC affiliates.
- Coordinate investment promotion activities with counterparts in the region.

Economic measures

This chapter has argued that economic factors are probably a *bigger constraint to FDI in Africa than policy ones* (in the narrow sense). However good and efficient the policy framework, sustained growth and upgrading of FDI needs the improvement of infrastructure, skills, technological capabilities, supplier networks and support institutions. The need for continuous investment in these is rising apace - liberalization, rapid technological change and the intensifying competition for new FDI are making it more and more important to make the location competitive by world standards. In addition, it is vital to put in place open trade and exchange regimes, and strong competition policies to ensure that newly opened markets stay competitive.

The economic measures needed have been amply analysed in many other studies. What is essential is to focus on the links between capability and competitiveness building and attracting FDI. In turn, FDI can itself provide a significant input into capability building - once it is attracted and enters activities where skill and technology development are possible. The way to get into the 'virtuous cycle' where local capabilities are strong enough to attract high quality FDI that in turn feeds into further upgrading is to get the right policy framework into place, target the appropriate investors and ensure that their essential factor and institutional needs are met. The exact way in which this should be done is very context specific, and needs more detailed analysis of each country's endowments, institutions and competitive needs.

NOTES

1. This means that many past investments undertaken to serve small fragmented markets will prove uneconomical and will be closed down, with a greater concentration of production sites in a few relatively advanced sites to serve entire regions. There are signs that this is already happening in Sub-Saharan Africa, for instance in the pharmaceutical industry, where Egypt and South Africa are being used as production sites to service most other countries. This is also noted for textile plants and auto assembly plants in African countries.
2. These countries are: Botswana, Cameroon, Côte d'Ivoire, Ghana, Guinea, Lesotho, Mauritius, Mozambique, Namibia, Senegal, Seychelles, South Africa, Tanzania, Uganda, Zambia and Zimbabwe.
3. This is based on an extensive compilation of material by Maura Liberatori in the Africa Region of the World Bank.
4. This review draws heavily on unpublished work by Kishore Rao of The Services Group. We are very grateful to him for letting us use this work.
5. The classification of various investment bureaucracies is made difficult by a number of factors. One problem is that more than one structure often exists within the same country. In Mexico and Turkey, for example, most investments are handled by a centralized approval agency; however, extremely large investments must be approved by inter-ministerial committees. Similarly, many countries establish separate approval and regulatory structures for 'strategic' or 'priority' sectors such as mining and petroleum, or EPZ operations. In addition, in considering alternative structures, it is important to note that the lines of regulatory authority and definition of responsibility are often implicit or can overlap in many

investment bureaucracies. The confusion is exacerbated by the fact that the guidelines for implementation are often unclear in the relevant laws and regulations. This is particularly true when investment programmes have evolved over time and are legally founded upon multiple pieces of legislation. Even when the laws and regulations are well formulated and clearly stated on paper, the reality of the investment approval process sometimes comes to include steps not specified in the legislation.

Bibliography

ADB (1997), 'Financing human development: lessons from advanced Asian economies', Manila, Asian Development Bank, ADB Theme Paper 5.

Albaladejo, M. (1999), 'A service centre approach to local innovative SMEs: the case of the Spanish "Toy Valley" cluster', Oxford, Queen Elizabeth House, draft.

Amsden, A.H. (2000a), *The Rise of the Rest: Late Industrialization outside the North Atlantic Region*, New York: Oxford University Press.

Amsden, A.H. (2000b), 'Industrialization under new WTO Law', paper presented at UNCTAD X, High-level Round Table on Trade and Development: Directions for the Twenty-first Century, Bangkok, 12 February.

APT-USSIA (1993), *Uganda Small Scale Industries Survey 1993*, by A. Tulip and M. Bitekerezo, Kampala: USSIA.

Archibugi, D. and Lundvall, B.-Å. (eds), (2000), *The Globalising Learning Economy: Major Socio-Economic Trends and European Innovation Policy*, Oxford: Oxford University Press.

Archibugi, D. and Pietrobelli, C. (2001), 'The globalization of technology and developing countries: new opportunities or further burden?', CNR-ISRDS Working Paper, Rome, processed.

Arthur Andersen, Invest in France Mission and UNCTAD (1998), *International Investment: Towards the Year 2002*, Geneva: United Nations.

Asante, Y. and Addo, S.E. (1997), 'Industrial development: policies and options', in V.K. Nyanteng (ed.), pp. 184–209.

Atkinson, K.C. (1999), 'MTS impact on the national economy and external trade policy adaptation of the East African countries, Uganda report', draft, JITAP (ITC/UNCTAD/WTO).

Ayiku, M.N.B. (1991), University-productive sector linkages: review of the state-of-the-art in Africa', Accra, for the IDRC, Canada. IDRC-MR280e.

Baah-Nuakoh, A., Jebuni, C.D., Oduro, A.D. and Asante, Y. (1996), *Exporting Manufactures from Ghana. Is Adjustment Enough?*, London: Overseas Development Institute, and Legon: University of Ghana.

Bank of Uganda (1998), *Annual Report 1997/98*, Kampala, Uganda.

Barro, R.J. and Lee, J.W. (1996), 'International measures of schooling years and schooling quality', *American Economic Review*, Papers and Proceedings, **86**(2), 218–23.

Battisti, G. and Pietrobelli, C. (2000), 'Intra-industry gaps in technology and investments in technological capabilities: firm-level evidence from Chile', *International Review of Applied Economics*, **14**(2), 253–69.

Benavente, J.M., Crispi, G., Katz, J. and Stumpo, G. (1997), 'New problems and opportunities for industrial development in Latin America', *Oxford Development Studies*, **25**(3), 261–78.

Best, M. (1990), *The New Competition: Institutions of Industrial Restructuring*, Cambridge: Polity Press.

Bhorat, H. (2000), 'The effect of trade flows on labour demand', *Trade and Industry Monitor*, South Africa, **13**, 6–10.

Biggs, T. and Ratauri, M. (1997), 'Productivity and competitiveness in African manufacturing', World Bank, RPED Discussion Paper No. 80.

Biggs, T. and Srivastava, P. (1996), 'Structural aspects of manufacturing in sub-Saharan Africa', World Bank Discussion Papers, Africa Technical Department Series, No. 346.

Biggs, T., Moody, G.R., van Leeuwen, J.-H. and White, E.D. (1994), 'Africa can compete! Export opportunities and challenges for garments and home products in the U.S. market', World Bank Discussion Papers, Africa Technical Department Series, No. 242.

Biggs, T., Shah, M. and Srivastava, P. (1995), 'Technological capabilities and learning in African enterprises', World Bank Technical Paper Number 288, Washington, DC, World Bank.

Bigsten A., Collier, P., Dercon, S., Fafchamps, M., Gauthier, B., Gunning, J.W., Isaksson, A., Oduro, A., Oostendorp, R., Pattillo, C., Soderbom, M., Teal, F. and Zeufack, A. (1998), 'Rates of return on physical and human capital in Africa's manufacturing sector', Centre for the Study of African Economies, WPS/98-12, University of Oxford, May.

Bigsten A., Collier, P., Dercon, S., Gauthier, B., Gunning, J.W., Isaksson, A., Oduro, A., Oostendorp, R., Pattillo, C., Soderbom, M., Sylvain, M., Teal, F. and Zeufack, A. (1999), 'Investment in Africa's manufacturing sector: a four country panel data analysis', *Oxford Bulletin of Economics and Statistics*, **61**(4), 489–512.

Bonaglia, F., Goldstein, A. and Richaud, C. (2001), 'Measuring reform', in J. Braga de Macedo and O. Kabbaj (eds), *Reform and Growth in Africa*, Paris: OECD Development Centre, pp.79–116.

Bongenaar, B. and Szirmai, A. (1999), 'The role of a research and development institute in the development and diffusion of technology', Eindhoven Centre for Innovation Studies (The Netherlands), Working Paper 99.9. Reprinted as 'Development and diffusion of technology, the case of TIRDO', in A. Szirmai and P. Lapperre (eds) (2001).

Booth, A. and Snower, D. (eds) (1996), *Acquiring Skills: Market Failures, Their Symptoms and Policy Responses*, Cambridge: Cambridge University Press.

Botchwey, K. (1998), 'Ghana', in *The Africa Competitiveness Report 1998*, World Economic Forum and Harvard Institute for International Development, Geneva.

Braunerhjelm, P. and Fors, G. (1995), 'The Zimbabwean manufacturing sector: current status and future development potential', Stockholm, The Industrial Institute for Economic and Social Research, report prepared for the Confederation of Zimbabwe Industries.

Bresnahan, T.F., Brynjolfsson, E. and Hitt, L.M. (1999), 'Information technology, workplace organisation and the demand for skilled labour: firm-level evidence', New York, National Bureau of Economic Research, NBER Working Paper No. W7136.

Bwisa, H.M. and Gacuhi, A.R. (1997), 'Diffusion and adaptation of technology from research institutes and universities in Kenya: an empirical investigation', Nairobi, African Technology Policy Studies, Kenya Chapter, *ATPS Policy Brief*, July.

Caputo, E. (1999), 'Poverty impact of macroeconomic reform and DFID programme aid in Uganda', DRN mimeo for DFID, Rome.

Caputo, E. and Rabellotti, R. (1990), *Beyond Structural Adjustment: the Experience of Ghana and Senegal*, Rome: Istituto Italo Africano.

Casson, M. and Pearce, R. (1987), 'Multinational enterprises in LDCs', in N. Gemmell (ed.), *Surveys in Development Economics*, Oxford: Basil Blackwell, pp. 90–132.

Caves, R.E. (1982), *Multinational Enterprise and Economic Analysis*, Cambridge: Cambridge University Press.

CBI (Cross-Border Initiative) (1999), 'Road map for investor facilitation', Paper for Fourth Ministerial Meeting in Mauritius, October 1999, prepared by co-sponsors (African Development Bank, European Union, IMF and World Bank).

Central Bureau of Statistics (1999), *Economic Survey 1999*, Nairobi: Central Bureau of Statistics, Government of Kenya.

Central Statistical Office (various), *Quarterly Digest of Statistics*, Harare: Central Statistical Office.

Chand, S.K. and van Til, R. (1988), 'Ghana: towards successful stabilization and recovery', *Finance and Development*, **25**(1), 32–5.

Chenery, H.B., Robinson, S. and Syrquin, M. (1986), *Industrialization and Growth: A Comparative Study*, Oxford: Oxford University Press for the World Bank.

Chhibber, A. and Leechor, C. (1993), 'Ghana: 2000 and beyond', *Finance and Development*, **30**(3), 24–7.

CloFed (1993), *Clothing Industry of South Africa: 1993 Product Directory and Handbook*, Clothing Federation of South Africa, Gardenview (South Africa).

Cohen, W.M. and Levinthal, D.A. (1989), 'Innovation and learning: the two faces of R&D', *Economic Journal*, **109**, 569–96.

Collier, P. and Gunning, J.W. (1999a), 'Explaining African economic performance', *Journal of Economic Literature,* **37** (March), 64–111.

Collier, P. and Gunning, J.W. (1999b), 'Why has Africa grown slowly?', *Journal of Economic Perspectives*, **13**(2), 3–22.

COSTECH (1998), *Priority Areas of Research and Development in Tanzania*, Dar es Salaam: Tanzania Commission for Science and Technology.

CSIR (1973), *The Role of the Council for Scientific and Industrial Research in Determining Science Policy and Research Priorities*, Workshop Proceedings, Accra.

CSIR (1990), *Science and Technology Plan Options*, Document presented to Ghana Government, Accra.

CSIR (1999), *CSIR Handbook*, Accra, Ghana, July.

CZI/FNF (1995), *Conference on ESAP II, A New Vision*, Harare: Confederation of Zimbabwe Industries and Friedrich Naumann Foundation.

David, P.A. and Foray, D. (1995), 'Accessing and expanding the knowledge-base in science and technology', *STI Review – Science, Technology and Industry*, Paris: OECD, 16, 13–68.

Deraniyagala, S. (1999), 'Comparative and pooled analysis of the three countries', in S. Lall (ed.), *The Technological Response on Import Liberalization in Sub-Saharan Africa*, London: Macmillan pp. 207–24.

Deraniyagala, S. and Semboja, H.H.H. (1999), 'Trade liberalization, firm performance and technology upgrading in Tanzania', in S. Lall (ed.), *The Technological Response on Import Liberalization in Sub-Saharan Africa*, London: Macmillan, pp. 112–47.

DFID (1999), *Uganda Country Strategy Paper*, Department for International Development, London: HMSO.

Dijkstra, A.G. and Van Donge, J.K. (2001), 'What does the "show case"' show? Evidence of and lessons from adjustment in Uganda', *World Development*, **29**(5), 841–63.

Doutriaux, J. and Barker, M. (1995), 'The university industry relationship in science and technology', Ottawa, Industry Canada, Occasional Paper Number 11.

Duijsens, R. and Lapperre, P. (2001), 'Technical education, knowledge and skills in the metal working industry in Tanzania', in A. Szirmai and P. Lapperre (eds).

Dunning, J.H. (1993), *The Globalization of Business*, London: Routledge.

Durevall, D. (1993), 'Trade liberalisation: the Zimbabwean way', in M. Blomström and M. Lundahl (eds), *Economic Crisis in Africa*: Perspectives on Policy Responses, London: Routledge.

Economist, The (1996), 'World Economy Survey', London, 28 September, p. 48.

Economist, The (1997), 'World Education League: Who's Top?', London, 29 March, pp. 25–7.

Edquist, C. (ed.) (1997), *Systems of Innovation: Technologies, Institutions and Organisations*, London: Pinter.

Enos, J.L. (1995), *The Pursuit of Science and Technology in Sub-Saharan Africa under Structural Adjustment*, London: Routledge.

Evenson, R.E. and Westphal, L.E. (1995), 'Technological change and technology strategy', in J. Behrman and T.N. Srinivasan (eds), *Handbook of Development Economics*, Vol. III, Amsterdam: Elsevier Science.

Financial Times (1999), 'Survey of Tanzanian Economy', London, 31 March.

Frempong, G.K. (1998), *Institutions Supporting Scientific and Industrial Development*, Technology Capacity Series No.1, STEPRI/CSIR, second edition, Accra.

Ghana Statistical Service (1998), *Quarterly Digest of Statistics*, Vol. XVI, No.1, Accra, Ghana.

Godfrey, M. (ed.) (1997), *Skill Development for International Competitiveness*, Cheltenham: Edward Elgar.

Gogo, J.O. (2000), 'Policies for technology transfer: Ghana', background paper prepared for UNCTAD-JITAP, Accra, May.

Gogo, J.O., Micah, J.A., Afful, K.N. and Goka, A.M. (1998), 'The development and management of science and technology policy in Ghana', Final Report on Phase 1 of the Carnegie Project on S&T Policy Dialogue, New York, Carnegie Corporation, February.

Government of Ghana (1958), *Research Act No. 21*, Accra: Government Printer.

Government of Ghana (1964), *Seven-year Development Plan, 1963/64 to 1969/70*, Accra: Office of the Planning Commission.

Government of Ghana (1968), *Council for Scientific and Industrial Research*, NLCD 293, 1968, Accra: Government Printer.

Government of Ghana (1977), *Five-year Development Plan 1975/76 to 1979/80*, Accra: Ministry of Economic Planning.

Government of Ghana (1978), 'Approach and guidelines for the preparation of a technology plan for Ghana', Draft Report of UNIDO Mission to Ghana, Vienna, UNIDO, United Nations.

Government of Ghana (1995), *Ghana Vision 2020 (The First Step: 1996–2000)*, Presidential Report to Parliament on Co-ordinated Programme of Economic and Social Policies, Accra.

Green, F., Ashton, D., James, D. and Sung, J. (1999), 'The role of the state in skill formation: evidence from the Republic of Korea, Singapore and Taiwan', *Oxford Review of Economic Policy*, **15**(1), Spring, 82–96.

Guerrieri, P., Iammarino, S. and Pietrobelli, C. (eds) (2001), *The Global Challenge to Industrial Districts: SMEs in Italy and Taiwan*, Cheltenham: Edward Elgar.

Guisinger, S. (1986), 'Host-country policies to attract and control foreign investment', in T. Moran et al., *Investing in Development: New Roles for Private Capital?*, Washington, DC: Overseas Development Council.

Gunning, J.W. and Mumbengegwi, C. (eds), (1995a), *The Manufacturing Sector in Zimbabwe: Industrial Change under Structural Adjustment*, RPED Survey, Amsterdam, Free University.

Gunning, J.W. and Mumbengegwi, C. (1995b), 'Regional program on enterprise development: report on round III (1995) of the Zimbabwe survey', Amsterdam, Free University and Harare, University of Zimbabwe (draft).

Harbison, F.H. and Myers, C.S. (1964), *Education, Manpower and Economic Growth*, New York: McGraw-Hill.

Harvey, C. and Robinson, M. (1995), 'Economic reform and political liberalisation in Uganda', Institute of Development Studies, Brighton, Research Report No. 29, June.

Helleiner, G.K. (ed.) (2001), *Non-Traditional Export Promotion in Africa: Experience and Issues*, Study for UN University World Institute for Development Economics Research (WIDER), Basingstoke: Palgrave.

Holmgren, T., Kasekende, L., Atingi-Ego, M. and Ddamulira, D. (1999), 'Aid and reform in Uganda', draft, Washington, DC, World Bank.

Husain, I. and Faruqee, R. (eds) (1994), *Adjustment in Africa*, Washington, DC: World Bank.

IFC/FIAS (1997), *Foreign Direct Investment*, Washington, DC: International Finance Corporation and Foreign Investment Advisory Service, World Bank.

ILO (1998), *World Employment Report 1998–99*, Geneva: International Labour Office.

ISO (1999), *The ISO Survey of ISO 9000 and ISO 14000 Certificates*, Geneva: International Standards Organization.

ISO (2000), *The ISO Survey of ISO 9000 and ISO 14000 Certificates - Ninth Cycle*, Geneva: International Standards Organization.

ISSER (Institute of Statistical, Social and Economic Research) (1999), *The State of the Ghanaian Economy in 1998*, Legon: University of Ghana, June.

Jansen, D. (1983), 'Zimbabwe: government policy and the manufacturing sector', Study for the Ministry of Industry and Energy Development, Larkspur, California, mimeo.

Jebuni, C.D., Oduro, A.D., Asante, Y. and Tsikata G.K. (1992), *Diversifying Exports. The Supply Response of Non-traditional Exports to Ghana's Economic Recovery Programme*, London: Overseas Development Institute, and Legon: University of Ghana.

Kaplinsky, R. (1994), *Easternization: The Spread of Japanese Management Techniques to Developing Countries*, Ilford: Frank Cass.

Kapur, I., Hadjimichael, M.T., Hilbers, P., Schiff, J. and Szymczak, P. (1991), 'Ghana: adjustment and growth, 1983-91', IMF Occasional Paper No. 86, Washington DC, IMF.

Kingoria, G.K. and Gacuhi, A.R. (1999), 'Basic sciences for the development of Kenya', Nairobi, NCST and Ministry of Research and Technology, prepared for the Conference of Basic Sciences for Development in Eastern and Southern Africa, draft.

KIRDI (1999a), *Policies and Strategies*, Nairobi: Kenya Industrial Research and Development Institute.

KIRDI (1999b), *National Industrial Research Programmes*, Nairobi: Kenya Industrial Research and Development Institute.

Knight, J.B. (1996), 'Labour market policies and outcomes in Zimbabwe', Oxford University, Institute of Economics and Statistics, draft.

Kosacoff, B. (1996), 'Business strategies and industrial adjustments: the case of Argentina', Buenos Aires, Economic Commission for Latin America and the Caribbean, Working Paper No. 67, LC/BUE/L.150.

KSA (1996), 'Consulting service for Zimbabwe garment and textile PHRD initiative', Dusseldorf, Kurt Salmon Associates, Report prepared for the World Bank.

Kumar, N. (ed.) (1998), *Globalization, Foreign Direct Investment and Technology Transfers*, London: Routledge, for United Nations University Institute for New Technologies.

Lall, S. (1978), 'Transnational, domestic enterprises and industrial structure in host LDCs: A survey', *Oxford Economic Papers*, **30**, 217-48.

Lall, S. (1990), *Building Industrial Competitiveness in Developing Countries*, Paris: OECD Development Centre.

Lall, S. (1992a), 'Structural problems of African industry', in F. Stewart, S. Lall and S. Wangwe (eds), *Alternative Development Strategies in Sub-Saharan Africa*, London: Macmillan, pp.103-44.

Lall, S. (1992b), 'Technological capabilities and industrialization', *World Development*, **20**, 165-86.

Lall, S. (1993a), 'Introduction', in S. Lall (ed.), *Transnational Corporations and Economic Development*, London: Routledge, The UN Library on Transnational Corporations, Vol. 3.

Lall, S. (1993b), 'Trade policies for development: A policy prescription for Africa', *Development Policy Review*, **11**(1), 47-65.

Lall, S. (1995), 'Structural adjustment and African industry', *World Development*, **23**, 2019-31.

Lall, S. (1996), *Learning from the Asian Tigers: Studies in Technology and Industrial Policy*, London: Macmillan.

Lall, S. (1997), 'Attracting foreign investment: new trends, sources and policies', London, Commonwealth Secretariat, Economic Paper 31.

Lall, S. (1998), 'Exports of manufactures by developing countries: emerging patterns of trade and location', *Oxford Review of Economic Policy*, **11**(2), 54–73.

Lall, S. (1999a), 'Promoting industrial competitiveness in developing countries: lessons from Asia', London, Commonwealth Secretariat, Economic Paper 39.

Lall, S. (1999b), 'Competing with labour: skills and competitiveness in developing countries', Issues in Development, Working Paper No. 31, Development Policies Department, ILO, Geneva.

Lall, S. (ed.) (1999c), *The Technological Response to Import Liberalization in Sub-Saharan Africa*, London: Macmillan.

Lall, S. (2000a), 'Evaluation of promotion and incentive strategies for FDI in Sub-Saharan Africa', Oxford, draft for the World Bank Africa Department, Washington, DC.

Lall, S. (2000b), 'Selective industrial and trade policies in developing countries: theoretical and empirical issues', in C. Soludo (ed.), *Economic Policymaking and Implementation in Africa*, Project for the International Development Research Centre (Canada).

Lall, S. (2001a), *Competitiveness, Technology and Skills*, Cheltenham: Edward Elgar.

Lall, S. (2001b), 'Competitiveness indices and developing countries: an economic evaluation of the Global Competitiveness Report', *World Development*, **29**(9), 1501–25.

Lall, S. and Rao, K. (1996), 'Indonesia: sustaining manufactured export growth', Report prepared for the Asian Development Bank, Manila.

Lall, S. and Wangwe, S. (1998), 'Industrial policy and industrialisation in Sub-Saharan Africa', *Journal of African Economies*, **7**, Supplement 1, 70–107.

Lall, S. and Wignaraja, G. (1994), 'Foreign involvement by European firms and garment exports by developing countries', *Asia-Pacific Development Journal*, **1**, 21–48.

Lall, S. and Wignaraja, G. (1996), 'Skills and capabilities in Ghana's competitiveness', in S. Lall (ed.), *Learning from the Asian Tigers: Studies in Technology and Industrial Policy*, London: Macmillan.

Lall, S. and Wignaraja, G. (1998), 'Mauritius: dynamising export competitiveness', London, Commonwealth Secretariat, Economic Paper 33.

Lall, S., Barba-Navaretti, G., Teitel, S. and Wignaraja, G. (1994), *Technology and Enterprise Development: Ghana under Structural Adjustment*, London: Macmillan.

Lall, S., Rao, K. and Wignaraja, G. (1996), 'Building Sri Lankan competitiveness: a strategy for manufactured export growth', Report for the National Development Council, Government of Sri Lanka.

Lall, S., Robinson, P., Sellek, M. and Wignaraja, G. (1998), 'Zimbabwe: enhancing export competitiveness', Study prepared for the Ministry of Industry, Government of Zimbabwe and the Commonwealth Secretariat, London.

Latsch, W. and Robinson, P. (1999), 'Technology and the response of firms to adjustment in Zimbabwe', in S. Lall (ed.), *The Technological Response to Import Liberalization in Sub-Saharan Africa*, London: Macmillan, pp. 148–206.

Leechor, C. (1994), 'Ghana: frontrunner in adjustment', in I. Husain and R. Faruqee (eds), pp. 153–92.

Lim, L. (1995), 'Foreign investment, the state and industrial policy in Singapore', in H. Stein (ed.), *Asian Industrialization and Africa*, London: Macmillan, pp. 205–39.

Lundvall B.-Å. (ed.) (1992), *National Systems of Innovation: Towards a Theory of Innovation and Interactive Learning*, London: Pinter Publishers.

Manzocchi, S. and Pietrobelli, C. (2001), 'The globalisation of financial markets and its implications for developing countries. Is FDI a panacea for developing economies?', in P. García Ruiz (ed.), *El Problema de la Deuda Externa*, Pamplona: Ediciones Universidad de Navarra.

McCormick, D. (1999), 'African enterprise clusters and industrialization: theory and reality', *World Development*, **27**, 1531–51.

McPherson, M.A. (1991), *Micro- and Small-Scale Enterprises in Zimbabwe: Results of a Country-Wide Survey*, Bethesda: GEMINI.

McPherson, M.A. (1998), 'Uganda', in *The Africa Competitiveness Report 1998*, World Economic Forum and Harvard Institute for International Development, Geneva.

Mead, D.C. and Kunjeku, P. (1993), *Business Linkages and Enterprise Development in Zimbabwe*, Harare: Confederation of Zimbabwe Industries.

MEST (1998), *Draft National Science and Technology Policy*, Ministry of Environment, Science and Technology, Accra, Ghana.

Middleton, J. and Dempsky, T. (1989), 'Vocational education and training: a review of World Bank investment', World Bank Discussion Paper 51.

Middleton, J., Ziderman, A. and Van Adams, A. (1993), *Skills for Productivity: Vocational Education and Training in Developing Countries*, Oxford: Oxford University Press, for the World Bank.

Ministry of Finance, Planning and Economic Development (1998), *Statistical Abstract 1998*, Kampala, Uganda.

Ministry of Industry and Commerce (1995), 'The future for industry in Zimbabwe: assessment of policies and strategies', Harare, Government of Zimbabwe, draft.

Ministry of Industry and Commerce (1997), 'Industrial policy and strategy - from 1996 to 2006', Harare, Government of Zimbabwe, draft.

Ministry of Science, Technology and Higher Education (1996), *The National Science and Technology Policy for Tanzania*, Dar-es-Salaam, Government of the United Republic of Tanzania.

MIST (1992a), *Industrial Policy Statement: A Strategy for Industrial Regeneration*, Ministry of Industries, Science and Technology, Government of Ghana, Accra.

MIST (1992b), *Science and Technology Policy Statement*, Ministry of Industries, Science and Technology, Accra, Ghana.

Mlawa, H.M. (1999), *Technology Policies for Sustainable Development in Eastern Africa: Kenya, Tanzania, Zambia and Zimbabwe*, Dar es Salaam: DUP Press.

Mokabi, G.N. (1999), 'Policies for the transfer of appropriate technology in Kenya', Nairobi, report for UNCTAD.

Moran, T. (1999), *Foreign Direct Investment and Development*, Washington, DC: Institute for International Economics.

MOTI (1994), *Uganda Industrialisation Policy and Framework 1994–99*, Kampala: Ministry of Trade and Industry, Government of Uganda.

Mowery, D.C. and Rosenberg, N. (1989), *Technology and the Pursuit of Economic Growth*, Cambridge: Cambridge University Press.

Muzulu, J. (1996), 'The structural adjustment implications of real exchange rate depreciation on the manufacturing sector in Zimbabwe', in C. Harvey (ed.), *Constraints on the Success of Structural Adjustment Programmes in Africa*, Basingstoke: Macmillan.

Mwamadzingo, M. and Ndung'u, N. (1997), 'Development of science and technology infrastructure in Kenya during periods of structural adjustment', Nairobi, African Technology Policy Studies, Kenya Chapter, *ATPS Policy Brief*, July.

Mwega, F.M. (2001), 'Promotion of non-traditional exports in Kenya, 1980–96', in G.K. Helleiner (ed.).

Mytelka, L.K. (ed.) (1991), *Strategic Partnerships and the World Economy*, London: Pinter Publishers.

Mytelka, L.K. and Teschafew, T. (1998), 'The role of policy in promoting enterprise learning during early industrialisation', Geneva: UNCTAD, African Development in a Comparative Perspective, Study number 7.

National Council for Science and Technology (1995), 'Working document on industrial technology policy and regulatory environment for development', Nairobi, National Council for Science and Technology, Republic of Kenya, NCST No. 34.

Ndulu, B., Semboja, J. and Mbellem, A. (2001), 'Promoting non-traditional exports in Tanzania', in G. K. Helleiner (ed.).

Nelson, R.R. (ed.) (1993), *National Innovation Systems: A Comparative Analysis*, Oxford: Oxford University Press.

Nelson, R.R. and Winter, S.J. (1982), *An Evolutionary Theory of Economic Change*, Cambridge, MA: Harvard University Press.

NSF (1998), *Science and Engineering Indicators 1998*, Washington DC: National Science Foundation.

Nyanteng, V.K. (ed.) (1997), *Policies and Options for Ghanaian Economic Development*, Second Edition, Institute of Statistical, Social and Economic Research: University of Ghana, Legon.

Obwona, M.B. (1998), *Determinants of Foreign Direct Investments and their Impact on Economic Growth in Uganda*, Economic Policy Research Centre, Research Series No. 4, Kampala, Uganda.

OECD (1997), *Main Science and Technology Indicators*, Paris: Organisation for Economic Cooperation and Development.

Pack, H. (1993), 'Productivity and industrial development in Sub-Saharan Africa', *World Development*, **21**(1), 1-16.

Pack, H. and Paxson, C. (2001), 'Is African manufacturing skill constrained?', in A. Szirmai and P. Lapperre (eds).

Paganetto, L. and Pietrobelli, C. (eds) (2001), *Scienza, Tecnologia e Innovazione: Quali Politiche?* (*Science, Technology and Innovation: What Role for Public Policies?*), Bologna: Il Mulino.

Pietrobelli, C. (1994a), 'Ghana: private sector development and employment generation under the structural adjustment program', report for Development Researchers Network and the European Union, July.

Pietrobelli, C. (1994b), 'Technological capabilities at the national level: an international comparison of manufacturing export performances', *Development Policy Review*, **12**(2), June, 115-48.

Pietrobelli, C. (1996), *Emerging Forms of Technological Co-operation: The Case for Technology Partnerships - Inner Logic, Examples and Enabling Environment*, Science and Technology Issues, Geneva: UNCTAD.

Pietrobelli, C. (1997), 'On the theory of technological capabilities and developing countries' dynamic comparative advantage in manufactures', *Rivista Internazionale di Scienze Economiche e Commerciali*, **44**(2), 313-38.

Pietrobelli, C. (1998), *Industry, Competitiveness and Technological Capabilities in Chile. A New Tiger from Latin America?*, London: Macmillan.

Pietrobelli, C. (2000), 'The role of international technology transfer in the industrialisation of developing countries', in M. Elena and D. Schroeer (eds), *Technology Transfer*, Aldershot: Ashgate.

Pietrobelli, C. (2001), 'National industrial systems in Africa. The nature and deficiencies of technological effort in African industry', background paper for the UNIDO *World Industrial Development Report 2002*.

Pietrobelli, C. and Samper, J. (1997), 'The measurement of Europe–Asia technology exchanges: asymmetry and distance', *Science and Public Policy*, **24**(4), August, 255–71.

Pigato, M. (1999), 'Foreign direct investment in Africa: old tales and new evidence', World Bank, Africa Region, draft.

Porter, M. (1990), *The Competitive Advantage of Nations*, New York: Basic Books.

Radosevic, S. (1999), *International Technology Transfer and Catch-Up in Economic Development*, Cheltenham: Edward Elgar.

Rao, K. (1999), 'Free trade zones in the Middle East: development patterns and future potential', Arlington, VA, The Services Group, draft.

Ratnayake, R. (1994), *Effective Protection of Manufacturing Industries in Zimbabwe*, Harare: Centre for International Economics/MIU.

Redding, S. (1999), 'Dynamic comparative advantage and the welfare effects of trade', *Oxford Economic Papers*, **51**(1), 15–39.

Reinert, E. (1995), 'Competitiveness and its predecessors – a 500 year cross-national perspective', *Structural Change and Economics Dynamics*, **6**, 23–42.

Reinikka, R. and Svensson, J. (1999a), 'Confronting competition: investment response and constraints in Uganda', Policy Research Working Paper No. 2245, Washington, DC, The World Bank.

Reinikka, R. and Svensson, J. (1999b), 'How inadequate provision of public infrastructure and services affects private investment', Policy Research Working Paper No. 2262, Washington, DC, The World Bank.

Republic of Kenya (1996), *Industrial Transformation to the Year 2020*, Nairobi: Government Printer, Sessional Paper No. 2 of 1996.

Republic of Kenya (1997), *National Development Plan 1997–2001*, Nairobi: Government Printer.

Republic of Uganda (1999), *Vision 2025: A Strategic Framework for National Development*, Ministry of Finance, Planning and Economic Development, Kampala, February.

Rhee, Y.W., Katterbach, K., Belot, T., Bowring, A., Jun, Y.W. and Lee, K.C. (1995), 'Inducing foreign industrial catalysts into Sub-Saharan Africa', World Bank, Private Sector Development Department, PSD Occasional Paper No. 1.

Riddell, R.C. (ed.) (1990), *Manufacturing Africa: Performance and Prospects of Seven Countries in Sub-Saharan Africa*, London: Curry.

Rodrik, D. (1996), 'Coordination failures and government policy: a model with applications to East Asia and Eastern Europe', *Journal of International Economics*, **40**(1/2), 1–22.

Rodrik, D. (2000), 'Can integration into the world economy substitute for a development strategy?', Paper presented to the World Bank's ABCDE-

Europe Conference in Paris, June 26–28 (http://www.worldbank.org/research/abcde/eu_2000/pdffiles/rodrik.pdf).

Rosenberg N. (1982), *Inside the Black Box: Technology and Economics*, Cambridge: Cambridge University Press.

Rush, H., Hobday, M., Bessant, J., Arnold, E. and Murray, R. (1996), *Technology Institutes: Strategies for Best Practice*, London: International Thomson Business Press.

Sachs, J. (1998), 'Foreign direct investment in Africa', in *The Africa Competitiveness Report*, Geneva: World Economic Forum.

Science and Technology Sector Committee of the National Development Commission (1981), *Science and Technology Policy Proposals*, Accra: National Development Commission.

Selvaratnam, V. (1994), 'Innovations in higher education: Singapore at the competitive edge', Washington, DC, World Bank, Technical Paper number 222.

Semboja, H.H. and Kweka, J.P. (2001), 'The form and role of innovativeness in enhancing firms' productivity: the case of selected manufacturing firms in Tanzania', in A. Szirmai and P. Lapperre (eds).

Skålnes, T. (1995), *The Politics of Economic Reform in Zimbabwe: Continuity and Change in Development*, London: Macmillan.

Soludo, C. (1998), 'Trade policy reforms and supply responses in Africa,' Geneva: UNCTAD, African Development in a Comparative Perspective, Study number 6.

Soon, T.W. (1993), 'Education and human resource development', in L. Lim et al. (eds), *Challenge and Response: Thirty Years of the Economic Development Board*, Singapore: Times Academic Press, pp. 235–69.

Sowa, N.K., Baah-Nuakoh, A., Tutu, K.A. and Osei, B. (1992), *Small Enterprises and Adjustment. The Impact of Ghana's Economic Recovery Programme on Small-Scale Industrial Enterprises*, London: ODI and Accra: University of Ghana.

Spar, D. (1998), 'Attracting high technology investment: Intel's Costa Rican plant', Washington, DC, Foreign Investment Advisory Service, IFC and World Bank, FIAS Occasional Paper 11.

Ssemogerere, G. and Ddamulira, D. (2001), 'Growth, external sector and the role of non-traditional exports in Uganda', in G.K. Helleiner (ed.).

Standard Chartered Bank Zimbabwe (1997), *Business Trends Zimbabwe*, Harare, No. 55, March.

Steel W.F. and Webster L.A. (1992), 'How small enterprises in Ghana have responded to adjustment', *World Bank Economic Review*, **6**(3), 423–38.

Stein, H. (1992), 'Deindustrialization, adjustment, the World Bank and the IMF in Africa', *World Development*, **20**(1), 83–95.

Stein, H. (1994), 'The World Bank and the application of Asian industrial policy to Africa: theoretical considerations', *Journal of International Development*, **5**(1), 1–19.

Stein, H. (ed.) (1995), *Asian Industrialization and Africa: Studies in Policy Alternatives to Adjustment*, London: Macmillan.

Stryker, J.D. (1994), 'Costs and benefits of eliminating institutional constraints on the expansion of non-traditional exports', presented at a seminar at the Department of Economics, University of Ghana, Legon, May.

Sverrisson, A. (1993), *Evolutionary Technical Change and Flexible Mechanisation: Entrepreneurship and Industrialisation in Kenya and Zimbabwe*, Lund: Lund University Press.

Szirmai, A. and Lapperre, P. (eds) (2001), *The Industrial Experience of Tanzania: A Case Study of Industrialisation in Sub-Saharan Africa*, Basingstoke: Palgrave.

Szirmai, A., Prins, M. and Schulte, W. (2001), 'Measuring manufacturing performance in Tanzania', in A. Szirmai and P. Lapperre (eds).

Tan, H.W. and Batra, G. (1995), *Enterprise Training in Developing Countries: Incidence, Productivity Effects, and Policy Implications*, Washington, DC, World Bank, Private Sector Development Department.

Teal F. (1999a), 'The Ghanaian manufacturing sector 1991–95: firm growth, productivity and convergence', *Journal of Development Studies*, **36**, 109–27.

Teal F. (1999b), 'Why can Mauritius export manufactures and Ghana not?', *The World Economy*, **22**, 981–93.

Technology Transfer Centre - CSIR (1991), *Report on Small and Medium Enterprises Sector Study,* Accra.

Teitel, S. (2000), *Technology and Skills in Zimbabwe's Manufacturing: From Autarky to Competition*, Basingstoke: Palgrave.

TIC (1998), *Investors' Guide to Tanzania*, Dar es Salaam: Tanzania Investment Centre.

Torp, J.E. (1995), 'Transnational corporations and industrial restructuring in developing countries: Zimbabwe case study', Copenhagen, Copenhagen Business School, Report prepared for UNCTAD, draft.

TSG (1997), *The Investor Roadmap of Tanzania*, Arlington, VA: The Services Group, Report for USAID, Prime Contractor: Coopers and Lybrand.

TSG (1998), *The Investor Roadmap of Kenya*, Arlington, VA: The Services Group, Report for USAID, Prime Contractor: Coopers and Lybrand.

TSG (1999), *Tanzania Investor Roadmap*, Arlington, VA: The Services Group, Report for USAID, Prime contractors: PricewaterhouseCoopers.

UIA (1998), 'A survey of technologies and skills in Uganda industries', Kampala, Uganda Investment Authority.

UIA (1999), *A Guide to Investing in Uganda*, Kampala, Uganda Investment Authority.

UK Cabinet Office (1996), *Competitiveness: Creating the Enterprise Centre of Europe*, London: Her Majesty's Stationery Office.

UNCTAD (1994), *World Investment Report 1994*, Transnational Corporations, Employment and the Workplace, Geneva: United Nations.

UNCTAD (1998a), *World Investment Report 1998: Trends and Determinants*, Geneva: United Nations.

UNCTAD (1998b), *Survey of Foreign Firms in Uganda*, Kampala: Inter-Africa Corporate Ltd for UNCTAD and UIA.

UNCTAD (1999a), *World Investment Report: Foreign Direct Investment and Development*, Geneva: United Nations.

UNCTAD (1999b), *Foreign Direct Investment in Africa: Performance and Potential*, Geneva: United Nations.

UNCTAD (2000), *Investment Policy Review of Uganda*, Geneva: United Nations.

UNDP (1995), *Human Development Report 1995*, Oxford: Oxford University Press.

UNDP (2001), *Human Development Report 2001: Making New Technologies Work for Human Development*, Oxford: Oxford University Press.

UNESCO (various), *Statistical Yearbook*, Paris: United Nations Educational, Scientific and Cultural Organization.

UNIDO (1999), *African Industry 2000: The Challenge of Going Global*, Vienna: UNIDO.

UNIDO (2002), *World Industrial Development Report 2002*, Vienna: UNIDO, forthcoming.

UNIDO (various), *Industrial Development: Global Report*, Vienna: UN Industrial Development Organization.

UNIDO/ILO (1992), *Industrial Sector Review and Programming Mission to Ghana*, August.

Velenchik, A. (1995), 'Labour markets', in J.W. Gunning and C. Mumbengegwi (eds) (1995a).

Verner, D. (1999), 'Wage and productivity gaps: evidence from Ghana', WPS 2168, Washington, DC, The World Bank.

Wanga, G. (2000), 'Analysis of selected macroeconomic indicators and technological development in Tanzania', Dar es Salaam, Economic and Social Research Foundation, report for UNCTAD.

Wangwe, S.M. (ed.) (1995), *Exporting Africa: Technology, Trade and Industrialisation in Sub-Saharan Africa*, London: Routledge.

Wangwe, S.M. (2001), 'Economic reforms, industrialisation and technological capabilities in Tanzanian industry', in A. Szirmai and P. Lapperre (eds).

Wangwe, S.M. and Diyamett, B. (1998), 'Cooperation between R&D institutions and enterprises: the case of the United Republic of Tanzania', in

UNCTAD, *New Approaches to Science and Technology Cooperation and Capacity Building*, Geneva, 193–210.

Wangwe, S.M., Musonda, F.M. and Kweka, J.P. (1997), 'Policies for manufacturing competitiveness: the case of Tanzania', Dar es Salaam, Economic and Social Research Foundation.

Wells, L.T. and Wint, A.G. (1990), *Marketing a Country: Promotion as a Tool for Attracting Foreign Investment*, Washington, DC: International Finance Corporation.

Wignaraja, G. and Ikiara, G. (1999), 'Adjustment, technological capabilities and enterprise dynamics in Kenya', in S. Lall (ed.), *The Technological Response to Import Liberalisation in Sub-Saharan Africa*, London: Macmillan, pp. 57–111.

Wint, A.G. (1993), 'Promoting transnational investment: organizing to service approved investors', *Transnational Corporations*, **2**(1), 71–90.

Wong, P.-K. (1996), 'From NIE to developed economy: Singapore's industrial policy to the year 2000', *Journal of Asian Business*, **12**(3), 65–85.

Wood, A. (1994), *North–South Trade, Employment and Inequality: Changing Fortunes in a Skill-Driven World*, Oxford: Clarendon Press.

Wood, A. and Mayer, J. (1998), 'African economic structure in comparative perspective', Geneva, UNCTAD, African Development in a Comparative Perspective, Study number 4.

World Bank (1986), Kenya: Policies and Prospects for Restoring Sustained Growth of Per Capita Income, Washington, DC: World Bank.

World Bank (1987), 'Zimbabwe: an industrial sector memorandum', Washington, DC, World Bank, Report No. 6349-Zim.

World Bank (1988), *Education in Sub-Saharan Africa: Policies for Adjustment, Revitalisation, and Expansion*, Washington, DC: World Bank.

World Bank (1989a), *Zimbabwe: The Capital Goods Sector, Investment and Industrial Issues*, Washington, DC: World Bank.

World Bank (1989b), 'Zimbabwe: private investment and government policy', Washington, DC, World Bank, Report No. 7646-Zim.

World Bank (1993), *Ghana 2000 and beyond: Setting the Stage for Accelerated Growth and Poverty Reduction*, Western Africa Dept., Washington, DC, February.

World Bank (1994), *Adjustment in Africa: Reforms, Results and the Road Ahead*, Oxford: Oxford University Press.

World Bank (1995), 'Zimbabwe: achieving shared growth', Volume II, Washington, DC, World Bank, Report No. 13540-ZIM.

World Bank (1996a), *Uganda: The Challenge of Growth and Poverty Reduction. A Country Study*, Washington, DC: The World Bank.

World Bank (1996b), 'Staff appraisal report Zimbabwe: enterprise development project', Washington, DC, World Bank, Report No. 15062-ZIM.

World Bank (1999), *World Development Report: Knowledge for Development*, Washington, DC: World Bank.

World Economic Forum (WEF) and Harvard Institute for International Development (HIID) (1998), *The Africa Competitiveness Report 1998*, Geneva: World Economic Forum.

Zimbabwe Clothing Council (1997), 'Zimbabwe clothing and textile chain policy framework and proposals for the way forward', Harare.

Zimbabwe Trade and Investment Consultants (1997), 'UK Investment in Zimbabwe', London, Report prepared for the Zimbabwe Investment Centre.

Zimconsult (1993), 'Industrial sub-sector studies', Harare, mimeo.

Index

Africa
export performance 23-6
export processing zones (EPZs) 213
FDI
attracting 202-40
economic and policy determinants 209-15
entry procedures and requirements 217-18
policies 216-232
policy implications 232-9
investment promotion agencies (IPAs) 228-32
ISO certification 43
legal systems 220-21, 238
loss carry-forward provisions 220
tax systems 220
technology systems 1
work permit regulations 220
Africa Project Development Facility (APDF) 135
Africa Regional Intellectual Property Organization (ARIPO) 117
African Regional Industrial Property Office (ARIPO) 61
Amsden, A.H. 4
Angola, investment incentives 219
Archibugi, D. 4
Asia, export processing zones (EPZs) 214
Asian Tigers 189
Atkinson, K.C. 119
autonomous strategies 31
Ayiku, N.M.B. 74

Baah-Nuakoh, A. 146
Batra, G. 180
Battisti, G. 7
Best, M. 6, 12
Biggs, T. 2, 13, 41, 51, 89, 132, 133, 179, 180, 181, 186, 187
Bigsten, A. 110, 143
Bongenaar, B. 98
Botchwey, K. 158
Botswana, FDI entry requirements 218
Bresnahan, T.F. 34
Bwisa, H.M. 71, 73

Cameroon, FDI entry requirements 218
capital goods imports, Uganda 49, 118
Caribbean Basin, FDI 234-6
Carson Products West Africa, Ghana 148
CBI (Cross-Border Initiative) 49, 209, 216, 218, 219, 220, 221, 230, 232
Chand, S.K. 141
Chenery, H.B. 2
China
exports 26
and Uganda 131
Codex Alimentarius Commission 127
Cohen, W.M. 7
Collier, P. 210
comparative advantage 209
competition
changing nature 6
'new competition' 12
competitiveness 2, 3-6, 12
corruption 49, 68, 230
Costa Rica, FDI 234-6
Cross-Border Initiative *see* CBI
customs systems 238

Deraniyagala, S. 85, 86
developing countries
empirical research 7
export growth 22
exports 29
industrial performance 13
DFID (Department for International Development) 109, 138
Dijkstra, A.G. 114
Diyamett, B. 101
Donge, J.K. van 114

East African Community 96, 130–31
East Asia 23, 25
  exports 26
economic policies, liberalization 15
The Economist 6
Edquist, C. 9
educational enrolment rates
  engineering 35, 37
  national 37–8
  regional 32, 34–7
  tertiary technical enrolments 34–6, 39
EMPRETEC Zimbabwe 196
engineers 122–3, 180–81
Enos, J.L. 1, 155, 166
enterprise-technology institution relationships 132–3
entrepreneurship 14
Euromoney 48
export processing zones (EPZs) 67, 69–70, 211–15
  Africa 213
  Asia 214
  changing concepts 212–13
  Ghana 147
  weaknesses 214–15
export structures 16–17
exports
  Ghana 145, 146–7
  global trends in 20–23
  manufactured export performance 16–32
  Tanzania 29, 85
  Uganda 29, 112, 113, 135–7
  world exports 1980-97 21
  Zimbabwe 29

Faruqee, R. 15
FDI 1, 2, 16, 30–31, 44–9
  Africa
    attracting 202–40
    economic and policy determinants 209–15
    entry procedures and requirements 217–18
    inflows 44, 46–8
    policies 216–32
    policy implications 232–9
  Caribbean Basin 234–6
  Costa Rica 234–6
  economic determinants 207
  and economic measures 239
  Ghana 48, 172–3, 218
  host country determinants 206
  host government policies 204
  inflows
    by region 44, 45
    and technology inflows 48
  and infrastructure 210–11
  Kenya 59, 63, 77
    attraction 80–81
    entry requirements 219
    inward 66–9
  and labour 210
  and liberalization 208–9
  location 202–9
    decisions by MNCs 203–4
    and technical change 205
  processing times 218
  resource-based 222
  and skills 210
  Sub-Saharan Africa
    attraction 236–9
    determinants 209–15
  Tanzania 48, 91–4, 106–7
  and technology activity 210
  Uganda 48, 114–15, 118–22, 218
  and the UK 233
  Zimbabwe 48, 187, 218
FDI dependent strategies 30–31
FDI policy, Africa 236–8
FDI promotion 238
  and Zimbabwe Investment Centre (ZIC) 228–30
Financial Times 91
firms
  linkages with universities 74
  Zimbabwe 191
foreign direct investment *see* FDI
free trade zones 211–15
Frempong, G.K. 152

Gacuhi, A.R. 71, 73
Gambia, FDI entry requirements 218, 219
garment industry
  labour costs 39–41
  Tanzania 89
  Zimbabwe 183
Ghana 141–75
  business associations 147

capital goods imports 49
Carson Products West Africa 148
Council for Scientific and Industrial Research (CSIR) 149-50, 157, 166, 167, 173
  financing 156
  objectives 153-4
Development and Application of Intermediate Technology (DAPIT) 170
direct investments 160
Economic Recovery Programme 141
EMPRETEC 169-70
export promotion 146-7
exports 145
FDI
  attracting 172-3
  entry requirements 218
  inflows 48
Food Research Institute (FRI) 166-8, 173
GDP 141, 142, 155
human capital 159, 161, 172
import liberalization 144
import substitution strategy 141
industrial background 142-9
industrial growth 142, 143
industrial investment 145-6
Institute of Industrial Research (IIR) 165-6
intellectual property regime 157-8
Investment Code 146
investment incentives 220
labour productivity 144-5
manufacturing 142, 143, 144-5
manufacturing value added (MVA) 142, 171
Ministry of Environment Science and Technology (MEST) 150-51, 152-3, 155, 172
Ministry of Industry Science and Technology (MIST) 150
National Research Council 149, 153
patents 157-8
Pioneer Food Cannery 148
policy framework for industry 145-9
policy recommendations 170-74
Private Sector Development Project (PSDP) 154
R&D 155, 157, 172
science and technology
  financing 155-7
  infrastructure 161-70
  policies 149-58
Science and Technology Policy Research Institute (STEPRI) 150 162, 171-2
science and technology system, co-ordination and planning 172
skills 37, 159, 172
standards 162-5
taxes 158-9
technological activity 158-9
technological capabilities 51
Technology Consultancy Centre (TCC) 170
technology infrastructure and institutions 173-4
technology strategy formulation 171-2
technology transfer 158-9
Technology Transfer Centre (TTC) 162
training 159, 161
Ghana Academy of Sciences 149
Ghana Export Promotion Council (GEPC) 146-7
Ghana Free Zones Board (GFZB) 147
  and TNCs 147-9
Ghana Investment Promotion Centre (GIPC), functions 146
Ghana Regional Appropriate Technology Service (GRATIS) 168-9
Ghana Standards Board (GSB) 162-3, 174
  activities 164-5
Ghana Vision 2020 171
global trends, in exports 20-23
globalization 8, 205, 206, 207-8
Gogo, J.O. 17, 150, 155, 158
Government of Ghana 149
Green, F. 182
Guerrieri, P. 8, 100
Gunning, J.W. 210

Harbison, F.H. 37
Harbison-Myers Index 37, 38, 39
Harvey, C. 109
Helleiner, G.K. 14
high-technology (HT) products 20, 22

Highly Indebted Poor Country (HIPC) initiative 114
Holmgren, T. 114, 115
Hong Kong 105
human capital 5
  Ghana 159, 161, 172
  Kenya 78–9
  Tanzania 104–5
  Uganda 122–6, 138
  Zimbabwe 186
human capital base 32, 34–41
Husain, I. 15

Ikiara, G. 56, 66, 67, 71, 73, 75, 133
ILO (International Labour Office) 5, 6
import liberalization 15
import substitution 6
import-substituting industries (ISIs), restructuring 31
imports, capital goods 49, 118
India, National Institute of Fashion Technology (NIFT) 185–6
industrial capabilities 3, 6–9
industrial development 2, 10
  weaknesses 14–16
industrial growth 4
industrial performance 32
  developing countries 13
Industrial Policy and Framework 1994-99, Uganda 113
industrial technology systems 1
infrastructure
  and FDI 210–11
  private sector investment in 221–2
infrastructure projects 208
innovation 8, 9, 22
  Uganda 137–8
Institutional Investor 49, 119
institutional linkages 132–3
integrated structures 205, 206, 207–8
intellectual property rights (IPR) 60–61
  Ghana 157–8
  Kenya 60–63, 79, 81
  Tanzania 88, 107
International Country Risk Guide Index 49, 216
International Standards Organization *see* ISO
investment incentives
  Angola 219
  Ghana 220
  Kenya 219, 220
  South Africa 220
Investment Policy Review of Uganda 119
investment promotion
  and private organizations 223–4
  and quasi-government organizations 223
investment promotion agencies (IPAs) 222–8
  Africa 228–32
  functions 224–5
  implementation 227
  investment regulation 227
  and the private sector 228
  techniques 225–6
ISO certification 41, 64
  Africa 43
  Kenya 70
  Tanzania 96
  Uganda 128, 129
  Zimbabwe 192, 193, 199, 200
ISSER (Institute of Statistical, Social and Economic Research) 164

Kenya 54–82
  capabilities 55
  Central Bureau of Statistics 57
  corruption 68
  export processing zones (EPZs) 67, 69–70
  FDI 59, 63, 66–9, 77
    attraction 80–81
    entry requirements 219
    impediments 68
    inward 66–9
  GDP 56–7
  human capital 78–9
  import-substituting industrial strategy 56
  industrial development 54–5
    background 56–7
  intellectual property rights (IPR) regime 60–63, 79
    strengthening 81
  investment incentives 219, 220
  ISO certification 70
  Jomo Kenyatta University of Agriculture and Technology (JKUAT) 73

manufacturing value added (MVA) 56
Ministry of Education, Science and Technology 58
Ministry of Labour and Human Resources Development 59
Ministry of Tourism, Trade and Industry 58-9
Nairobi University 73
National Development Plan (1970-74) 57
patents 61, 62-3
policy implications 75-81
Power Technics 64-5
protection 56
R&D 54-5, 66, 67, 71-3, 79-80
in universities 73-4
Science and Technology Act 58
science and technology policies 57-63
skills 37, 76, 78-9
standards 70-71
technological activity 63-6
technological capabilities 51, 52, 75-81
technology 55
technology imports 63-6, 79
technology infrastructure 70-75, 80
technology institutions 80
technology policy 58-60
technology strategy formulation 77-8
trade liberalization 56, 57, 59, 64, 66, 75-6
training 76, 78-9
universities 72, 73-4, 75
Kenya Bureau of Standards (KEBS) 70-71, 74-5, 80
Kenya Industrial Research and Development Institute (KIRDI) 57, 71-3, 75
internal constraints 72, 90
reorganization 71-3
services 72
Kenya Investment Promotion Centre (KIPC) 59, 67, 69-70, 80
Kenya Polytechnic 73
Kenyan Intellectual Property Office (KIPO) 61, 62-3
Knight, J.B. 178, 179, 180, 183
knowledge, use of 8
KSA 183
Kweka, J.P. 89

labour, and FDI 210
labour costs 18
Lall, S. 2, 3, 4, 5, 13, 14, 15, 18, 37, 41, 44, 48, 55, 76, 89, 99, 100, 105, 119, 144, 155, 159, 163, 166, 170, 171, 173, 180, 189, 190, 202, 210
Latsch, W. 133, 187
Leechor, C. 141
legal systems
Africa 220-21, 238
Tanzania 93
Levinthal, D.A. 7
liberalization 44, 202
and FDI 208-9
licence payments 44
loss carry-forward provisions, Africa 220
low-technology (LT) products 18, 22
Lundvall, B.-A. 9

McCormick, D. 168
McPherson, M.A. 114, 119
managerial performance 16
manufactured export performance 16–32
manufacturing 2, 12-13
Ghana 142, 143, 144-5
manufacturing value added (MVA) 32, 33
Ghana 142, 171
Kenya 56
Sub-Saharan Africa 12, 13
Tanzania 86
Zimbabwe 177
Manzocchi, S. 182
medium-technology (MT) products 18, 20, 22
mergers and acquisitions 208
Mlawa, H.M. 87, 103
MNCs 30
FDI location decisions 203-4
Mowery, D.C. 10
multinational corporations *see* MNCs
Myers, C.S. 37

national innovation systems 9
national technology systems 9-11
effectiveness 10
Nelson, R.R. 7, 8, 9, 10
'new competition' 12
Nigeria, FDI entry requirements 218

Obwona, M.B. 115, 120, 138

Pack, H. 37, 44
Patent Cooperation Treaties (PCT) 61
patents
  Ghana 157–8
  Kenya 61, 62–3
  Tanzania 88
  Uganda 116–17
Paxson, C. 37, 44
Pietrobelli, C. 2, 4, 7, 31, 142, 170, 182
Pigato, M. 47, 48, 49, 208, 209, 217
Pioneer Food Cannery, Ghana 148
policy failure 14–15
policy liberalization, and FDI 208
policy reform 4
Power Technics, Kenya 64–5
private organizations, and investment promotion 223–4
private sector
  investment in infrastructure 221–2
  and investment promotion agencies (IPAs) 228
privatization 44, 47, 208, 237
productivity, impact of skills 37–8
productivity growth 13
protective barriers 3, 4

quasi-government organizations, and investment promotion 223

R&D 7, 41, 42, 129–33, 138
  Ghana 155, 157, 172
  Kenya 54–5, 66, 67, 71–4, 79–80
  Tanzania 83–4, 89, 94, 95, 102, 105
  Zimbabwe 186–7, 189–90, 193–5, 199, 200
Rao, K. 215
Ratauri, M. 13, 41, 89
Reinert, E. 3
Reinikka, R. 110, 112, 118, 134
relocation
  of processes 29
  of production 22
Republic of Congo, FDI entry requirements 218
Republic of Kenya 54
Republic of Uganda 112
research and development *see* R&D
resource-based (RB) products 18, 22
risk ratings 48–9
Robinson, M. 109
Robinson, P. 133, 187
Rosenberg, N. 10
RPED study 187
Rush, H. 99

Semboja, H.H.H. 85, 86, 89
Siemens 233–4
Singapore 234
  training system 182
Singapore Economic Development Board 227, 228
skill levels, index 37
skills 5–6, 34
  and FDI 210
  Ghana 37, 159, 172
  impact on productivity 37–8
  Kenya 37, 76, 78–9
  Sub-Saharan Africa 51
  Tanzania 104–5
  Uganda 122–6, 134, 138
  Zimbabwe 177–86, 197–9
SMEs (small and medium enterprises) 119
  Tanzania 100, 106
  Uganda 116, 131
  Zimbabwe 188, 191, 193–7, 199, 200
Soludo, C. 31
Soon, T.W. 182
South Africa, investment incentives 220
Srivastava, P. 13
standards
  Ghana 162–5
  Kenya 70–71
  Tanzania 95–6
  Uganda 127–9
  Zimbabwe 191–3
Stein, H. 15
Sub-Saharan Africa
  educational enrolment rates 34
  export of primary products 25–6
  FDI
    attraction 236–9
    determinants 209–15
  manufacturing value added (MVA) 12, 13
  risk ratings 48
  skills 51
  technological base 51

technological competitiveness 31–2
Svensson, J. 110, 112, 118, 134
Szirmai, A. 86, 98

Tan, H.W. 180
Tanzania 83–108
'Basic Industrial Strategy' 84
Centre for the Development of Science and Technology (CDTT) 87
COSTECH 94–5, 102, 104
functions 94–5
employment 92
exports 29, 85
FDI
attracting 106–7
inflows 48
inward 91–4
procedural problems 92–3
garment industry 89
GDP 84–5
and Germany 101
human capital 104–5
import substitution 84
industrial background 84–6
industrial base 83
Institute of Production Innovation (IPI) 87, 100–101
institutions 87–8
intellectual property rights 88, 107
'Investor roadmap' exercise 91, 92–4, 221
ISO certification 96
labour productivity 86
legal system 93
manufacturing performance 85–6
manufacturing value added (MVA) 86
Ministry of Science, Technology and Higher Education (MSTHE) 83
National Fund for the Advancement of Science and Technology (NFAST) 87
patents 88
policy recommendations 103–7
private industry 102
R&D 83–4, 89, 94, 95, 102, 105
science and technology
plan 83–4
policies 86–8, 94
'Sister Industrial Programme' 99
skills 104–5
Small Industries Development Organization (SIDO) 87, 99–100, 102, 106
SMEs 100, 106
standards 95–6
and Sweden 99
taxes 91
technological activity 88–90, 105
technological capabilities 51, 52
technological upgrading 103–4
technology imports 103, 105
technology infrastructure 94–102, 105–6
technology institutions 105–6
technology strategy formulation 104
trade liberalization 85
Tanzania Award for Science and Technological Achievement (TASTA) 87
Tanzania Breweries 89
Tanzania Bureau of Standards (TBS) 95–6, 105
Tanzania Cigarette Company 89, 90
Tanzania Investment Centre (TIC) 91
Tanzania National Scientific Research Council (TNSRC) 86–7
Tanzanian Engineering and Manufacturing Design Organization (TEMDO) 87
Tanzanian Industrial Research and Development Organization (TIRDO) 87, 96–9, 102, 106
services 97–8
technology projects 98–9
tax systems, Africa 220
taxes 237
Ghana 158–9
Tanzania 91
Uganda 115
Teal, F. 145, 171, 173
technical change, and FDI location 205
technological activity 41–3
and FDI 210
Ghana 158–9
Kenya 63–6
Tanzania 88–90, 105
Uganda 115
Zimbabwe 186–8
technological capabilities

Ghana 51
Kenya 51, 52, 75–81
Tanzania 51, 52
Zimbabwe 51, 52, 186–8
technological competitiveness
strategies 30–32
Sub-Saharan Africa 31–2
technological exports 20, 22
technological performance 16
technology 4
technology inflows 44–9
and FDI inflows 48
technology institutions 10–11
technology policies 10
technology systems, Africa 1
technology-intensive activities 17
Technoserve 169
Thai Board of Investment, information provision 231–2
Thailand, investment promotion 227
Til, R. van 141
TNCs 4, 5, 8, 9, 22, 60
and Ghana Free Zones Board (GFZB) 147–9
training and skill development by 121–2
trade barriers 3
training 121–2
Uganda 123–4, 139
Zimbabwe 197–8
transnational companies *see* TNCs
TRIPs agreement 61, 117
TSG 68, 91, 219

Uganda 109–40
bilateral treaties 216
Business Uganda Development Scheme (BUDS) 116
capital goods imports 49, 118
and China 131
economy 109, 110, 134
education 138–9
engineers 122–3
exports 29, 112, 113
of roses 135–7
FDI 114–15, 118–22
entry requirements 218
inflows 48
foreign investment 138
GDP 109, 110
GNP 109
human capital 122–6, 138
Income Tax Act of 1997 115
index of industrial production 111
industrial background 109–12
Industrial Policy and Framework 1994-99 113
industrial structure 134
industry-university linkages 138
innovation 137–8
intellectual property regime 116–17
investment 110, 112
Investment Code 114–15, 119
investor confidence index 119
ISO certification 128, 129
liberalization 114
life expectancy 109
long-term strategic policies 137–8
macroeconomic framework 134
Makerere University 124–6
Management Training and Advisory Centre (MTAC) 124, 139
manufacturing production 109–10
Ministry of Finance 109
Ministry of Trade and Industry (MOTI) 113, 128
National Agricultural Research Organization (NARO) 126, 129–30
patents 116–17
policy framework, and the private sector 114–16
primary exports 26
Private Sector Foundation (PSF) 116
R&D 138
R&D institutions 129–33
rose exports 135–7
science and technology policy 112
skills 122–6, 134, 138
SMEs 116, 131
standards 127–9
strategic policy statements and objectives 112, 114
tariffs 114
taxes 115
technological activity 115
technology development 112–17
technology system, lack of 135–7
technology transfer to 118–22
training 123–4, 139

Transfer of Knowledge through Expert Nationals (TOKTEN) 115
Unilever Uganda Ltd. 121-2
Uganda Exporters' Association (UEA) 116
Uganda Gatsby Trust 126
science and technology infrastructure 126-33
Uganda Industrial Research Institute (UIRI) 130, 131-2, 139
Uganda Investment Authority (UIA) 119, 120, 122, 123
Uganda Manufacturers Association Consultancy and Information Services (UMACIS) 115
Uganda Manufacturers Association (UMA) 115
Uganda National Bureau of Standards (UNBS) 127-9, 139
functions 128
Uganda National Chamber of Commerce and Industry (UNCCI) 116
Uganda National Council for Science and Technology (UNCST) 126, 127
Uganda Registration Services Bureau (URSB) 117
Uganda Small-Scale Industry Association (USSIA) 115-16
UK, attraction of FDI 233-4
UNCTAD 4, 44, 114, 118, 119, 120, 121, 122, 196, 206
UNDCP 164
UNDP 109, 115
UNIDO 12, 13, 15, 56, 57, 100
Unilever Uganda Ltd. 121-2
universities, linkages with firms 74, 191, 199
USAID 92

Verner, D. 159

wage costs 38-41
wages, international comparison 184
Wangwe, S.M. 13, 29, 84, 88, 89, 94, 101
Washington consensus 15
WEF 91
Wells, L.T. 206, 224
Wignaraja, G. 56, 66, 67, 71, 73, 133, 159
Wint, A.G. 206, 224
Winter, S.J. 7, 8
work permit regulations, Africa 220
World Bank 67, 109, 114, 130, 141, 145, 177-8, 187, 196, 204, 216
World Economic Forum 68, 159
World Intellectual Property Organization (WIPO) 117
WTO (World Trade Organization) 61, 63

Zambia, FDI entry requirements 218
Zimbabwe 176-201
Biotechnology Research Institute 193
Building Research Institute 194
Business Extension and Advisory Service (BESA) 196
Clothing Design and Technical Institute (CDTI) 183
Economic Structural Adjustment programme (ESAP) 176-7, 187
education system 177-9
Electronics Technology Institute 195
employee training 179-83
EMPRETEC Zimbabwe 196
Energy Technology Institute 195
Environment and Remote Sensing Institute 194
exports 29
FDI 187
entry requirements 218
inflows 48
firms, and universities 191, 199
GDP 176
human capital 186
industrial competitiveness 183
industrial development 176
ISO certification 192, 193, 199, 200
liberalization 187
Manpower Development Fund 198
manufacturing value added (MVA) 177
National Metrology Institute 192, 195
policy recommendations 197-200
Production Engineering Institute 194-5
R&D 186-7, 199, 200
promotion in industry 189-90
R&D institutions 193-5
science and technology infrastructure

190–91
Scientific and Industrial Research and Development Centre (SIRDC) 193
skills 177–86, 197–9
skills levels 37
Small Business Support Unit (SBSU) 196–7
Small Enterprise Development Corporation (SEDCO) 196
SME support systems 195–7, 199, 200
SMEs 188, 191, 193, 194–5
standards 191–3
Standards Association of Zimbabwe (SAZ) 191–3
functions and financing 192
technological activity 186–8
technological capabilities 51, 52, 186–8
technological performance 186–8
technological priorities 188–9
technology finance 190
technology imports 186–8
technology index 187
and technology institutions abroad 200
technology support 199–200
Technology Transfer Centres, proposed 200
tertiary technical enrolments 178
textile and clothing industry 183
training 197–8
Unilateral Declaration of independence (UDI) 178, 189
Venture Capital Company of Zimbabwe (VCCZ) 197
vocational education 179
wages 183
Zimbabwe Enterprise Development Programme 196
Zimbabwe Investment Centre (ZIC)
and FDI promotion 228–30
shortcomings 229–30
Zimbabwe Manpower Development Fund 182
Zimbabwe Productivity Centre, proposed 200